A Priest's Guide for the Great Festival

SOUTH ASIA RESEARCH

SERIES EDITOR
Patrick Olivelle

A Publication Series of
The University of Texas South Asia Institute
and
Oxford University Press

THE EARLY UPANISADS
Annotated Text and Translation
Patrick Olivelle

INDIAN EPIGRAPHY
A Guide to the Study of Inscriptions in Sanskrit,
Prakrit, and the other Indo-Aryan Languages
Richard Salomon

A DICTIONARY OF OLD MARATHI
S. G. Tulpule and Anne Feldhaus

DONORS, DEVOTEES, AND DAUGHTERS OF GOD
Temple Women in Medieval Tamilnadu
Leslie C. Orr

JIMUTAVAHANA'S *DAYABHAGA*
The Hindu Law of Inheritance in Bengal
Edited and Translated with an Introduction and Notes by
Ludo Rocher

A PORTRAIT OF THE HINDUS
Balthazar Solvyns & the European Image of India 1740–1824
Robert L. Hardgrave

MANU'S CODE OF LAW
A Critical Edition and Translation of the Manava-Dharmasastra
Patrick Olivelle

NECTAR GAZE AND POISON BREATH
An Analysis and Translation of the Rajasthani Oral Narrative of Devnarayan
Aditya Malik

BETWEEN THE EMPIRES
Society in India 300 BCE to 400 CE
Patrick Olivelle

MANAGING MONKS
Administrators and Administrative Roles in
Indian Buddhist Monasticism
Jonathan A. Silk

SIVA IN TROUBLE
Festivals and Rituals at the Pasupatinatha Temple of Deopatan
Axel Michaels

A PRIEST'S GUIDE FOR THE GREAT FESTIVAL
Aghorasiva's Mahotsavavidhi
Richard H. Davis

A Priest's Guide for the Great Festival

Aghorasiva's Mahotsavavidhi

Translated with Introduction
and Notes by
RICHARD H. DAVIS

OXFORD
UNIVERSITY PRESS
2010

OXFORD
UNIVERSITY PRESS

Oxford University Press, Inc., publishes works that further
Oxford University's objective of excellence
in research, scholarship, and education.

Oxford New York
Auckland Cape Town Dar es Salaam Hong Kong Karachi
Kuala Lumpur Madrid Melbourne Mexico City Nairobi
New Delhi Shanghai Taipei Toronto

With offices in
Argentina Austria Brazil Chile Czech Republic France Greece
Guatemala Hungary Italy Japan Poland Portugal Singapore
South Korea Switzerland Thailand Turkey Ukraine Vietnam

Published by Oxford University Press, Inc.
198 Madison Avenue, New York, New York 10016

www.oup.com

Library of Congress Cataloging-in-Publication Data
Aghorasivacarya, 12th cent.
[Mahotsavavidhi. English]
A priest's guide for the great festival : Aghorasiva's Mahotsavavidhi / translated and with introduction and notes by Richard H. Davis.
p. cm.
In English and Sanskrit; includes translation from Sanskrit.
Includes bibliographical references.
ISBN 978-0-19-537852-8
1. Saiva Siddhanta—Rituals—Texts—Early works to 1800. 2. Siva (Hindu deity)—Cult—India, South—Early works to 1800. 3. Fasts and feasts—India, South—Saiva Siddhanta—Early works to 1800. I. Davis, Richard H. II. Title.
BL1281.855.A37513 2009
294.5'38—dc22 2008055636

9 8 7 6 5 4 3 2 1

Printed in the United States of America
on acid-free paper

Acknowledgments

I date the beginning of this project to December 1999, when Vidya Dehejia asked me to contribute an essay to a catalogue for an exhibition of Chola bronzes that would open at the Arthur M. Sackler Gallery in Washington in November 2002. The topic Vidya suggested was the "original ritual context" of the bronze images. Medieval Chola bronzes, as is well known, were not originally fabricated as sculptures for museum display (though this is sometimes forgotten in the world of art), but were intended for religious purposes, most notably to serve as processional icons of the Hindu gods during festivals. I found this an attractive subject for research and agreed to take it on. In summer of 2000, I was able to travel to Tamilnad to begin work on this topic.

In India two scholars whom I greatly esteemed, N. R. Bhatt and R. Nagaswamy, both suggested I take a look at the *Mahotsavavidhi* of Aghoraśiva for my research. My brief essay for the Sackler catalogue (Davis 2002) led me to look at a variety of different source materials, but as I read through Aghoraśiva's text, I decided that this Āgama text would be worthy of more sustained attention. I also began to think that this might lead to a broader project on festival processions as a widespread form of "cultural performance" in India and elsewhere.

In 2002 I returned to India, and at that time I was fortunate enough to be able to read through the *Mahotsavavidhi* with N. R. Bhatt. This guided reading formed the center of my translation. Other parts of this publication, such as the annotations and the introduction, have taken shape subsequently through my attempts to understand more fully Aghoraśiva's terse guidelines and to place these guidelines in a broader religious context.

I am aware of many debts that I have amassed over nine years of working on this project, and the *balidāna* I offer here can only be partial repayment. My greatest debt is to N. R. Bhatt, most erudite of all modern scholars of Śaiva Āgamas. His patient guidance through what were to me often obscure terms and passages in the *Mahotsavavidhi* provided the basis of this translation. In a broader sense, I would like to pay tribute to the French Institute at Pondicherry, where Bhatt served for many years as chief pandit. In 1956 Jean Filliozat launched a project to recover and document the immense religious literature of the south Indian Śaiva tradition, particularly the Sanskrit Śaiva Āgamas, and he assigned N. R. Bhatt to begin the process of collecting manuscripts and producing critical editions of the key Āgama texts. This project laid the groundwork for a tremendous wealth of scholarly editions and translations over five decades. All scholarly work in the field of Āgama studies rests on the foundation established at the French Institute. Over the years, I have profited greatly from the Institute's hospitality and from conversation with scholars working there, including Hélène Brunner, Bruno Dagens, T. Ganesan, Dominic Goodall, Françoise L'Hernault, and P. R. Srinivasan. It will be evident in the translation how often I have relied on the expertise of these scholars in my own work.

Other scholars and institutions in India have also directly assisted me. The late S. S. Janaki, former director of the Kuppuswami Sastri Research Institute, initiated me into the study of Śaiva Āgama literature, and I was fortunate to work with her on the *nityakarman* section of Aghoraśiva's *Kriyākramadyotikā*, which has proven essential to understanding the *Mahotsavavidhi*. The Kuppuswami Sastri Research Institute has been a supportive base for several research stays in Chennai, and I am grateful to the current director V. Kameswari and to my friends there. The late Śaiva ācārya K. A. Sabharatna Sivacarya served as an expert practitioner and consultant on Āgama based rites. In numerous conversations and by his own example, R. Nagawamy has pushed me to think of Āgama teachings in their broader historical context. I am also grateful to Rashmi Poddar, who has smoothed the way for me in Mumbai and encouraged my interest in ritual aesthetics.

In trying to understand the twelfth-century guide of Aghoraśiva, I have found it extremely valuable to observe modern temple festivals and to speak with modern temple priests about contemporary practices. In Madurai, for observations of the festivals of the Minakshi-Sundareshvara temple, I am particularly grateful to two priests who have patiently answered my many questions, S. Sathasiva Bhattar and S. Sankaran Sivachariyar. I have also benefited from the helpful assistance of Dr. S. Bharathy, head of the American Institute of Indian Studies Tamil Language Program, and from the welcome of Minakshi temple officials, including Karumuttu T. Kannan, chairman of the temple Board, and B. Raja, its executive officer. In Madurai, I enjoyed conversations and guidance from R. Venkataraman and T. Damodaran. At the Kapalishvara temple in Mylapore, Chennai, Arundasundaram Gurukkal gave me valuable advice on Śaiva festivals early on in this project. And closer to home in New York, the chief priest at the Maha Ganapathi Temple in Queens, New York, Bhairava Moorthy, provided expert guidance for a temple festival adapted to a North American setting.

Throughout my work on this project I have been able to give talks exploring various of the *Mahotsavavidhi* and festival processions more generally. I am grateful to the audiences at Bombay University, Bowdoin College, the University of California Berkeley, the University of Chicago, Columbia University, Cornell University, University of Delhi, University of Michigan, St. Lawrence University, the Tamil Arts Academy, Thyagaraja College, Vassar College, and Yale University for their many observations, suggestions, and criticisms. It would not be possible to perform *balidāna* for all the many individuals whose questions and observations have proven valuable to this project, but I would like to single out for special tribute (*viśeṣabali*): Ginni Ishimatsu, Leslie Orr, Indira Peterson, Karen Prentiss, Martha Selby, Archana Venkatesan, and Blake Wentworth.

Institutional support for research is fundamental to any project of this sort. I am deeply grateful to Bard College for its support throughout this project, in the significant forms of a research leave and a sabbatical. I have also profited immensely from the lively intellectual atmosphere of the college and from ongoing conversations with many colleagues: Sanjib Baruah, Jon Brockopp, Bradley Clough, Bruce Chilton, Paul Murray, Jacob Neusner, and more recently Carolyn Dewald and Kristin Scheible. At Yale University I was happy to be made a research affiliate of the Council for South Asian Studies for several years, which allowed me access to the wonderful Yale library.

Major fellowships for this project came from the John Simon Guggenheim Foundation and the National Endowment for the Humanities. Grants from the American Institute of Indian Studies, the Asian Cultural Council, and the Bard Research Fund enabled research trips to India.

At Oxford University Press, I am grateful to Patrick Olivelle for his interest in taking on this volume in the South Asian Studies series, and to two anonymous readers for their valuable suggestions. I thank also the various editors who have assisted in transforming the manuscript into a book: Margaret Case, Brian Desmond, Meechal Hoffman, Cynthia A. Read, and Justin Tackett.

I owe gratitude also to Mark Dyczkowski and to the Muktabodha Indological Research Institute for their work in the creation of a digital version of the *Mahotsavavidhi*, from which the devanagari text in this volume was generated.

In any Śaiva procession, members of the family march closest to the deity. My son Matthew helped as research assistant for one trip to Madurai, and Gaṇeśa-like, removed the obstacles from my computer-generated diagrams. My wife Rita McCleary has been an encouraging and conscientious interlocutor throughout this project, and deserves my tribute always.

Contents

List of Abbreviations, xi

List of Tables and Diagrams, xiii

Notes on Text, Author, and Translation, 3

Introduction, 15

Translation, 59

Text (in devanagari), 147

References, 173

Index, 185

Abbreviations

AĀ	*Ajitāgama*
KKD	*Kriyākramadyotikā* of Aghoraśiva
KKDP	*Kriyākramadyotikāprabhā* of Nirmalamaṇi
MĀŚ	*Mahotsavavidhikrama Āgamaśekhara*
MM	*Mayamata*
ML	*Mudrālakṣaṇa*
MṛĀ	*Mṛgendrāgama*
MV	*Mahotsavavidhi* of Aghoraśiva
PKĀ	*Pūrvakāmikāgama*
RĀ	*Rauravāgama*
RV	*Ṛgveda*
SP	*Somaśambhupaddhati* of Somaśambhu
ŚPM	*Śaivāgamaparibhāṣāmañjarī* of Vedajñāna
ŚPV	*Śivalingapratiṣṭhāvidhi* of Aghoraśiva
Tai Br	*Taittirīya Brāhmaṇa*
UKĀ	*Uttarakāmikāgama*
UKārĀ	*Uttarakāraṇāgama*

List of Tables and Diagrams

Tables

1. Divisions of the Festival, 62
2. Types and Durations of Mahotsavas, 63
3. Tālas in Nityotsava and Mahotsava, 90
4. Elements of *Bherītāḍaṇa*, 91
5. Daily Presiding Deities (*Dinādhipas*), 102
6A. Processional Vehicles and Events (Nine-day Festival), 108
6B. Processional Vehicles and Events (Thirteen-day Festival), 135
6C. Processional Vehicles and Events (Nine-day Goddess Festival), 136

Diagrams

1. Flagpole and Deities, 69
2. Design of Nandin Banner, 73
3. Trident and Deities, 84
4. *Bherī* Drum and Deities, 87
5. Vāstumaṇḍala: *Paramaśayin* Type, 94
6. Solar Calendar and Māsotsava, 140

A Priest's Guide for the Great Festival

Notes on Text, Author, and Translation

Text

The *Mahotsavavidhi* is a Śaiva ritual guidebook, composed in Sanskrit by the *ācārya* Aghoraśiva in 1157 C.E., during the reign of the south Indian Chola ruler Rajaraja II. It is a Śaiva Paddhati, a relatively brief text of rules or prescriptions (*vidhi*) intended to guide a priest in the performance of a nine-day temple festival (*mahotsava*).

This translation of Aghoraśiva's *Mahotsavavidhi* is based on a text published in 1910 by the Civañānapōtayantracālai (Sivajnanabodha Press) in Chintadripet, Chennai. In 1901, Mayilai Alagappa Mudaliyar, a pious Śaiva layman, established the press in order to bring out inexpensive editions of important Śaiva Āgama works, for the practical use of priests. In fact, these appear to have been the first mechanically reproduced copies of a genre of Sanskrit texts that had up to then circulated only in the form of hand-copied palm-leaf manuscripts. They were printed in grantha script, an enhanced form of Tamil script for rendering Sanskrit. Alagappa Mudaliyar first published primary Āgamas such as the *Kāmikāgama*, *Kāraṇāgama*, and *Suprebhedāgama*, and later went on to publish also important Paddhatis, priestly manuals based on the Āgamas, including *Siddhāntasārāvali*, *Kriyākramajyotikā*, *Śivaliṅgapratiṣṭhāvidhi*, and *Aparakriyāvidhi*.

The work he called the *Mahotsavavidhi* of Aghoraśiva was one of these Paddhati works.[1]

Beginning in the 1960s, the Teṉṉintiya arccakar acōcīyēṣaṉ (South Indian Archakar Association), also based in Chennai, reprinted many of the original Sivajnanabodha Press publications, again for the most part in grantha script. These too were inexpensive volumes published by Śaiva priests and intended for the use of Śaiva priests. Generally they followed the earlier editions closely, although in some cases the Archakar editors saw fit to interpolate additional passages. The South Indian Archakar Association brought out a new edition of the *Mahotsavavidhi* in 1974, edited by S. Swaminatha Sivacarya.

Neither the early twentieth-century grantha editions of the Sivajnanabodha Press nor the later ones of the South Indian Archakar Association were critical editions in the modern scholarly sense. The aim was to provide practical guidance for Śaiva temple priests and other pious initiates in their devotional and ritual activities, not to reconstruct a historical text at some stable moment in its transmission (often taken as the time of its composition), as part of a larger project of religious or cultural history (Goodall 2000: 214). Alagappa Mudaliyar's texts lack the apparatus that scholars have come to expect: use of multiple manuscript sources, citations of alternate readings and textual variations among the sources, and so on. The first true critical editions of Śaiva Āgama texts were produced only in the 1960s, beginning with N. R. Bhatt's editions of the *Rauravāgama* (1961–1988), *Mṛgendrāgama* (1962), and the *Ajitāgama* (1964–1991) under the auspices of the French Institute of Pondicherry (Filliozat 1994). However, it should be said that Alagappa Mudaliyar evidently took the trouble to avail himself of good manuscripts of the texts he published and to provide knowledgeable and generally reliable readings of these manuscript sources.

For this translation I have used a devanagari transcript of the 1910 Alagappa Mudaliyar edition, prepared at the Kuppuswami Sastri Research Institute under the direction of S. S. Janaki. Copies of the original, printed nearly a hundred years ago on cheap paper, are rare and fragile. I have compared this transcript with the 1974 South Indian Archakar Association publication in grantha, and have also used a copy of the original 1910 edition (or rather, a xerox of a copy of the original) housed in the library of the French Institute of Pondicherry. Since these printed editions are not easily available (neither appear in a WorldCat search of research libraries), I append the Sanskrit text of the *Mahotsavavidhi* in this volume. The devanagari text

[1] The fullest account of the history of Āgama publications may be found in the introduction by N. R. Bhatt to Varadachari 1986, vol. 1, pp. viii–x.

included is based on an e-text produced under the supervision of the Muktabodha Indological Texts project, working from the transcript and the 1974 grantha publication. I have made no attempt to produce a critical edition.

Alagappa Mudaliyar's edition of *Mahotsavavidhi* consists in three parts. The first part he identifies, in the Tamil table of contents, as "Akoracivācāriyār Utcavapattati," the *Utsavapaddhati* of preceptor Aghoraśiva. This portion takes up sixty pages of text, and concludes with a colophon that identifies the composition as that of the preceptor Aghoraśiva, also known as Parameśvara, and states that it is part of a work called the *Kriyākramadyotikā*, the "Light on Ritual Procedures." It is written largely in prose and consists in succinct step-by-step instructions for a priest's performance of a nine-day *mahotsava* and also for more modest festivals held monthly, fortnightly, and weekly. It presents itself as a self-standing work, and does not explicitly cite other works.

The second portion Alagappa Mudaliyar calls the "Utcavaviti Ākamacēkaram" in the table of contents, while at the start of the section he identifies it as *Mahotsavavidhikrama Āgamaśekhara*, the "crown of Āgamas pertaining to festival rules and procedures." In contrast to the first part, this section of the publication is composed primarily in verse and incorporates citations from numerous Āgamas. (A list of Āgamas quoted in the *MĀŚ* includes *Kāmikāgama, Yogajāgama, Cintyāgama, Kāraṇāgama, Ajitāgama, Dīptāgama, Sūkṣmāgama, Sahasrāgama, Amśumadāgama, Svāyambhuvāgama, Vīratantra, Rauravāgama, Makuṭāgama, Candrajñānāgama, Lalitāgama, Kiraṇāgama*, and *Vātulāgama*. The Upāgamas quoted are *Mṛgendrāgama, Bhīmasamhitā, Kumāratantra*, and *Vidyeśvarasamhitā*.) In some cases the citations correspond to passages in the published editions of these Āgamas, while in others it has not been possible to locate cited passages in extant works. The compiler of this portion also draws from several ancillary Śaiva works, most extensively a composition he calls the *Sakalāgamasaṅgraha*, the "Collection of All Āgamas." This is a common name for many Śaiva digests, but here it appears to refer to a text or portion of a larger text devoted to the topic of *mahotsava*. Overall, the second section of Alagappa Mudaliyar's edition is a 363 page Āgama digest that follows Aghoraśiva's primary text quite closely topic by topic, and provides much valuable exposition that explains and expands Aghoraśiva's more concise directions. Accordingly, I have drawn upon this part of the book extensively in understanding Aghorasiva's text and in annotating my translation.

There is no reason to suppose that this second section is the work of Aghoraśiva. It does not have a colophon identifying authorship, but two benedictory verses at its beginning provide a helpful clue. The first verse honors the god Gaṇeśa, while the second offers verbal worship to the author's preceptor, one Sadāśiva of Kanchipuram. The same verses also appear in a commentary on another work of Aghoraśiva, by Kacchapeśvara, a Śaiva exegete of the seventeenth century. It is a reasonable hypothesis, then, to view the *Mahotsavavidhikrama Āgamaśekhara* as the later digest of Kacchapeśvara, intended to amplify the succinct Paddhati work of Aghoraśiva with more extensive quotations from the Āgamas available to him.[2]

For convenience I refer consistently to the first section of the book as the *Mahotsavavidhi* (abbreviated *MV*) of Aghoraśiva, and the second as *Mahotsavavidhikrama Āgamaśekhara* (abbreviated *MĀŚ*).

Alagappa Mudaliyar includes a brief third section in his publication, entitled the *Gotrasantati*, or "the genealogy of [Aghoraśiva's] clan of teachers." A colophon identifies this also as the work of Aghoraśiva, alias Parameśvara, and states that it too is a portion of the *Kriyākramadyotikā*. This verse composition of forty-three stanzas provides an account of the various Śaiva lineages, monastic networks, and disciplic successions to which Aghoraśiva related himself. Notably it also gives a date of composition, equivalent to 1157 C.E.

Mahotsavavidhi and *Kriyākramadyotikā*

In the colophon to *Mahotsavavidhi*, Aghoraśiva states clearly that this text is a portion of the *Kriyākramadyotikā*. On the title page of his edition, Alagappa Mudaliyar takes this a step further and identifies the *Mahotsavavidhi* as the "sixth part" (*āṟām pākam*) of the *Kriyākramadyotikā*. This raises an intriguing question about the relationship of the *Mahotsavavidhi* with Aghoraśiva's well-known work on ritual procedures.

The *Kriyākramadyotikā*, also known as the *Aghoraśivapaddhati*, aims, in Aghoraśiva's own words, "to clarify the daily and other rituals." The commentator Nirmalamaṇi argues that one should use this Paddhati rather than any other, because Aghoraśiva clarifies what other Paddhatis have left unclear or unsaid. Apparently many South Indian Śaivas have agreed with Nirmalamaṇi. It has been probably the most influential work pertaining to Śaiva ritual practice in Tamilnad, as Hélène Brunner and N. R. Bhatt have both observed. This work has been published in several editions, starting with that of Alagappa Mudaliyar, but the best so far is a 1927 edition of 487 pages in grantha script published by the Jnanasambandhan Press. Editors K. Krishna Sastri and P. Srirama Sastri based their publication on four manuscripts held by Śaiva teachers in Jaffna, Vedaranya, Cidambaram, and Suryanarkoyil, and included

[2] I thank T. Ganesan at the French Institute of Pondicherry for first drawing my attention to the significance of this verse. See Goodall 1998: xiii.

the excellent commentary of the sixteenth century Śaiva Siddhāntin of Tiruvarur, Nirmalamaṇi. The seventeenth century Śaiva pandit Kacchapeśvara also commented on part of the *Kriyākramadyotikā*, but this commentary has not been published. More recently, the late S. S. Janaki at the Kuppuswami Sastri Research Institute completed a critical edition of the first section of the text, under the auspices of the Indira Gandhi National Centre for the Arts. Publication plans for this critical edition, combined with a translation by Ginnette Ishimatsu and myself, are uncertain at present. Working with Dr. Janaki, Wayne Surdam translated the third major section, on *dīkṣā*, in his 1984 dissertation at the University of California, Berkeley.

In its published versions, the *Kriyākramadyotikā* (abbreviated *KKD*) covers three fundamental topics. First, it discusses the daily rites (*nitya-karman*) to be performed by a pious Śaiva initiate on his own behalf (*ātmārtha*). These rites include the worship of the Sun identified as a form of Śiva (*sūryapūjā*), the daily worship of Śiva in the form of a Śiva-liṅga (*nityapūjā*), and a small sacrifice into a fire identified as a form of Śiva (*nityahoma*), as well as other ancillary observances. Nirmalamaṇi points out that Aghoraśiva discusses daily observances first because they are the prerequisites for all other rituals. Second, Aghoraśiva sets out instructions for several occasional rites (*naimittika-karman*), generally of an expiatory nature, including *pavitrotsava* and *damanotsava*. Third, he prescribes a sequence of transformative rituals that cumulatively initiate an individual into the Śaiva community (*samayadīkṣā, viśeṣadīkṣā*), remove his bondage (*nirvāṇadīkṣā*), consecrate him either as a priest (*ācāryadīkṣā*) or as a mantra- adept (*sādhakadīkṣā*), and release his soul finally at the time of bodily cremation (*antyeṣṭi*). Nirmalamaṇ;i's commentary carries through all these matters.

In this arrangement of topics, Aghoraśiva's Paddhati corresponds closely with an earlier work in verse composed in the eleventh century by Somaśambhu, the *Kriyākaṇdakramāvali* or *Somaśambhupaddhati*. This succinct Paddhati work was first edited by Subrahmanya Sastri (1931) and Zadoo (1947), and has been authoritatively translated in four hefty annotated volumes by Hélène Brunner-Lachaux (hereafter simply Brunner). It is probable, as Brunner suggests, that Aghoraśiva modeled his *Kriyākramadyotikā* on the Paddhati of his North Indian predecessor. Somaśambhu did not end his work with the topic of *antyeṣṭi*, and there are good reasons to suppose that Aghoraśiva also continued his Paddhati beyond that final topic. Several texts attributed to Aghoraśiva, and identifying themselves as portions of the *Kriyākramadyotikā*, may well have constituted an original, larger work that I will provisionally call the *Mahā-kriyākramadyotikā*, to distinguish this hypothetical reconstruction from the published *Kriyākramadyotikā*.

In the *Somaśambhupaddhati*, after the transformative rituals comes a fourth section dealing with the ritual consecration or "establishment" of a Śiva-liṅga (*liṅgapratiṣṭhā*) and other consecrated objects meant for private or public worship. In 1921 Alagappa Mudaliyar published as a self-standing volume the *Śivapratiṣṭhāvidhi*, which was republished by the South Indian Archakar Association in 1964. The first page of this work identifies it as a part of Aghoraśiva's *Kriyākramadyotikā*. Nirmalamaṇi mentions at one point in his commentary that Aghoraśiva did indeed write on the subject of *pratiṣṭhā*. However, we need to be cautious in accepting the identification of this publication as a continuation of Aghoraśiva's Paddhati. Some portions of the published text appear consonant with the existing *Kriyākramadyotikā*, but as Brunner (*SP* 4, p. lv) has noted, the published *Śivapratiṣṭhāvidhi* departs in several fundamental respects from the style of Aghoraśiva as we know it from the *Kriyākramadyotikā*. The published *Śivapratiṣṭhāvidhi* abounds in Vedic mantras, whereas Aghoraśiva almost always prefers Āgamic ones, and it is stuffed with direct citations from primary Āgamas. In the *Kriyākramadyotikā*, Aghoraśiva seldom cites other texts explicitly.

Quite possibly the original core of Aghoraśiva's discussion of *śivapratiṣṭhā* in the *KKD* has been expanded upon by later transmitters, in accord with changes in practice and new needs for explication, through the incorporation of ancillary passages from other texts. The result, we might suppose, is a published *Śivapratiṣṭhāvidhi* that is one part Aghoraśiva, three parts added digest—but without the separation between the two parts that we find in the published *Mahotsavavidhi*. If this is the case, it would take a critical effort to separate out the portion composed by Aghoraśiva in the *Śivapratiṣṭhāvidhi* from the later additions, though it is possible that some manuscripts may adhere more closely to an Aghoraśiva original.

There are other published works that are attributed to Aghoraśiva and linked to the *Kriyākramadyotikā*. These include a *Subrahmaṇya Pratiṣṭhāvidhi* (published 1920), said to be the "fifth portion" of the *KKD*, and a *Prāyaścittavidhi* (n.d.), supposed to be the "seventh portion." These publications have the same composite quality as the published *Śivapratiṣṭhāvidhi*. Integrating these with the other existing texts, we can imagine a hypothetical *Mahā-Kriyākramadyotikā* of seven parts:

1. *Nityakarman* (published Cidambaram 1927)
2. *Naimittikakarman: pavitra and damana* (Cidambaram 1927)
3. *Dīkṣāvidhi, Abhiṣeka, and Antyeṣṭi* (Cidambaram 1927)
4. *Śivapratiṣṭhāvidhi* (Chintadripet 1921)
5. *Subrahmaṇya-pratiṣṭhāvidhi* (Chintadripet 1920)

6. *Mahotsavavidhi* (Chintadripet 1910)
7. *Prāyaścittavidhi* (Chintadripet, n.d.)

The *Gotrasantati* included at the end of the published *Mahotsavavidhi* would make a fitting conclusion to this ritual magnum opus of Aghoraśiva. Alagappa Mudaliyar at least was aware of a Śaiva tradition linking all these works together, and the order of presentation appears logical and appropriate. However, this will remain purely a hypothetical connection until someone undertakes the research necessary to substantiate or disprove it.

With the *Mahotsavavidhi* I believe we are on firmer ground than with the other later works attributed by Alagappa Mudaliyar to Aghoraśiva. The style of exposition and the procedural orientation in the *Mahotsavavidhi* are fully consonant with that of the *Kriyākramadyotikā* or *Aghoraśiva-paddhati* commented on by Nirmalamaṇi. In the *Mahotsavavidhi* Aghoraśiva frequently uses phrases like *pūrvokta* ("as previously stated") that refer back to the treatments of topics located in other parts of the *Kriyākramadyotikā*. I see no reason to doubt that the first section of the published *Mahotsavavidhi* is the composition of the twelfth-century *ācārya* Aghoraśiva.

Author

In the *Gotrasantati* appended to the published *Mahotsavavidhi*, Aghoraśiva speaks of the completion of his work in the year 1157 C.E. This date has long served as a fixed point in the turning world of Śaiva Siddhānta chronology. But the *Gotrasantati* does more than supply a date. Aghoraśiva here locates himself within a complex tradition of lineages, monastic networks, and preceptors. Aghoraśiva's own spiritual genealogy begins with Durvāsas, the legendary and irascible Śaiva sage, and continues through twelve *ācāryas* in all, concluding with Sarvātmaśiva, also known as Hṛdayaśambhu, the guru who initiated Aghoraśiva.[3]

Scholars have devoted considerable effort and ingenuity in attempting to sort out the lineages of Śaiva teachers in this and other texts, and to coordinate this information with known Śaiva works and with references to Śaiva preceptors and ascetics in early medieval inscriptions. This remains inconclusive, in part due to the extremely fragmentary character of the evidence, and also (as

[3] The *Gotrasantati* is not altogether clear, and a critical edition of the brief text would be most valuable. Dominic Goodall has located portions of the text in other manuscripts within the French Institute collection (personal communication). I have discussed some of the *Gotrasantati* material in Davis 1992. I am grateful to the late Hélène Brunner for her helpful comments and corrections of this article.

Dominic Goodall has observed) due to the initiatory naming practices of the medieval Śaivas. The same names may be borne by several distinct Śaiva teachers, and the same person may be identified by more than one name (Goodall 2000: 207). I do not propose to clear up that muddle here, but the *Gotrasantati* does alert us to a point of importance about the author's background.

Aghoraśiva places himself in the theological school of Śaiva Siddhānta, and he clearly depicts his tradition as a pan-Indian school. Among his lineage of teachers he mentions: Uttuṅgaśiva, a Gujarati living in Kalyāṇanagarī; Brahmaśiva also from Gujarat; two teachers who served as royal preceptors to rulers in Varanasi, Pūrṇaśiva and Vidyāntaśiva; Śrīkaṇṭhaśiva described as a "bull among the Bengalis"; Dhyānaśiva also from Bengal; and Somaśambhu, author of *Somaśambhupaddhati*, who was probably based either in the Dahala region near Tripuri or in Kashmir. This point needs to be highlighted because there is a long-standing scholarly misrepresentation that portrays Śaiva Siddhānta as an exclusive product of the Tamil region (Davis 1992, Goodall 2004: xiii–xxxiv). While Aghoraśiva did live and teach in Tamilnad, his own training and purview were much broader.

In particular Aghoraśiva looked towards Śaiva Siddhānta teachers in Kashmir. In a recent authoritative outline of Kashmiri Śaiva literature, Alexis Sanderson (2007) speaks of the tenth century as a "golden age" for Kashmiri theological exegesis within the dualistic Siddhānta school. The line of "kaṇṭha" teachers, starting with Bhaṭṭṇa Rāmakaṇṭha and including Vidyākaṇṭha, Śrīkaṇṭha, Nārāyaṇakaṇṭha, Rāmakaṇṭha II, and Vidyākaṇṭha II, produced a rich corpus of commentaries on Āgamas and self-standing theological works that articulated Śaiva Siddhānta principles in considerable depth (Goodall 1998). It is clear that Aghoraśiva studied these works carefully, for he wrote his own commentaries on several of the Kashmiri works, and in one work he explicitly declared his great respect for Rāmakaṇṭha II (while punning on the *kaṇṭha* part of his name).

> Following faithfully the footsteps of that strong-voiced (*mahākaṇṭha*) lion (*kaṇṭhīrava*) Rāmakaṇṭha, I do not fear the trumpetings of those rutting elephants, the sophists (*kutārkika*) (*Mṛgendrāgamavṛttidīpikā vidyāpāda* v. 4)

By all indications Aghoraśiva was a successful Śaiva preceptor who wrote on a variety of topics. He speaks of himself as a master of grammar and logic, and as knowledgeable in areas like Vaiśeṣika and Veda. According to the *New Catalogus Catalogorum* (Raghavan 1958: 1. 58–59), he was author of several literary works, including two works identified as *kāvya*, one dance-drama (*nāṭaka*), and a work apparently on poetics.

Abhyudaya ("Sunrise," "The Sunrise Ceremony"), a *nāṭaka*
Āścaryacāra ("The astonishing trip"), a *kāvya*
Pāṣaṇḍāpajaya ("Defeat of the heretics"), a *kāvya*
Kāvyatilaka ("Ornament of Literature")

None of these works has yet been located.

Aghoraśiva was much more prolific as a teacher within the field of Śaiva Siddhānta theology and practice. We can divide his Śaiva works into three types:

(1) commentaries or subcommentaries on existing Śaiva Āgamas,
(2) commentaries on Śaiva Siddhānta theological or philosophical works, and
(3) independent works on Śaiva ritual practice.

As the words of Śiva himself, the Śaiva Āgamas naturally enjoyed great authority among Śaiva Siddhāntins, and composing a commentary on one of the Āgamas was a good place for any aspiring Śaiva exegete to begin. It may be that Aghoraśiva's first purely Śaiva work was a subcommentary (*dīpikā*) on the commentary (*vṛtti*) by the Kashmiri author Nārāyaṇakaṇṭha on the philosophical portion (*vidyāpāda*) of *the Mṛgendrāgama*. This has been published and translated. He also composed several other Āgama commentaries, not yet published.

Mṛgendrāgama-vṛtti-dīpikā (Subrahmanya Sastri 1928; Hulin 1980)
Dviśatikālottarāgama-vṛtti
Sarvajñānottarāgama-vṛtti
Mohaśurottarāgama-vṛtti

Scholars affiliated with the French Institute in Pondicherry are currently editing the *Dviśatikālottarāgamavṛtti* and the *Sarvajñānottarāgamavṛtti*.

The clearest and most systematic expositions of the metaphysical and theological premises (*jñāna*) of the Śaiva Siddhānta order in Sanskrit are found not in the Āgamas themselves, but rather in a series of works ascribed to human authors who wrote in the ninth through eleventh centuries. The earliest and most important of these Śaiva philosophical system-builders was Sadyojyoti, but other important authors include Bhojadeva and several of the Kashmiri authors in the Kaṇṭha lineage. Eight of their brief works were bundled together as the *Aṣṭaprakaraṇa*, the "Eight Treatises." Aghoraśiva wrote commentaries on six of them.

Aṣṭaprakaraṇa (Dvivedi 1988)

(1) *Tattvaprakāśa* of Bhojadeva, with *vṛtti* of Aghoraśiva (Filliozat 1971, Gengnagel 1996)
(2) *Tattvasangraha* of Sadyojyoti, with *ṭīkā* of Aghoraśiva (Filliozat 1988)
(3) *Tattvatrayanirṇaya* of Sadyojyoti, with *vyākhya* of Aghoraśiva (Filliozat 1991, Davis 2000)
(4) *Nādakārikā* of Bhaṭṭa Rāmakaṇṭha, with *vrtti* of Aghoraśiva (Filliozat 1984)
(5) *Bhogakārikā* of Sadyojyoti, with *vṛtti* of Aghoraśiva (Borody 2005)
(6) *Ratnatrayaparīkṣā* of Sadyojyoti, with *vṛtti* of Aghoraśiva

In the Śaiva Siddhānta perspective, correct knowledge (*jñāna*) is necessary for efficacious action (*kriyā*), just as correct action reciprocally gives rise to a more effective understanding of things. So it was natural for a preceptor like Aghoraśiva to compose both theological works and practical guides to ritual action.

Aghoraśiva's works on ritual practice employ a straight-forward, step-by-step exposition and a technical vocabulary with little or no elaboration or argumentation. They appear as the works of a well-established mature teacher offering practical guidance to other worshipers of Śiva. The *Kriyākramadyotikā* stands as his major comprehensive work in this genre, and with its additions as the *Mahā-Kriyākramadyotikā* this would constitute a comprehensive ritual Paddhati covering the major liturgical procedures in the Śaiva system.

Evidently this was not his only work in the area of ritual practice. Scholars at the French Institute have recently recovered a work of Aghoraśiva devoted to the meditative visualization of Sadāśiva, the highest visible form of Śiva.

Pañcāvaraṇastava (Goodall et al. 2005)

As an eminent author in the area of Śaiva Siddhānta, the name of Aghoraśiva has also been a magnet for spurious works. Compositions by later authors have been attributed to Aghoraśiva, such as the *Parārthanityapūjāvidhi* (Brunner 1999). As we have seen, other works identified as works of Aghoraśiva, such as the published *Śivaliṅgapratiṣṭhāvidhi* probably consist in Aghoraśiva's original composition mixed with later interpolations.

A more complete study of this central figure in the development of Śaiva Siddhānta as an integrated system of theology and ritual practice would make a major contribution to the historical study of Indian religions.

Translation

In his ritual works Aghoraśiva addresses a select audience of pious initiated worshipers of Śiva, who follow the Śaiva Siddhānta school of knowledge and action. To this audience he seeks to provide guidance as to the proper or best method of ritual practice or *kriyā*. In the *Mahotsavavidhi* he speaks to an even more restricted audience: one who is qualified to act as a chief priest in a Śaiva temple festival, an *ācārya* or preceptor. Such a priest would be a male qualified by birth in an appropriate Śaiva brāhmaṇa *gotra*, and would have undergone a sequence of initiations and a consecration (*ācāryābhiṣeka*) that confer on him the capacity to perform Śaiva ritual "on behalf of others" (*parārtha*). In addition to these genetic and initiatory qualifications, the *ācārya* would have acquired a significant practical education as a working priest, by performing the countless ritual actions that make up the liturgical program of a Śaiva temple.

Aghoraśiva was himself an *ācārya*, and he composed his text for those who were competent in the shared ritual culture of the medieval Śaiva temple. The *Mahotsavavidhi* is, as its title implies, a text of injunctions or prescriptions (*vidhi*) leading to action. The characteristic verb form is the third person singular optative. The addressee or priest "should" or "ought to" do such and such an action. Occasionally he adopts causative optative forms. The priest should direct others to perform such and such a rite. Aghoraśiva provides guidance for an ideal nine-day *mahotsava* to an ideal priest capable of putting the advice into practice himself and directing others to do so.

Having an ideal priest as an intended audience makes the text far from ideal from a translator's point of view. Aghoraśiva assumes that his addressee will be able to turn terse technical directions into ritual activity. The author and his audience share a technical code, a highly specific vocabulary of ritual practice. The translator is not an ideal priest, however, and the scholarly audience for which this translation is intended has (I am reasonably certain) no intention of putting Aghoraśiva's directives for a great festival into practice. The task of the translator in such a case is intelligibility, and to become comprehensible the technical vocabulary needs to be unpacked. One needs to fill in, for a non-expert reader, at least some of the tacit knowledge that Aghoraśiva's original audience would have brought to their hearing or reading and practical employment of the text.

To explicate the terms and procedures of the *Mahotsavavidhi* in this translation, I make extensive use of footnotes. In this I follow the lead of the great pioneer in translating Śaiva ritual texts, Hélène Brunner. The goal is not simply to translate the words, but to provide at least some sense of the practices to which those words point. This requires locating other texts that explain or amplify what Aghorasiva's text leaves unstated. My aim has been to select works that are close in outlook to Aghoraśiva. The chronology of Śaiva Siddhānta ritual texts is still at a relatively preliminary stage of study, so it is not always possible to be certain what texts would have been available or known to a twelfth-century priest in southern India. To find explanatory materials I have preferred two starting points: the earlier portions of the *Kriyākramadyotikā* and the anthology of Āgama texts in *Mahotsavavidhikrama Āgamaśekhara*. The others works I have found most valuable have been Brunner's richly annotated volumes of the *Somaśambhupaddhati* and the Chola-period *śilpaśāstra*, the *Mayamata* translated by Bruno Dagens. I have also made use of the excellent critical editions of Āgamas of N. R. Bhatt and others at the French Institute as needed.

Lawrence Hoffman, a scholar of Jewish liturgical studies, has urged others in his field to move beyond a fixation with textual studies, and to seek to recover also "the worshiping community that lives beyond the text (1987: 19)." In the field of Śaiva studies, an enormous amount of fundamental textual work remains still to be done. My annotated translation of the *Mahotsavavidhi* is intended as one contribution to this basic presentation of texts. But I am also sympathetic to Hoffman's call. Aghoraśiva articulated his textual vision of an ideal nine-day Śaiva temple festival within a world of South Indian temple Hinduism of the twelfth century. The general Introduction that precedes the translation is an effort to reimagine the relationship between the *Mahotsavavidhi* and the medieval Śaiva "worshiping community" toward which Aghoraśiva originally directed it. In particular I wish to highlight the role of the festival procession as a form of public ceremonial and as a central feature in medieval South Indian temple ritual. I hope this can be seen as a contribution to a fuller historical understanding of Indian religious culture.

Introduction

In southern India, the most dramatic manifestations of public religiosity are the great annual temple festivals, known in Sanskrit as *mahotsava* or *brahmotsava* and in Tamil as *tiruviḻā*. During these immense cultural performances, gods resplendent in bright silk garments, brilliant gold ornaments, and colorful garlands of flowers parade forth from their stone temple sanctums like the splendid lords of the cosmos that their devotees believe them to be. The deities, physically present in bronze icons, process through the surrounding streets in palanquins carried on the shoulders of temple servants, or in grand wooden chariots drawn by hundreds of devoted laborers pulling on thick hemp ropes. Decorated oxen, elephants, and camels lead the way. Musicians proclaim the coming of the divine with rumbling drum beats and the piercing melodies of the double-reeded *nadasvaram*. Priests cool the deity with fans made of yak tails. Along the way the deities pause in their regal progress to receive the adulation and the presentations of their prosperous and grateful votaries. Welcoming the gods' visit on their streets, townsfolk light oil lamps, fold hands, and offer up coconuts, bananas, and flower garlands.

At major south Indian temples such as the Minakshi-Sundareshvara temple in Madurai, the Ranganatha temple in Sri Rangam, or the Nataraja temple at Chidambaram, festivals may last up to fifteen days with two processions each day. Each morning and evening the principal deities emerge from the temple shrines atop different "vehicles" (*vāhanas*) such as lion, bull, and elephant. These culminate in the great chariot processions (*ratha-yātrā*), where gods ride in gigantic carts that appear like moving shrines as they traverse the city streets. Crowds in the hundreds of thousands attend the largest of these chariot processions.[1]

Festival processions such as these have been a striking feature of southern Indian temple culture for over a millennium. In the time of the Pallavas of Kanchipuram and the Pandyas of Madurai, who ruled much of the Tamil region in the eighth and ninth centuries, devotional poet-saints like Campantar sang hymns of praise to the gods Śiva and Viṣṇu as they presented themselves during processions.

> The Lord of Cittīccaram shrine in Naṟaiyūr
> who has the river in his hair,
> the poison stain on his throat,
> and the Veda on his tongue,
> goes resplendent in ceremonial dress,
> as his devotees and perfected sages
> sing and dance his widespread fame,
> and the sound of festival drums
> beaten on the streets where the temple-car is pulled
> spreads on every side. (Peterson 1989: 183)

Under the Pallavas, devotional worship directed toward the great pan-Indian gods Śiva and Viṣṇu, organized around temples built of permanent stone, displaced earlier Vedic and heterodox ritual forms as the dominant mode of elite public religious practice in the Tamil region. Pallava-period bronze images meant for festival processions, and several inscriptions likewise indicate that the foundations for the distinctive south Indian forms of temple festivals were being established by the ninth century.

When the Chola dynasty controlled the Tamil regions in the tenth through the thirteenth centuries, however, the scale of Hindu temple construction increased significantly, and so too did the level and organization of worship conducted in these temples. By all indications, temple festivals expanded dramatically during this period as well. In his wide-ranging study of modern religious festivals in southern India and Sri Lanka, Paul Younger observes that hundreds of temple festivals follow a similar pattern. "Almost all are 10-day festivals," notes Younger (2002: 60), "they begin with the raising of the temple

[1] There are many ethnographic accounts and studies of modern south Indian temple festivals and processions. A brief list would include: De Neve 2000, Diehl 1956: 158–180, Good 2004, Harman 1989, Kaali 1999, L'Hernault and Reiniche 1999, Martin 1982, Pillay 1953, Waghorne 1992, and Younger 2002. Also see "Wedding of the Goddess," a documentary film of the Madurai Chittrai festival, filmed in 1972.

flag and the cutting of a sapling or the planting of a variety of grains in a pot of carefully mixed soils. In large temples, the daily processions of the deities on different *vāhanas* or carts climax on the final day with the pulling of a grand chariot with long hempen ropes." Because most of these festivals are celebrated in temples that date back to the Chola period, Younger postulates that the Chola administrators must have encouraged the new uniform patterns of festival practice. Promulgated broadly in the expanding temple culture of medieval south India, temple festivals of this type continue to be celebrated right up to the present day in many temples, albeit with myriad changes over time and adaptations to local circumstances.[2]

The World of Aghoraśiva

The *Mahotsavavidhi*, or "Procedures for the Great Festival," of the Śaiva preceptor Aghoraśiva offers a particularly rich depiction of south Indian temple festival practice from the Chola period. Composed by an eminent south Indian teacher of the mid-twelfth century, this work aims to convey clear and authoritative guidance for the Śaiva priests who would officiate at temple rites. In his brief Sanskrit text, Aghoraśiva articulates a priest's-eye vision of how an ideal festival should be enacted within any Śaiva temple. We cannot know the exact relationship this medieval text bore to existing temple practices, of course, but it is my view that this prescriptive work played a significant role in institutionalizing and disseminating a shared pattern for Śaiva temple festivals in medieval south India.

Temple Culture in Twelfth-Century Tamilnad

The first half of the twelfth century C.E., when Aghoraśiva lived and wrote, was an auspicious time for the development of Śaiva temple culture in central Tamilnad. The political consolidation of a large imperial polity under the eleventh-century Chola rulers Rajaraja I (r. 985–1012 C.E.) and Rajendra I (r. 1012–1044), and its relative dynastic stability following the accession of Kulottunga I in 1070, allowed for a lengthy period of cultural elaboration

[2] Historical studies of precolonial-period festivals of south India are relatively rare: see Hudson 1977 and 1982, and Younger 1995. A promising recent approach involves the use of inscriptions to trace developments in medieval south Indian temple culture, such as Orr 2004. Another approach, as here, is to use medieval litergical works. For south Indian Vaiṣṇava festivals, see Colas 1996. The unpublished dissertation of Barazer-Billoret (1999) is the most comprehensive survey to date of festival prescriptions in medieval Śaiva Āgama literature.

and institutionalization of Śaiva ritual practices and literatures. Succeeding Kulottunga I (r. 1070–1122), his son Vikrama Chola (r. 1118–1135), grandson Kulottunga II (r. 1130–1150), and great -grandson Rajaraja II (r. 1146 –1172) presided over a flourishing Chola domain for a century marked less by expansion or innovation than by consolidation and refinement.

Much of this cultural development centered around the god Śiva, Śaiva devotional literature, and the temples dedicated to his regular worship. We can see the results of this Śaiva consolidation, still today, in the physical remains of the massive stone temples and temple complexes of twelfth-century Tamilnad (Balasubrahmanyam 1979, Meister and Dhaky 1983) and in the elegant bronze images of the Śaiva deities that populate many museums (Dehejia 2002, Nagaswamy 1983, 2002). The enormous corpus of inscriptions carved onto the stone walls of the religious structures likewise serves as a sign of the abundance and diversity of Śaiva religious practice of the period (Orr 2006). Just as compelling are the written texts. The epic *Periya Purāṇam*, composed by the poet Cēkkiḻār at Chidambaram during the reign of Kulottunga II, narrates in Tamil verse the lives of the earlier *nāyanmārs*, Śaiva saints (Ramachandra 1990), at a time when the Tamil devotional songs of these saints, and their images, were being increasingly incorporated into temple liturgy (Orr 2007). At the same time, Aghoraśiva and other Śaiva preceptors sought to organize the varied Sanskritic Āgama tradition into a coherent program of ritual practice both for pious individual practitioners worshiping on their own behalf (*ātmārtha*) and for temple priests conducting services for others (*parārtha*). As scholars such as Karen Prentiss (1999) and Whitney Cox (2005) have noted, the Sanskritic Āgama-based and Tamil *bhakti*-oriented forms of Śaivism constituted a diverse and no doubt often contentious religious formation in twelfth-century Tamilnad. A full cultural or religious history of the period remains to be written, but here I wish to sketch a few relevant aspects for reimagining the religious landscape within which Aghoraśiva composed his work on *mahotsava*.

Chola rulers of this period evidently considered Śiva to be the "family god" (*kulanāyakar*) of the ruling lineage, especially in his form as Naṭarāja at Chidambaram. In the standard eulogy that introduces inscriptions of his reign, Vikrama Chola takes pride in his patronage of the great Śaiva temple at Chidambaram.

> [Vikarama Chola] covered with fine gold the enclosure, the gate-towers, ...lls and buildings surrounding the shrine of pure gold where his ...ly-god practices the *taṇḍava* dance . . . ; covered with splendid gold ...r on which offerings abound, so that the light of heaven was

> reflected; covered with pure gold and adorned with numerous strings of large round pearls the sacred car temple, in order that, conferring long life on the delighted people, the miraculous dancer [Nataraja] who occupies the golden hall might be drawn in procession at the great festival called the "festival of the great name" on the great days of Puraṭṭādi and Uttiraṭṭādi, so as to cause prosperity on the great earth and joy to the gods; was pleased to build a long temple street of mansions with jewels and called it after his royal prosperous name; and made numberless splendid insignia, beginning with dishes cut of fine gold, together with a Kalpa tree of pure gold. (Krishna Sastri 1929: 185)

It is clear that Vikrama directed much of his largesse toward the festivals of the temple. Vikrama is probably taking credit here for actions initiated by one of his ministers. Naralokaviran was a general in the Chola army during the reign of Kulottunga I, fought in several military campaigns, and became a subordinate fief-holder and court minister under Vikrama. He also engaged in vigorous benefactions at a number of important Śaiva temples, most notably at Chidambaram. He was responsible for the construction of two large temple gateways and for the expansion of the Goddess shrine within the Nataraja temple complex. It appears he took particular interest in the program of Nataraja festivals, for among his contributions are provisions for lamps on the processional routes, watering the streets during festivals, a pavilion near the ocean and a broad road leading to it for the bathing festival in Masi month, several bronze images meant for procession, a "bull-vehicle" for the deity to ride during the Bhikshatana procession, and a bugle inlaid with gold to herald the arrival of Śiva.[3] Vikrama Chola and Naralokaviran must have collaborated to promote the Nataraja temple at Chidambaram as the primary Śaiva center of south India.

While Vikrama Chola helped adorn the sacred car at Chidambaram so that Śiva might be drawn through the streets in procession, the Chola ruler also conducted his own festival-like royal processions. Vikrama's court-poet Oṭṭakkūttar composed a lengthy Tamil *ulā*, or processional poem, to celebrate such a royal procession through the Chola capital, the *Vikkiramcōḻaṉulā*. Subsequently Oṭṭakkūttar wrote two more for Vikrama's successors, Kulottunga II (*Kulōttuṅkacōḻaṉulā*) and Rajaraja II (*Irācarācacōḻaṉulā*) (Hart and Pai 2003,

[3] Naralokaviran's own inscription at Chidambaram details much of this: ARE 120 of 1888, published in Krishna Sastri 1923: 31–34. See Nilakanta Sastri 1932: 176–200 for a comprehensive study of Naralokaviran. Nagaswamy 2002 discusses the icons commissioned by Naralokaviran. Also see Younger 1995: 52 on his contributions to Chidambaram.

Irācārām 2000). As Daud Ali has observed, such poetic evocations of rulers on parade reflect important political practices of the period. "Early medieval kings," he observes, "performed much of their political action through processions. Their conquests were essentially processions around the quarters of the earth. When at peace, they spent much of their time travelling, in full array, within their kingdoms—a fact that required a number of palaces available to the royal family" (Ali 1996: 187). At the same time, the royal *ulās* of the twelfth century Chola rulers point to a cultural practice shared by Śaiva temple and Chola court, in which the visual display of lordship was realized most powerfully within the public procession of god and king.

While Chidambaram received the pious attention of the Chola court, many other temples throughout the Chola dominion also expanded through local patronage. Under Rajaraja II, a major new imperial temple was constructed at Darasuram, near Kumbhakonam. Smaller than the massive royal temple structures built a century or more earlier at Thanjavur and Gangaikondacholapuram, the Darasuram Rajarajaesvara temple illustrates several of the main tendencies in Chola architecture and sculpture of the twelfth century, as do the additions to the existing Nataraja temple at Chidambaram. Twelfth-century temple construction showed a greater emphasis on ornamentation and sculptural embellishment. Shrines devoted to the Goddess grew in size and prominence. Outlying temple gateways rose in height and importance, and in many cases began to overshadow the main *vimānas* at the center. Ancillary pavilions around the primary sanctuaries proliferated. Śaiva temples became temple complexes. As Crispin Branfoot (2001: 191) observes, "Tamil temples from the twelfth or thirteenth century onwards were often large walled complexes of structures rather than individual buildings, with multiple shrines, long corridors, several concentric walled enclosures entered through towering pyramidal gateways (*gopurams*) and various pillared halls (*maṇḍapas*)." Many of these new structures were designed specifically to serve the needs of festivals.

On an outer wall of the royal temple at Darasuram stands a row of ninety-five small images of Śaiva priests. Each stands with hands folded in homage to the god inside the temple. The sculpted priests are individually identified; inscriptions give their names, often both birth-name and initiatory name, and the villages or towns from which they hailed. The priests' names clearly identify them as Śaiva *ācāryas*. There are twenty-four Īśānaśivas, nineteen Aghoraśivas, six Hṛdayaśivas, and other repeating *dīkṣā-nāmas* typical of the Śaiva Siddhānta order. Why have these figures been enshrined here? The archeologist P. R. Srinivasan (1987: 20–21) suggests that the human prototypes of all these Śaiva preceptor images may have participated in the consecration of Rajaraja's imperial temple. Such a grand enterprise must have drawn the foremost Śaiva priests of the Chola region. We can imagine Aghoraśiva, author of the *Mahotsavavidhi*, as one of the nineteen Aghoraśivas attending the event, whose small images are fixed in permanent worship at Darasuram.

Aghoraśiva's Guide for Priests

Aghorasiva was a Śaiva-brāhmaṇa *ācārya* (preceptor) of the Kauḍinya clan. He traced his spiritual lineage back to the legendary sage Durvāsas, through a series of Śaiva teachers in many parts of India, up to his initiating guru Sarvātmaśiva, also known as Hṛdayaśambhu. Aghoraśiva identified himself in one work as a teacher "who adorns the Chola region," and a persistent tradition links him with the Śaiva center of Chidambaram. According to one legend, Durvāsas himself appeared before Aghoraśiva at Chidambaram to officiate at his priestly consecration (*ācāryābhiṣeka*) there. On the outskirts of Chidambaram is an Aghoraśivācārya Matha, supposedly founded by the master himself (Davis 1992, Goodall 1998, Surdam 1984).

Aghoraśiva composed numerous works, including commentaries on Āgamas and explications of philosophical works. These works adhere to the dualistic school of Śaiva knowledge and action known as Śaiva Siddhānta, or "Perfected Śaivism." Several works of poetry and a drama are attributed to Aghoraśiva as well, though no manuscripts have been found of these works. Most important for our purposes, he composed a lengthy ritual manual entitled the *Kriyākramadyotikā*, or "Light on Ritual Procedures," also known as the *Aghoraśiva Paddhati*. The *Mahotsavavidhi* translated here identifies itself as part of Aghoraśiva's larger Paddhati.

Aghoraśiva states at the outset of the *Kriyākramadyotikā* (hereafter *KKD*) that his purpose in composing the Paddhati is "to clarify the daily and other rituals." The use of the word *dyotikā*, light or illumination, in his title likewise points to Aghoraśiva's desire to elucidate a program of proper practice, within the large and varied corpus of Śaiva ritual literature. He bases his work on the Śaiva Āgamas, a corpus of Sanskrit works that spelled out Śaiva ritual practices in profuse detail. The Āgamas present themselves as the direct teachings of Śiva himself. Paddhatis like that of Aghoraśiva, by contrast, are works by human authors that seek to articulate a more unified Śaiva system of ritual practice amid the diverse teachings of the Āgamas. Aghoraśiva writes in prose, rather than the verse of most Āgamas, and he sets forth procedures in a straightforward sequential manner. He does not generally comment on the significance of these actions within the *KKD*, though one can gain a strong sense of the larger Śaiva Siddhānta theology within which he grounded his ritual work from his philosophical commentaries.

The commentator Nirmalamaṇi glosses "daily and other rituals" as denoting the three categories of ritual: daily or regular (*nitya*) actions such as bathing rites and daily worship of the Śiva-liṅga, occasional (*naimittika*) acts such as initiation or consecration of icons or temples, and optional rites to gain desired ends (*kāmya*) such as a ritual for procuring a son. The published *KKD*, including Nirmalamaṇi's commentary, covering some 487 pages, encompasses daily ritual (*nityakarman*), annual rites of completion and expiation, and several types of spiritual initiations (*dīkṣā*). However, it appears that the *KKD* was originally still larger, for several other works of a similar style by Aghoraśiva also identify themselves as portions of the *KKD*. The colophon of the *Mahotsavavidhi* states unambiguously that it is a part of the *KKD* composed by the preceptor Aghoraśiva.

The *Mahotsavavidhi* addresses itself to an initiated Śaiva preceptor acting as chief priest or master of ceremonies at a Śaiva temple festival. Aghoraśiva refers to this master as *guru* (teacher), *ācārya* (preceptor), and *deśika* (guide). He sets forth the procedures such a priest should follow in conducting a nine-day festival. Although he recognizes *mahotsavas* of other lengths, Aghoraśiva considers the nine-day festival as "the best of all types" of *mahotsava*.

Aghoraśiva's prescriptions are not specific to a particular temple, but rather are intended to provide general guidelines for Śaiva festivals at any temple with the necessary resources. During the time of Aghoraśiva, as we have seen, major temple complexes like Darasuram and Chidambaram were being constructed or expanded. The *mahotsava* that Aghoraśiva prescribes could be performed at one of these Śaiva centers, but it could just as readily be adapted to smaller temples or local shrines. The author uses phrases such as *yathāśakti* ("according to one's capacities") to indicate the need to adjust the scale of festival activities to the institution and the resources available. Throughout the procedures, he emphasizes the need to construct new ritual spaces, often temporary structures that exist only for the duration of the festival.

Aghoraśiva assumes that his priestly audience is knowledgeable in the basic procedures of Śaiva ritual practice, and frequently employs technical shorthand for complex actions, with confidence that the competent priest will know how to carry out the appropriate acts. At the same time, because Aghoraśiva focuses his attention on the conduct of priests during the festival, he omits from his prescriptions many aspects of festival activity about which we might like to know more. Presumably these were matters outside of the control of priests, or issues best left to local choice or negotiation. As large-scale social events, festivals require the active contributions and participation of many persons, who bring their own forms of specialized knowledge and their own perspectives. Within the complex agency of a festival, the chief priest's voice may be important, but it is by no means the only one.

Although we cannot use Aghoraśiva's priestly guide uncritically as a description of any actual festival performances of the twelfth or any other century, we can see in the *Mahotsavavidhi* the procedural guide of an erudite and influential Śaiva preceptor of the Chola period as to how a chief priest ought ideally to conduct a temple festival. He writes within the tradition of Śaiva Āgama literature, restating and at times reformulating procedures prescribed by Śiva in existing Āgamas. At the same time, I would argue, he composes with an awareness of the varied temple practices that existed around him throughout the Chola dominions. In my view, Aghoraśiva seeks to articulate a systematic and comprehensive outline of festival activities, to guide an officiating Śaiva priest, that could be realized and adapted to local circumstances prevalent in the twelfth century, and that would at the same time put into practice certain universal Śaiva Siddhānta principles.

Whether Aghoraśiva would realize these practical aims in composing the *Mahotsavavidhi* would depend on his audience, of course. Aghoraśiva uses the term *vidhi* (rule, ordinance) in his title, pointing to an injunctive force in his prescriptions. However, we must leave open the question of how fully the *Mahotsavavidhi*, or any Āgama procedural guide, actually informed the practices of priests or other Śaiva initiates in the Chola period or any other time. The Āgamas at least had the authority of Śiva's authorship to recommend them. A human-authored Paddhati like Aghoraśiva's *KKD* had to rely on its clarity of presentation and on the prestige of its author. Aghoraśiva certainly did enjoy the esteem of other Śaivas. One pupil extols the teacher's comprehensive knowledge:

> the supreme *deśika*, Aghoraśivācārya, who is known on this earth by the other great name of Parameśvara, skilled in all the *śāstras*, beginning with those of the Vaiśeṣika school, the master of the Vedas, possessed of complete knowledge of Nyāya, full of wisdom, considered as the foremost of those whose names are equated with Śiva. (Surdam 1984: 271 n. 175)

The ritual works of Aghoraśiva have indeed had, as Hélène Brunner has observed, a remarkable impact on temple practices of southern India over centuries. "It is in reciting this manual [the *KKD*]," she noted, "that Śaiva priests of Tamilnad even today still carry out the actions of their ritual (1977: 110)." Scholars of south Indian Śaivism such as Brunner, N. R. Bhatt, and S. S. Janaki have recognized Aghoraśiva's ritual manual as the single most influential guide for the modern performance of Śaiva worship.

I would like to suggest that the *Mahotsavavidhi* is more than just a procedural guide for practicing priests. The text presents a vision of the *mahotsava* as a congregative event that brings together masses of human devotees and multitudes of gods. As Aghoraśiva presents it, the festival enacts an orderly hierarchical cosmos orbiting around the central lord Śiva, activated by the ritual practices of priests and other knowledgeable specialists, and filled with the devotional joy of all beings able to participate in Śiva's world. For a time, the festival transforms the surrounding community into a veritable Śiva-city.

In the remainder of the Introduction, I discuss some of the central categories and key themes in Aghoraśiva's prescriptions for the nine-day festival, as an orientation to the translation of his text., I begin with the term I have been translating as "festival."

Utsava and *Mahotsava*

In his fourteenth-century hagiography of the Chidambaram Nataraja temple, *Koyil Purāna*, the Śaiva teacher Umāpati praises the annual celebration of *Maci Makam*.

> When the Lord goes in procession the devotees feel joy and shed tears of joy. Setting aside heavenly bliss the gods long to come for Śiva's procession, and praising it worship with hands folded. . . . As the procession passes by, the clouds, which had been sleeping in the pine trees, suddenly rise up and the pine needles fall onto the flowers below, spilling honey like rain upon the road below. The humming of the bees in the flowers blends in with the chatter of the birds in every direction. The assembly of worshipers grows continually, and the tears from their eyes hang like strings of pearls. Around the trident of the Lord are the rulers of all the earth with their weapons and their armies. The gods play their musical instruments, and all the people of the earth perform their different duties as they worship. (Younger 1995: 53)

Describing Śiva's procession to the sea, Umāpati glorifies the special atmosphere of devotional joy and congregative celebration characteristic of south Indian temple festivals. When Śiva comes forth from the temple, as Umāpati would have it, all humans, kings, gods, and even nature itself seek to participate and lend their particular talents in honoring the Lord.

The most common term for these occasions, *utsava* is generally translated as "festival." The English word festival derives from the Latin word for a feast, and then comes to connote the festive mood of joy and plentitude that accompanies such special meals. The Sanskrit *utsava* likewise refers to various special celebrations associated with that festive mood, both secular and sacred.[4] But in the Āgamas the term is employed more specifically to denote a set of temple ceremonies. While the south Indian temple *utsava* does at times involve grand feasts and the sharing of food among a broad community, this is not its defining feature. The characteristic mark of the *utsava*, as Umāpati indicates, is the procession of the deity, when god becomes accessible to all. The living presence of the gods, rather than the pleasures of eating, is the principal cause of joy and festivity.

Though less descriptive than Umāpati, the Śaiva Āgamas extol the *utsava* for its many benefits. *Kāraṇāgama* (*pūrva* 141.1–2) links the term *sava*, from the root *su* (to set in motion), with Śiva's fundamental activity of *sṛṣṭi*, emanation or creation. *Ut-sava*, then, is that by which Śiva's creative activity is manifested or made visible (*ud-bhūta*). The *Vijayottarāgama* defines the term by its enlightening effects on those who perform it: "The *utsava* is that which extricates the creatures who have fallen into the stain of ignorance from their bondage, and thereby it brings about the manifestation of their power of knowledge" (Ganesan 2005: 4). Or, as *Ajitāgama* (25.1) puts it more broadly, the *utsava* prevents all misfortunes and brings prosperity to the worlds.

The Śaiva Āgamas provide procedures for several different types of *utsava*. The most common is the regular "daily festival" (*nityotsava*), performed as a concluding part of daily worship one or more times each day. Other units of time also have their own festivals. In a later section of *Mahotsavavidhi*, Aghoraśiva speaks of weekly festivals (*varotsava*), fortnightly festivals (*pakṣotsava*), monthly festivals (*māsotsava*), and festivals coordinated with particular alignments of the stars (*ṛkṣotsava*). Finally, there are the annual "great festivals" (*mahotsava*), which may last as many as fifteen days, according to the *Ajitāgama* (27.2–7), or still longer, according to other Āgama texts. Aghoraśiva's central

[4] See Gonda 1975 for a general exploration of the term *utsava*. Anderson 1993 offers an interesting sustained inquiry into the classical "Spring Festival" (*vasantotsava*) of India. Here, as generally in northern India, *utsava* refers to a great variety of festive ceremonies, for the most part not associated with temples. However, Anderson also describes a south Indian text of the Vijayanagara period, Ahobala's *Virūpākṣavasantotsavacampū*, where the *vasantotsava* has been adapted as a Śaiva temple *mahotsava* (1993: 171–97).

aim in *Mahotsavavidhi* is to set out an ideal method for temple priests in conducting a nine-day *mahotsava.*

Daily *Utsava*

Aghorasiva does not describe the daily festival in his *Kriyākramadyotikā*, but many Āgamas that deal with temple worship do discuss it.[5] One should consider the daily festival, states the *Kāmikāgama*, as a part or "limb" of daily worship (*nityapūjā*) in Śaiva temples (*UKĀ* 5.1). After the priest has completed his ritual services directed toward Śiva present in the Śiva-liṅga (called the *acalamūrti* or "immobile body") fixed within the central sanctum of the temple, he shifts his attention to another icon imbued with the presence of Śiva. This is a mobile body (*calamūrti*) made of metal, most often in the form of Paśupati, Śiva as "Lord of All Creatures." Śiva's manifestation in this image, and in other portable icons, enables the Lord to move beyond the restricted space of the temple sanctum. During *nityotsava*, Śiva Paśupati goes out in procession. The icon makes a circumambulatory tour (*pradakṣiṇa*) around the outer precincts of the temple complex or beyond the walls of the temple through the surrounding community. Śiva's movement outward is the defining feature of the *nityotsava* and of all other Śaiva temple *utsavas*. Through his movement Śiva makes himself present and visible to all devotees, including those ordinarily unable to enter the temple.[6] As *Kāraṇāgama* sees it, Śiva undertakes *utsava* processions "for the rogues, birds, and animals who are not initiated, as well as for initiates and devotees " (Sabharatna Sivacarya 1988: 93).

According to *Ajitāgama's* account of *nityotsava*, Paśupati is the main daily processional form of Śiva, but other icons and implements may also accompa-

[5] Aghorasiva does not treat *nityotsava* in KKD's *nityakarman* section because his concern in that portion of the text is to specify "worship on one's own behalf" (*ātmārthapūjā*), rather than the public worship conducted by priests in temples "on behalf of others" (*parārthapūjā*). Private worship does not require *nityotsava*, as does public worship. There is an interesting account of *nityotsava* in the *Parārthanityapūjāvidhi*, a text that has traditionally been attributed to Aghoraśiva. However, both Hélène Brunner (1999) and Ginnette Ishimatsu (2000) show convincingly that this is not a composition of the twelfth-century Aghoraśiva. See Brunner 1999: 307–11 for a French translation of the *nityotsava* account in *Parārthapūjāvidhi.*

[6] Some medieval Śaiva texts such as *Suprabhedāgama* and Rāmakaṇṭha's *Jātinirṇayapūrvakālayapraveśavidhi* depict temple entry regulations according to an elaborate hierarchy of space.

> Śaiva brāhmaṇa priests worship in the sanctum. Initiatied non-Ādiśaiva brahmins worship in the entry-passage. Common brahmins reciting the Vedas worship in the fore-pavilion. Sacrificers, ascetics, and renouncers worship in the main pavilion. *Kṣatriyas* and *vaiśyas* worship in the door pavilion. *Śūdras* who have received liberating initiation worship in the outer pavilion. *Śūdras* who have received common initiation worship in the dance pavilion. And initiates of other classes should worship at the door of the entry tower. (*Suprebhedāgama*, quoted in Bhatt, n.d. p. 2)

See also Filliozat 1975. Davis 1991: 69–72 discusses temple space in terms of Śaiva Siddhānta principles.

ny Śiva in his tour. Depending on the scale of the ceremony, the members of Śiva's entouage may include Gaṇeśa, Umāmāheśvara (Śiva seated with Umā), the Trident, a Śiva-liṅga made of rice, the metal liṅga-covering (*golaka*), Śiva's sandals (*paduka*), the bull Nandin, and Caṇḍeśa (*AĀ* 27.3–4). The text goes on to rank *nityotsava* rites in nine gradations, from best to worst, according to the number of figures in the entourage. The best has all nine participants, while the minimal one features only Paśupati. The priest and temple servants raise each onto an appropriate conveyance, and carry them forth with pomp and celebratory noise.

> With a tumult of conches and kettle-drums, accompanied by incense and lamps, with parasols and yak-tail fans, accompanied by peacock-feather fans and banners, with song and dance accompanied by auspicious rhythms, and all the rest, the Lord should leave the temple and make a circumambulation outside. (*AĀ* 27.25–26)

Ajitāgama recommends both an outside procession and an inside procession, with visits to each of the eight directions inside the temple walls. At each stop, the drummers accompanying the procession play a distinctive rhythm suited to the divine guardian of that direction. At the completion of the *nityotsava*, the mobile icons return to their accustomed places inside the temple.

Monthly and Other *Utsavas*

The daily festival may form the simplest paradigm for *utsava* practices in Śaiva temples, but it is not the only type of festival by any means. In his section on "Monthly and Other Festivals," Aghoraśiva provides brief guidelines for several other categories of festivals linked to specific temporal units or transitions:

1. festivals at solar transitions (*saṅkrānti*), as when the sun shifts from its northern to southern courses and from southern to northern;
2. monthly festivals (*māsotsava*);
3. fortnightly festivals (*pakṣotsava*) on days of lunar transition, that is, the new-moon festival (*amāvāsyotsava*) and the full-moon festival (*paurṇamāsotsava*);
4. festivals related to the stars (*ṛkṣotsava*), specifically held at the moon's transition from one constellation or lunar mansion (*nakṣatra*) to another; and
5. weekly festivals (*varotsava*) linked to the day of the week on which Śiva's star, Ardra, falls.

Aghoraśiva includes technical instructions for calculating the timing of each of these, drawn probably from other specialist astronomical literature.

Aghoraśiva only outlines the conduct of these relatively simple festivals. In general they involve honoring the deities with special baths (*abhiṣeka, snāpana*) and sumptuous feeding, processions of the portable icons either within the temple complex or beyond it through the town, and final concluding rites of illumination (*nīrājana*). Officiating priests would be required to fill in the details from their own practical knowledge and from other texts.

For the conduct of special baths (*snāpana*), priests might rely on an Āgama such as *Rauravāgama* (chs. 20–24), which provides a clear account for baths with nine pots up to those with 1009. In each case the priest should mark out a geometrical design with the set number of squares. In each square he would set up a decorated water pot, and add specific substances to the water in each pot. He recites mantras to invoke different deities or powers into each one. The officiant honors all of them, and then has each pot poured over the central Śiva-liṅga, or over some other designated recipient. According to *Rauravāgama*, a bath of 108 pots would be particularly suitable on occasions of solar transitions.[7]

Aghoraśiva gives only brief guidelines for the conduct of processions in these festivals. For the festival of the full moon, to take one example, the priest has a group of processional icons that includes Gaṇeśa, Somāskanda, and other deities—probably the five icons that constitute the standard processional set—ornamented and led on a circumambulation either of the temple or the larger community, accompanied by musical instruments. The primary processional form of Śiva is specified as Somāskanda for the festivals of solar transition. For festivals involving the moon's movements such as *pakṣotsava*, Aghoraśiva does not say which processional form of Śiva should make the procession, but modern temple practice suggests it may be Candraśekhara, Śiva wearing the moon in his crown.

The Āgamas also describe a number of special festival observances that may be performed at particular times of the year. For example, in the springtime month of Māsi the *ḍolotsava* involves placing decorated images of Śiva and his consort on a swing for their pleasure. The *Sūkṣmāgama* describes a festival where images of Śiva and the Goddess are taken to the sea or another body of water to go fishing (*matysalīlā*), and another where the divine couple go to collect pearls from the sea (*mauktigrahaṇa*).[8]

---

[7] *RĀ* 23.1–2. For a brief procedural discussion, see Davis 1991: 64–69. For more detailed diagrams and discussion of substances and deities for the 108-pot bath, see *Rauravāgama*: Dagens and Barazer-Billoret 2000 1: 101–4.

[8] See Ganesan 2005 for a sketch of many such festivities. I am grateful to him for sharing this unpublished lecture manuscript with me.

Of all festivals, the *mahotsava* or annual "great festival" is the grandest by far. It stretches over many days, up to fifteen days or even longer, according to some Āgamas. During this festival time a complex set of ritual activities is performed: twice-daily processions, raising and lowering the festival banner, regular fire oblations in a special sacrificial hall, bathing ceremonies, special offerings of tribute, performances of dance and music, recitations of mantras and hymns, honoring of myriad deities, giving of gifts and honoraria, and much else. In its organization, the *mahotsava* encompasses the entire system of Śaiva ritual within itself.

In the *Mahotsavavidhi*, Aghoraśiva provides paradigmatic instructions for a nine-day *mahotsava*. It can be celebrated in any month, and performed at any Śaiva temple. No doubt priests would have adapted Aghoraśiva's guidelines to the specific circumstances of their local temples.

The Structure of the *Mahotsava*

The *mahotsava* takes place during a set amount of time, ranging from one day up to seventeen days. Aghoraśiva selects nine days as the preferred duration. The *mahotsava* may take place in any month, but within each lunar month Aghoraśiva specifies a particular *nakṣatra* or lunar asterism on which the festival ought best to conclude. However, he also acknowledges that local temple circumstances—such as the temple's location, the date of its founding, or the *nakṣatras* of significant personages—may also be used to determine the timing of the festival.

Festival time, once determined, is set apart from ordinary time in many ways. The temple and its environs are to be renovated for the festival. For the duration of the *mahotsava*, priests and other key participants are expected to observe an ascetic regimen. They should limit their meals to one per day, sleep on the ground, abstain from sexual intercourse, and bathe three times per day, Aghoraśiva recommends. Many of the participants wear special protective wristlets during that period. Further, Aghoraśiva specifies that other types of new ceremonial undertakings, such as weddings or the foundation of villages or temples, should not occur during festival time.

Āgamas generally organize the myriad complex actions of the *mahotsava* into eighteen principal rites or divisions (*bheda*). At the start of *Mahotsavavidhi*, Aghoraśiva cites one such list of constituent parts of the festival from the *Kāmikāgama*. These divisions correspond to the section divisions in the published edition of the *Mahotsavavidhi* of Aghoraśiva, and I follow them in the translation. Marie-Luce Barazer-Billoret usefully suggests that the festival may be further organized around four major ritual cycles: (1) inaugural rites, (2) twice-daily ritual activities, (3) the *tīrtha* cycle, and (4) rites of closure. A few events fall outside this organization, which she labels "additional ceremonies" (Barazer-Billoret 2000: 107).

Inaugural Rites

A special flag marks the beginning and end of the festival period. It is raised (*dhvajārohana*) to open the festival and lowered (*dhvajāvarohana*) to conclude it. In Aghoraśiva's time, raising the flag involved first of all the careful selection, preparation, and erection of a wooden pole to serve as flagstaff (sections 3–4). In the centuries since, most large temples have erected permanent metal flagpoles, and so they no longer require this annual installation rite for the pole. For *mahotsavas* devoted to Śiva, the central insignia on the temple flag will be Nandin, Śiva's bull mount. Aghoraśiva provides careful instructions for designing the banner, and then for invoking the divine presence of Nandin into his painted image (section 7). The actual raising of the flag is a dramatic moment, accompanied by auspicious mantras and the sounds of drums, conches, and other resounding instruments (section 8). When the flag is raised, the chief priest announces, "the festival that is to be done is now taking place."

In addition to the raising of the Nandin banner, other rites assist in setting the festival in motion. One is the sprouting of auspicious seeds (*aṅkurārpana*), a ceremony intended to insure the fruitfulness and success of the entire festival. This simple ritual requires gathering earth in vessels (section 5), and planting seeds in them (section 6). The germinated sprouts are later incorporated into other festival rites, such as the final bathing ceremony.

Another inaugural ceremony, to which Aghoraśiva devotes considerable attention, features drumming and dancing. Texts call this the *bherītāḍana* (beating of the *bherī* drum) or the *navasandhinṛtta* (dance at the nine corners), and they prescribe that it be performed in the evening after the raising of the flag (section 9). After the priest consecrates the main festival drum, the chief drummer receives it and taps out a particular rhythmic pattern, the *nanditāla*. The priest then issues invitations to all deities, all living beings, and even the oceans and mountains to attend the festival. The high-raised banner, the resounding drum, and the proclamations of the priest all broadcast the advent of the festival as an inclusive, congregative event. The priest, the drummer, and the temple dancers then make a circuit of the temple grounds. At a central location (*brahmasthāna*) and then at all eight corners of the temple grounds, the priest honors the guardians of the directions, the drummer beats different rhythms, and the dancers perform distinctive dances at each one. The festival is fully in motion.

Daily Festival Observances

The central and most conspicuous ritual events over the course of the festival are the regular twice-daily processions (section 14). These are the defining acts of the south Indian temple festival. Each morning and evening the deities, in the form of mobile processional icons (*utsavamūrtis*), take a journey outward (*yāna, yātrā*) from the temple, make a circumambulation (*pradakṣiṇa*) of the surrounding community, and then return to the temple. The primary divine figure of the procession is Śiva, most often in his familial form as Somāskanda, or "Śiva with Umā and Skanda." The god is ornamented with a full suite of jewelry and dressed in beautiful colored cloth, then adorned with garlands of flowers. Further, Śiva goes out surrounded by the familiar Indic insignia of royalty, namely, the parasol, the yak-tail fan, and the banner. Those who see the procession should be reminded of Śiva's cosmic sovereignty.

The Lord Śiva does not parade alone. Accompanying Somāskanda are the closest members of his household or court: his sons Gaṇeśa and Skanda, his wife Pārvatī, and his favored devotee Caṇḍeśa. These are the standard set of five for south Indian Śaiva temple processions, but Aghoraśiva adds to this group the bull mount Nandin, Śailādi, and the Devotees. Aghoraśiva also specifies the humans who should accompany the procession: chief priest, ruler, temple priests, Vedic brahmins, musicians and dancers, temple servants, and various members of the Śaiva community. Aghoraśiva observes that it is highly beneficial to walk with Śiva's procession.

During the processions, deities encounter worshipers outside the controlled environment of the temple sanctum. It is a moment of inclusion, since even those normally excluded from worshiping inside the temple may gain a direct view of the gods. It is also, as Umāpati's celebration of the Chidambaram procession suggests, an occasion for excitement, joy, and intense emotional devotion. Writing a practical guide for priests, Aghoraśiva does not consider devotional responses to the advent of the Lord outside temple walls to be his concern. However, in the procedures he prescribes there are indications that these divine processional journeys, in addition to all the opportunities for emotional connection they provide devotees, are also felt to pose dangers for the deities. Before the processions, priests tie special protective cords (*rakṣasūtras*) around the wrists of the festival icons (section 12). At the end of each procession, they perform a rite of illumination (*nīrājana*) for the returning deities as a purification or protection from any ill effects of the journey (section 15). At the close of the festival the priest offers a final pacification (*śānti*) consisting of three separate fire-rites, to ward off any lingering ritual errors or other undesirable consequences contracted during the festival (section 28). These concluding rites insure that Śiva and the other deities return to the inner sanctum in a proper state of purity and self-possession.

During each procession, Śiva rides a different conveyance. These may be palanquin, swing, or chariot, or they make take the form of animals (lion, swan, snake, bull, elephant, horse), other beings (*bhūta*, Rāvaṇa), or a variety of other vehicles (*vāhana*). Aghoraśiva sets out a specific program of conveyances for the nine days and eighteen processions, which add variety and color to the daily routines of the festival.

Within the program of processions, the festival also includes special events that supplement the regular pattern and provide further variety. On the fourth night, Aghoraśiva prescribes that the deity be taken on a perambulation (*pariveṣaṇa*) through a pleasant garden or forest grove, accompanied by song and dance, to give the Lord pleasure (section 14a). On the sixth day, and again on the ninth day, there is a festival of powder (*cūrṇotsava*), involving the preparation of special colored powders that are then sprinkled or smeared on icons and human participants (section 17). On the eighth evening, the troupe of temple women known as Rudragaṇikās accompany Śiva on a military-like march or, in other Āgamas, on a mock hunting expedition (*mṛgayātrā*).

The most dramatic of all the special events is the chariot procession (*rathayātrā*), which in Aghoraśiva's schedule occurs on the seventh morning (section 23). The chariot is a large wooden base on wheels, upon which temple servants erect a temporary festival superstructure of poles, cloth, and banners, such that it resembles a massive mobile shrine. (Chariots currently in use at venerable south Indian Śaiva temples like Tiruvarur and Madurai weigh several hundred tons. Some may date back to the Vijayanagara period, but none to my knowledge dates back to Chola times.) The chief priest prepares the chariot ritually by invoking a series of deities onto its different parts, and then has the deity raised onto it. Devotees pull the chariot through the streets with ropes. At the completion of this special procession, recommends Aghoraśiva, gifts should be given to all who have helped with the chariot and food should be distributed to all.

During the time of the festival, priests perform other regular, continuing rites. The most notable ongoing practices are the fire-rites carried out in a special sacrificial hall (*yāgaśālā*). Before the festival flag is raised, directs Aghoraśiva, the priest should have a temporary sacrificial pavilion constructed inside the temple complex, with altar and fire-pits (section 10). During the course of the festival, priests regularly honor a large group of deities who have been invoked into a set of water pots arranged on the altar, and they make sacrificial offerings into the fires maintained in the pavilion (section 11). Aghoraśiva calls this the Trident ceremony, since Śiva's essential weapon (*astra*) is also kept and honored in the sacrificial pavilion.

The offering of tribute (*bali*) to ancillary deities and guardian spirits is a common rite of Śaiva temple practice, and during the festival tribute is given on a grand scale. Processions each day circle the temple to present tribute to the World-guardians at the eight directions. During festival time, each day has a presiding deity (*dinādhipa*), and these presiding lords are also eligible to receive particular tribute offerings of delicious rice preparations (section 13). In addition, Aghoraśiva suggests that still other suitable recipients beyond the confines of the temple, in such locations as cowpens, grass storehouses, rivers, tanks, and the gateway towers, be given special festival tribute (section 13a).

The Tīrtha Cycle

The conclusion of the festival proper is marked by the lowering of the flag, as we have seen. But there are additional ceremonies that help bring the festival to a conclusion, which have to do with final bathing of those deities and humans who have participated in it. Aghoraśiva recommends that a final bathing rite (*tīrthasnāna*) be performed on the final day of the festival, prior to the flag-lowering. Modeled as a pilgrimage to a holy bathing place (*tīrthayātra*), this rite is intended to remove any pollution contracted during the festival and to bring about various auspicious results as well. On the penultimate day, the priest should have water from a holy water-source collected in pots. He then invokes river goddesses into each water vessel (section 16). Next morning the processional icons, the ceremonial trident, the pots with germinated sprouts, and the water pots containing invoked river goddesses all make a journey to the bathing place. There the priests perform an *abhiṣeka* affusion for the processional icons by pouring the water from the pots over them, and the priests along with other devotees who have accompanied them on this pilgrimage bathe in the waters of the *tīrtha* (section 18).

Aghoraśiva also prescribes a second ceremony of bathing on the final day of the festival. In the bath with pots (*ghaṭasnāna*), priests first bring to a conclusion the fire-rites that have been performed in the sacrificial pavilion over the course of the festival. Then temple attendants carry the special pots that have been honored in the pavilion throughout the festival to the temple sanctum, and the priest uses them to perform a special *abhiṣeka* bath for the Śiva-liṅga, the principal support of Śiva in the temple (section 19). The various divine beings and energies that have been honored as separate figures throughout the festival are thereby reabsorbed into the temple's most fundamental divine source.

Rites of Closure

During the evening of the ninth day comes the lowering of the flag (section 20). This concluding ceremony largely mirrors the acts of raising the flag, along with the ceremonial drumming of *bherītādana*. The priests also honor the processional icons a final time before returning them to the places they normally reside within the temple. Lastly, the chief priest makes a final offering of tribute, in complete silence (*maunabali*). If many actions of the festival have been characterized by a tumult of myriad voices and cacophonous sounds, its concluding act involves only the silent internal recitation of mantras. This brings the festival to a contemplative close.

Additional Ceremonies

There are additional rites and ceremonies, both before and after, that spill over the boundaries of the official nine-day duration of the festival. Many of these allow for the honoring of additional deities and persons. Some fit with the rites of inauguration or closure. Before the festival begins, in addition to the many preparations temple personnel must make for Śiva's *mahotsava*, Aghoraśiva recommends they also offer a festival for Gaṇeśa, lasting from one to nine days (section 2). This would be apt recognition of Gaṇeśa's common task of removing obstacles prior to major undertakings. After the main *mahotsava* of Śiva concludes with the flag-lowering, Aghoraśiva specifies that Caṇḍeśa, Śiva's fierce devotee, be honored with a brief rite of an expiatory purpose (section 21). Likewise, the chief priest receives his own festival after the close of Śiva's, which mainly consists of his being carried in procession through the town (section 22).

Aghoraśiva describes still other festival ceremonies that do not fit so clearly within the nine- day *mahotsava*. The most elaborate of these is the festival of Dancing Śiva, which commences with the preparation of the Naṭarāja processional icon on the eighth night. The next night this ceremony continues with the preparation of a special black balm that is applied to icons and priests alike, and with other ceremonies honoring Śiva as Lord of Dance (section 24). Aghoraśiva mentions, but does not describe, a marriage ceremony (*vaivāha*) in which Śiva and the Goddess are wed (section 25). He provides also a brief account of a festival for the Goddess, identified as Vīraśakti, which may take place on the second day after the conclusion of the nine-day Śiva *mahotsava*, or may be extended as a self-standing festival lasting as many as nine days itself (section 26). There is also a festival held for the Devotees, presumably the south Indian Tamil poet-saints, during which icons of these eminent worshipers of Śiva themselves receive special honors and make their own circumambulation of the city (section 27). It is not clear how these additional events fit into the festival structure as Aghoraśiva envisions it. Their inclusion in the *Mahotsavavidhi* may well reflect developing festival practices during Aghoraśiva's own time, or possibly later interpolations into the text. The later digest *Mahotsavavidhikrama Āgamaśekhara* (hereafter *MĀŚ*) speaks also of a thirteen-day festival program, whose expanded time frame would allow for the inclusion of these added rites.

The *mahotsava* that Aghoraśiva prescribes, then, is an immensely complex ritual event, or "meta-performance" as John MacAloon (1984) would put it, made up of a plethora of component rites, filling and stretching beyond the nine official days of festival time. The *mahotsava* invokes, honors, and celebrates Śiva and a whole host of gods, who make themselves present at the festival in a great variety of physical and nonphysical forms. It calls upon the expertise of Śaiva priests and many other specialists and performers, and it allows for the participation of still larger numbers of human celebrants. As a temporary gathering of gods and humans in shared activities and attitudes of devotion and celebration, it remakes the world, for that time, into the divine realm of Śiva.

Divinity

Śaiva Siddhānta theology insists on the oneness and unique divine character of Śiva. He is the One, incomparable, ubiquitous, eternal, and unfathomable. In some ultimate sense Śiva remains transcendent. Yet at the same time Śaiva Siddhānta avers that Śiva is "master of the world." He is the "unique seed of the cosmos," says Aghoraśiva, because Śiva is the instrumental cause of all creation (*Tattvaprakāśavṛtti* 1). Śiva acts in myriad ways within and upon the world, animating it through his five fundamental activities of creation (*sṛṣṭi*), maintenance (*sthiti*), destruction (*samhāra*), veiling (*tirobhāva*), and grace (*anugrāha*).

Śiva carries out his manifold activities in the world both through his own manifest forms (*mūrtis*), and through energies (*śaktis*) and divine agents (*adhikārins*) who enact his will. The most comprehensive manifestation of Śiva, according to Śaiva Siddhānta, is known as Sadāśiva, the "Eternal Śiva." Sadāśiva has a "body of mantras," most notably the five *brahmamantras* that correspond to Śiva's five fundamental activities. The cylindrical Śiva-liṅga at the center of nearly all south Indian Śaiva temples is worshiped, several times a day, as the support for Śiva's most complete presence as Sadāśiva. In addition, Śiva takes on many other manifestations to accomplish his worldly purposes. These are the forms made known to us through anthropomorphic images and through narrative accounts of his deeds in the Purāṇas and other literature: Śiva as the Lord of Dance, as the Beggar, as Half-Female, as Conqueror of the Triple City, as Lord of all Creatures, and so on. The Āgamas denote these manifestations of Śiva collectively as Maheśvara, the "Great Lord," and provide descriptions of as many as twenty-five such forms. Some are classified as auspicious and gentle (*saumya*), others as formidable and fearsome (*ugra*), and still others as mixed (*miśra*).

Śiva does not work alone, however. The cosmos is populated by other powers and deities who carry out his will under his direction. Most integral among these are Śiva's Śaktis, energies or powers often conceived as female divinities who arise intrinsically from Śiva. The Āgamas speak of multitudes of Śaktis who accomplish Śiva's myriad tasks within a variegated cosmos. Śiva also acts through other divinities. These gods include Vedic gods such as Indra and Agni, Brahman, Gaṇeśa, Skanda, Pārvatī, and hosts of others. In the Śaiva Āgamas these divinities—many of whom enjoy their own devoted followings—appear as subordinate agents whom Śiva instigates to act on his behalf, much as an emperor might assign lesser kings to perform the tasks of rule within smaller, encompassed parts of an imperial domain. Thus the so-called polytheism of Hinduism is visualized, within the theology of the Śaiva Siddhānta school, as a cosmic court assembly, with Śiva as the central figure presiding over a court of subordinate lords and attendants who bow to Śiva and extend his cosmic sovereignty. So too in the topography of medieval Śaiva temples in south India, gods throng the palace-dwelling of Śiva, covering the walls of the temple and residing in their own subsidiary shrines.

Some rituals within the Śaiva system focus more on the unitary character of Śiva. Daily worship (*nityapūjā*), for instance, centers around the worshiper's invocation of Sadāśiva within the Śiva-liṅga and the transactions between the worshiper and the comprehensive form of Śiva that follow. Of all the major rituals in the Śaiva system, the *mahotsava* places greatest emphasis on the multiplicity and dynamic extension of Śiva's divine agency. During the *mahotsava* Śiva appears most evidently not in the unitary unmoving liṅga fixed at the center of the temple, but in mobile processional icons embodying his visible worldly manifestations that emerge from the temple and process through the streets. Other deities parade along with Śiva. And processions are not the only expressions of divine effulgence. On the first day of the festival, recommends Aghoraśiva, the priest should invite all the deities to attend the festival, and throughout the events of the ensuing days priests invoke multitudes of gods and goddesses into icons, diagrams, pots, fires, banners, and many other ritual objects. Celebrants extend their offerings of worship, of praise, and of tribute far beyond Śiva to encompass scores of other deities. The *mahotsava* in its comprehensive and congregative character aims at a celebration of the divine activity of all the gods and goddesses, understood to be subordinate agents in the exercise of Śiva's divine overlordship extended throughout the world of humans and all creatures.

Śiva's Festival Appearances

Within a south Indian Śaiva temple, Śiva's primary presence is concentrated in the fixed stone Śiva-liṅga located in the "womb-room" (*garbhagṛha*) or sanctum at the center of the temple. That liṅga is called the root-manifestation (*mūlamūrti*). During the construction of the temple, the ritual installation (*pratiṣṭhā*) of the Śiva-liṅga is fundamental to animating the temple, and the regular liturgical actions of daily worship in the temple center upon the liṅga.

The Śiva-liṅga does not go unworshiped during the festival. Several festival rites occur within the sanctum, in the presence of the Śiva-liṅga, with the liṅga receiving first honors. It never loses its priority or divine presence. However, the noteworthy feature of the festival is the prominence given to other manifestations of Śiva. This is most evident in the mobile, anthropomorphic metal icons of Śiva that circulate through the world of the festival. If the stone Śiva-liṅga is an immobile manifestation (*acalamūrti*), say the texts, the metal festival icons are mobile ones (*calamūrti*). These portable images receive installation rites similar to those of the Śiva-liṅga, which animate them also as living supports of Śiva's divine presence, and in the temple they receive limited worship on a daily basis. During festival time, however, the mobile icons come into their own.

For the *mahotsava*, the foremost icon embodies Śiva in the form of Somāskanda, the Lord seated pleasantly with wife Umā and son Skanda. In this icon Śiva appears domestic and placid, and the Āgamas aptly classify Somāskanda as one of Śiva's benign (*śānta*) forms. This is appropriate for the festival, which is seen as a joyful and celebratory event rather than a challenging or fearsome one. During the festival's twice-daily processions, the icon is carefully adorned with its jeweled ornaments, garlanded with fresh flowers, and shielded with a nimbus. It is raised onto a suitable conveyance, and the priest then invokes the special presence of Śiva into the image and briefly worships it with flowers. Once prepared, Somāskanda emerges from the temple, surrounded by royal insignia like parasol and yak-tail fan, accompanied by a retinue of other divine figures and an entourage of human votaries, to make a stately circumambulation through the streets of the surrounding community, very much the regal lord touring his sovereign domain. For each procession Somāskanda rides in or on a different vehicle.

On certain occasions during the festival Śiva processes in other forms as well. Aghoraśiva describes a special Dancing Śiva procession that takes place on the tenth day, after the official conclusion of the festival (section 24). According to other Āgama texts, though not the *Mahotsavavidhi*, Śiva may also tour in the form of the Wandering Beggar (Bhikṣātana), on the eighth day of the festival. During the hunting expedition he may appear in the form of a Mountain Hunter (Kirāta) or as the Conqueror of the Three Cities (Tripurāntaka).

These anthropomorphic processional icons of Śiva serve as the devotional center of the festival, but they are not the only forms in which Śiva becomes manifest during it. Potentially Śiva can manifest himself anywhere, the theological texts stress. In practice, the Āgamas make clear, he does make his presence available in a great variety of material objects. For example, *Kāmikāgama* lists some of the forms suitable for the daily worship of Śiva:

> A circular diagram, a painting on a cloth, a sketch on a wall, a pedestal-shaped stone consecrated by mantras, fire, water, guru, tree, and so on, a book on its stand, especially a naturally-occurring liṅga-shaped stone or gem, a liṅga formed from sand or some such substance, and other objects also are said to be suitable for use as liṅgas. According to circumstances one may prepare any of these individually in order to worship Śiva. (*PKĀ* 4.270–72)

This divine profusion is even more apparent during the *mahotsava*. Over the course of the festival, Śiva appears not only in the Śiva-liṅga and the mobile festival icons but also in the flagpole, in a sacrificial fire, in the Trident, in a consecrated pot of water, in the festival *bherī*-drum, within the chariot Śiva will also ride, and in rice mixed with ghee and yogurt and molded into the shape of a liṅga. Priests even invoke Śiva into a bowl of moist paste that is smeared on the liṅga, the icons, and the devotees just before the great chariot procession on the seventh day. Some Āgamas describe the priest himself as a form of Śiva, a "mobile liṅga" (*calaliṅga*). It is as if the festival were designed to offer a practical demonstration of Śiva's ubiquity.

Some of these manifestations are more comprehensive than others. In his outline of ritual procedures, Aghoraśiva pays special attention to the wooden flagpole. The flagpole of course serves a necessary supporting role in the raising of the festival banner, the rite that commences the festival itself, but its significance goes well beyond this function. With its tall cylindrical shape, the flagpole resembles a liṅga that has shot up into the air, and some Āgama texts say that it is in fact a liṅga, an "instrumental liṅga" (*kāraṇaliṅga*) as distinct from the "subtle liṅga" (*sukṣmaliṅga*) inside the temple sanctum. A third liṅga, they add, is the temple tower (*vimāna*) itself, designated as the "gross liṅga" (*sthūlaliṅga*).

Before the festival begins one must select a tree for the pole, following procedures like those used to select a stone for a Śiva-liṅga (section 3). The artisan carefully cuts down the tree and brings it to the temple, where the priest purifies it. Like a liṅga, it is formed into three vertical portions, square, octagonal, and circular. The artisan affixes the ancillary parts of the pole, such as the cross-bars and supporting struts, bells, and a bundle of *darbha* grass. The pole is then set upright in a masonry support, termed a *vedika* or altar. Before raising the flag, the priest ritually transforms the altar into a "throne" (*āsana*) saturated with powers "from Ādhāraśakti up to Parāśakti," and then invokes Sadāśiva into the flagpole itself, following the same procedures one uses when invoking Sadāśiva into the liṅga. The flagpole becomes, for the limited period of the festival, a tall looming manifestation of Śiva in his highest manifest form, accessible to all.

In such comprehensive forms, Śiva encompasses multiple deities within his own being (*layāṅga*). So it is appropriate that the priest recognize and honor other divinities on the other parts attached to the pole. The three cross-bars are identified with Śiva's three principal Śaktis: Kriyāśakti, Jñānaśakti, and Icchāśakti. The two supporting struts are Sun and Moon, and the rope used to hoist the banner is the divine snake Takṣa.

In other festival manifestations, Śiva may appear as a central lordly being surrounded by other subordinate deities (*bhogāṅga*). During the *mahotsava*, officiants must construct a special "sacrificial pavilion" (*yāgaśālā*) somewhere within the temple complex, where fire oblations and other forms of ritual honoring can be carried out over the course of the ceremony (section 10). This begins with the laying out of an eighty-one-square *vāstumaṇḍala* and the honoring of a group of fifty-three deities occupying the *maṇḍala* and its periphery, following ritual procedures common to the construction of any new sacred site. Within the pavilion, Aghoraśiva specifies, will be a central altar, a set of up to nine fire-pits, and space around the periphery for additional paraphernalia. At the center of the altar are placed two water-pots, one designated the Śiva-pot (*śivakumbha*) and the other a pot for Śakti (*vardhanī*). The officiant performs a full invocation for Śiva, in the form of Yāgeśvara, Lord of the Sacrifice, in the Śiva-pot, and for his consort Yāgeśvarī in the Śakti pot. Śiva Yāgeśvara's role here is to preside over and protect the sacrificial rites that will be performed in the pavilion during the festival. Surrounding Yāgeśvara and his consort on the altar are pots for the eight Vidyeśvaras, and further around the outer circuits of the pavilion will be still other groups of deities. Further, in the principal fire-pit the priest kindles a fire identified as Śiva-Agni. Throughout the festival, priests are to make sacrificial fire-oblations in the fire pits twice daily, and they also honor the deities present in the pots. At the conclusion of the festival, the pots that have been worshiped throughout the ceremony are used to give a final consecrating bath to the principal Śiva-liṅga (section 19). Water from the Śiva-pot is poured directly over the liṅga, and water from the Śakti-pot over the pedestal, thereby reabsorbing one manifestation of Śiva back into another more permanent and encompassing one.

Śiva's Household

As the preeminent Lord of the Cosmos in his multiplicity of forms, Śiva is undisputed lord of the festival, but he is certainly not the only deity present. The festival begins with invitations to all the gods, and throughout the ceremony multitudes of divinities are on hand every step of the way. The most esteemed are those closest to Śiva, members of his family and inner circle: wife Umā, sons Gaṇeśa and Skanda, bull-mount Nandin, and favored devotee Caṇḍeśa. Those deities process with him, embodied in their own icons and transported in their own vehicles. More intimately, Umā and Skanda share in the Somāskanda image as well. In most cases they also preside over their own ceremonies within the *mahotsava*.

Gaṇeśa receives his own festival before the start of the main *mahotsava*, as is appropriate for the deity who removes obstacles (section 2). During the Gaṇeśa festival time, says Aghoraśiva, temple workers should renovate the processional conveyances and decorate the temple and the surrounding town in preparation. All the icons to be used in the upcoming festival are honored and ornamented. Gaṇeśa makes a circumambulatory procession around the town, accompanied by the Trident, Śiva's primary weapon, and Caṇḍeśa, Śiva's favored devotee.

Śiva's bull mount Nandin, an exemplar of devoted attentiveness, is invariably present in Śaiva temples as a fixed stone image always facing the central Śiva-liṅga. In Aghoraśiva's procedures for the *mahotsava*, a mobile metal icon of Nandin accompanies Śiva's procession. During some of the processions, the Somāskanda image is also placed on its bull mount. Nandin appears most prominently during the festival in the banner (sections 7 and 8). A two-dimensional image of Nandin occupies the center of the festival flag, surrounded by auspicious insignia. After the artisans have inscribed the design on the banner-cloth, the priest performs an elaborate installation to bring the full presence of Nandin into his drawn image. Modeled on the procedure for the installation of divine presence in three-dimensional images, this includes the rites of opening the bull's eyes, showing it auspicious objects, and taking it in procession around the town. Finally, officiants raise the banner onto the flagpole with all possible fanfare. This fluttering Nandin remains present throughout the festival, and Aghoraśiva directs the priests to worship him there two or three times a day during that period. At the festival conclusion, the flag is lowered and the flag-Nandin is reabsorbed into the more permanent stone image of Nandin in the temple sanctum.

The Goddess appears most often in various forms as Śiva's partner. She is Umā in the Somāskanda icon, Śivakāmī accompanying Naṭarāja, and Yāgeśvarī to Śiva's Yāgeśvara in the sacrificial pavilion. In her identity as Vīraśakti, however, she is also honored in her own festival, either as an adjunct rite scheduled on the eleventh day of the Śiva *mahotsava* or as an independent *mahotsava* of up to nine days, held after the conclusion of the Śiva festival (section 26). During the independent Goddess festival, as *MĀŚ* describes it, the rites parallel those of the Śiva *mahotsava*, but with significant alterations. On the flagpole, for instance, forms of the Goddess (Parāśakti, Bhuvaneśvarī, Mahālakṣmī, Manonmanī) substitute for the aspects of Sadāśiva. Processions for the Goddess festival are led by Gaṇeśa and Skanda, with Caṇḍeśa bringing up the rear. At the center of the divine parade is an autonomous mobile icon of the Goddess, and Śiva is nowhere to be seen.

Multitudes of Divinities

Like the sculpted walls of a medieval south Indian temple, the world of the festival is covered over in gods. It starts with the general invitation (*āhvāna*): "The priest then announces the festival and invites all the deities, starting with Śiva, including the eighteen members of Śiva's retinue, the World-guardians (Lokapālas) beginning with Indra, the oceans, mountains, underground regions, and all beings." Over the course of the festival, multitudes of deities are honored, fed, and praised. At its conclusion they are dismissed.

One way divinities are honored during the festival is through the offering of tribute (*bali*). These offerings are part of daily worship as well, and of most Śaiva public rituals, but they are carried out on an expanded scale during the festival (section 13). To offer tribute the priest circulates to a series of pedestals located around the temple complex and beyond, and gives food to the deities present at each one. As Aghoraśiva recommends, this becomes a procession in itself, with all the usual pomp, dance, music, and recitations. In Śaiva ritual, tribute normally goes especially to the World-guardians, a group of eight or ten deities who carry out the important task of protecting the world in every direction, under the broad supervision of Śiva. The World-guardians include some well-known Vedic and Hindu divine figures: Indra, Agni, Yama, Nirṛti, Varuṇa, Vāyu, Kubera, Īśāna (in circumambulatory order, starting in the east), Brahman above, and Viṣṇu below. During the festival priests offer tribute, in addition to the usual recipients, also to deities identified as the "daily deities" (*dinādhipas*), and to still other deities of a less exalted character who are located further afield beyond the temple, in rivers and tanks, in cowpens and storehouses and treasuries.

This only begins to suggest the thick texture of divine presences throughout the festival. These start with individual identifications of ritual paraphernalia as divine forms: the protective wristlets worn by icons, priests, and other ritual actors are identified as the cosmic snake Vāsuki or Ananta, the mortar and pestle used in the powder festival are the Earth and Mount Meru, and so on. They include organized groupings: the pots for the sprouts are assimilated to the Sun, Moon, and the twelve Ādityas, water-pots for the final bathing of icons are Manonmanī and the eight Rivers, and elsewhere we encounter groups of seven Mothers, eight Nandins, eight Nāgas, nine Planets, eighteen Gaṇas, and so on.

Important ritual objects themselves become, over the course of the festival, sites infused with multiple divinities. The trident, the flagpole, and the processional chariot all host myriad gods, as does the festival *bherī* drum. Near the start of the festival, Aghoraśiva directs the priest to invoke and honor a series of gods on the drum and drumstick: the seven Mothers on its hooks, the nine Planets on its handle, the snake Vāsuki on the string, Skanda on the drumstick, and Śiva in his Rudra form at its center. Only then should the priest hand it over to the chief drummer for the beating of the rhythms that help set the festival in motion.

Likewise new ritual spaces are constructed during the festival that offer place to many gods. Foremost of these constructed spaces is the sacrifical pavilion (*yāgaśālā*), a temporary hall put up before the festival begins and used throughout the festival. Before construction can begin, the Āgamas direct priests first to perform a pacification of the site (*vāstuśānti*) that the pavilion will occupy. They are to draw a geometrical diagram of eighty-one squares, and invoke into it a host of fifty-three deities, with Brahman as "Lord of the Site" occupying the central nine squares. Once the site and its resident deities are happily pacified, actual construction may begin. In the pavilion priests place pots in a determinate order, starting on the central altar with those for Śiva and Śakti, here identified as the Lord and Lordess of the Sacrifice. Around them are other pots, for the eight Vidyeśvaras, Sūrya, the four *kalās*, the eight

Gaṇeśvaras, Brahman as Lord of the Site, Lakṣmī, the ten World-guardians, Gaṇeśa, and the seven Preceptors.

Śaiva Siddhānta theology recognizes a great plentitude of divine powers populating the cosmos, and here they make their presence known in the temporary world of the festival. But they do not do so as a wild horde. In Śiva's cosmos they appear as ranked orderly subordinate powers. Likewise in the festival, the priest's ability to summon the deities with mantras, and his knowledge of where they belong, are meant to insure that the gods attend the ceremonies in their proper places.

Humans

Just as the *mahotsava* assembles a host of divinities in the course of its festivities, it also brings together multitudes of humans.[9] Both local residents and pilgrims from afar congregate to share in the special activities of the festival. All may observe the processions or march in the parades of the deities, they may partake of the food and other gifts distributed during the festival, and they may join in the purifying bath at its close. Many do more than simply participate, however. Since the *mahotsava* calls for numerous ritual activities, it requires the coordinated contributions of many specialists. Of all those who act within the festival, by far the most important in Aghoraśiva's view is the chief priest, who acts as master of ceremonies throughout the *mahotsava*.

Master of Ceremonies and Other Priests

The *mahotsava* is a large and complex ceremonial activity and requires the contributions of many ritual actors, but in Aghoraśiva's view, initiated Śaiva priests act as the primary agents in conducting the festival. In particular, Aghoraśiva addresses his advice to a single person, the chief priest who acts as master of ceremonies throughout the festival.

Aghoraśiva refers to the chief priest as the *ācārya*, and also as *guru* and *deśika*, always in the singular. The chief priest is necessarily a male Śaiva brāhmaṇa or Ādiśaiva by birth, and he must have undergone the sequence of ritual initiations (*dīkṣā*) and priestly consecration (*ācāryābhiṣeka*) that cumulatively confer upon the recipient the ritual competence (*adhikāra*) to perform

[9] Some of this section has appeared in Davis 2006. For an attempt to compare the actors in festivals as described by Aghoraśiva in the *Mahotsavavidhi* with the personnel mentioned in inscriptions of the Chola period, see Davis and Orr 2007.

Śaiva ritual on behalf of others (*parārtha*) (Brunner 1988). Some Āgamas provide additional qualifications to consider in choosing an *ācārya* for a public ritual. Says *Rauravāgama* (57.12–14), one should select as ācārya "one born in an Ādiśaiva lineage, learned in the meanings of the Āgamas, calm, patient, with all his anger subdued, a householder, healthy, conversant with the words of the Vedas and Śāstras, and wise in the ways of the world." In *Mahotsavavidhi*, Aghoraśiva views the chief priest as the implicit agent of all festival activities, much as Śiva is the underlying agent of all cosmic action.

During the course of the festival the chief priest is called upon to observe a special regimen, as we have seen. Moreover, within the festival the chief priest repeatedly performs the common rite of self-purification (*ātmaśudhhi*), which reiterates his state of ritual readiness or Śiva-ness (*śivatva*) (Brunner 1988, Davis 1991: 83–111). Throughout the festival the chief priest officiates, either directly or indirectly, at all the principal rites. Aghoraśiva often uses causative verb forms to indicate that the chief priest directs actions even when he does not personally carry them out. His principal role is acknowledged at the conclusion of the festival, in the form of an honorarium (*dakṣinā*) and even more in the special "Festival of the Priest" (*ācāryotsava*), where the priest is placed on a palanquin and carried in procession around the city, just as Śiva has been throughout the festival (section 22).

For a multifaceted ceremony such as the *mahotsava*, the chief priest requires ritual assistance. Aghoraśiva refers to the assisting priests in the festival collectively as the *ṛtvijs*, always in the plural. The term *ṛtvij* derives from the Vedic system, where it is used as the general category of sacrificial priests, subdivided into four subdivisions according to Vedic training and ritual function. In *Mahotsavavidhi* and Āgama usage, *ṛtvij* is a general term for assisting priests who are, like the chief priest, initiated and consecrated Śaiva brāhmaṇa *ācāryas*, and who act within the festival as extensions of the chief priest. They too should observe an ascetic regimen over the course of the festival, and they also receive an honorarium at the festival's close, though it may be smaller than that of the chief priest.

Aghoraśiva does single out one special category of assisting priests, the *mūrtipas* or "image-protectors." The image-protectors carry out several distinct functions: they assist in the ceremonial raising and lowering of the flag that mark the beginning and conclusion of the festival, and they perform the fire-oblations in the sacrificial pavilion throughout the festival. Aghoraśiva does not specifiy the number of image-protectors or their special significance in the *mahotsava*. However, the image-protectors play an important role in another major Śaiva ritual, the establishment of the liṅga (*liṅgapratiṣṭhā*), where eight *mūrtipas* incarnate the eight forms of Śiva disposed around the liṅga (*SP* 4 pp. ix–x).

Reciters

A Śaiva temple festival necessarily draws upon the specialized skills and contributions of many persons. One dramatic illustration of this lies in the multiplicity of sounds that accompany the processions and other principal rites of the *mahotsava*. In addition to instrumental music, Aghoraśiva refers to three different types of recitations that may also surround the processions of the gods: recitations of Śaiva mantras (*japa*), Vedic recitations (*vedaghoṣa, brahmaghoṣa*), and devotional hymns (*bhaktastotra*). In *Mahotsavavidhi* Aghoraśiva does not discuss the identities of those who perform these recitations.

Within the Āgama system, the recitation of Śaiva mantras is considered the most efficacious form of verbal activity, and in festivals the continuous recitation of certain mantras serves important ritual ends (*SP* 1 pp. xxx–xxxvi). According to Aghoraśiva, the chief priest himself should recite key mantras continuously as he accompanies the principal deities during processions. In other ritual contexts, a priest referred to as the mantra-reciter (*jāpin*) may recite the protective "weapon" mantra, ASTRA (*SP* 4 p. x). The recitation of Śaiva mantras within the setting of a public ritual such as *mahotsava* requires an initiated Śaiva brāhmaṇa.

The sounds of the Vedas likewise form part of the aural surrounding of processions and other festival activities, though they are considered to be auspicious adjuncts, rather than ritually efficacious, in the Śaiva Siddhānta system. Aghoraśiva does not specify what Vedic texts are to be recited, nor does he say anything about the identity of the Veda-reciters. Presumably this was the special province of Vedic brahmins, who had undergone their own procedures of ritual training and qualification, and who contributed their own specialized knowledge to the overarching festival program.

Less frequently Aghoraśiva calls for devotional hymns (*bhaktastotra*). For the regular processions Aghoraśiva speaks simply of "the sounds of the Vedas, etc." (*vedaghoṣādi*), and other Āgama texts indicate that the *ādi* (etcetera) here may well be filled out with the sounds of *bhaktastotra*. The most unambiguous reference to devotional hymns in *Mahotsavavidhi*, however, comes in the "festival of the Devotees" (*bhaktotsava*), which takes place after the completion of the regular nine-day festival. In this ceremony, icons of the Devotees are honored and praised with devotional hymns, though Aghoraśiva does not specify what those hymns are. Further, "those who know the Śaiva songs" receive cloth and other special gifts at this festival event. It is likely that Aghoraśiva has in mind specialist singers of the Tamil Śaiva hymns of the *Tevaram*.

Musicians and Entertainers

In addition to those who carry out specific ritual activities and recitations, there are many more who perform during the temple festival. These performers include dancers, musicians, singers, and other entertainers. Each category of performer would contribute their own specialized skills and training to the overall celebration of the *mahotsava*. By and large Aghoraśiva does not provide detailed information about these festival performers. Often the *Mahotsavavidhi* simply gives formulaic recommendations that an activity should be "accompanied by song, music, and dance," or by the "triple symphony" (*tauryatrika*) of vocal music, instrumental music, and dance, without further specification. We need to refer to other Āgama texts to learn about the qualifications expected of these performers. *Kāmikāgama* specifies that masters of music may be born in any of the four *varṇas* or in a mixed caste, and that they must have dedicated themselves to the knowledge of dance. They should be knowledgeable about musical instruments, as well as composition, song, recitation, and the like, and they should know the nine moods of drama. Further, they should be devoted to Śiva, and be without moral failings (*ŚPM* 5.180–85).

The festival is replete with dance. Dancers accompany every procession of the gods during the festival, and there are several rites within the festival where the *Mahotsavavidhi* specifies a special group of dancers. The Rudragaṇikās, "Śiva's female troops" or " Śiva's courtesans," the female temple dancers, play a prominent role in the festival, in Aghoraśiva's account. They occupy a position in Āgama texts parallel to that of the Devadāsīs in later south Indian temple culture, but the historical relation between the two categories of temple women remains uncertain (Kersenboom 1987, Orr 2000). *Ajitāgama* (27.157) speaks of the Rudragaṇikās as "lovely-bodied women of Śiva's abode, who wear garlands and ornaments," and *Rauravāgama* (ch. 19) adds that they should be pure, calm, beautiful, young, not covetous, and well trained in dance. Specifically, they perform the form of dance known as *śuddhanṛtta*, the "pure dance" based on movements coordinated with rhythmic phrases but not employing mimetic gestures (Janaki 1988: 52–54). According to *Mahotsavavidhi*, the Rudragaṇikās perform throughout the festival and often carry out key ritual actions. They dance in front of the deity during the daily processions, they wave lamps before the deity in *nīrājana*, they grind substances for the powder festival, and during the drum-beating ceremony (*bherītāḍaṇa*, also called *navasandhinṛtta*) they perform distinct dance patterns in coordination with the drummer's rhythms at each of the eight directions.

The festival requires instrumental music, as well as vocal recitations and song. Aghoraśiva often refers to the musicians as a collectivity, as *vādyakas* or *suvādikāras*, and for processions and other festival activities he may specify simply that "all the instruments" (*sarvavādya*) should be played. In some instances Aghoraśiva does name specific instruments, including the conch (*śaṇkha*), lute (*vīṇā*), flute (*veṇu*), and three kinds of drums (*bherī, mardala,* and *dundubhi*). Other Āgama texts provide longer lists of suitable instruments, and *Ajitāgama* (27.128–31) recommends that instruments of four categories be employed in the festival: skin-percussion drums, stringed instruments, metal percussion, and hollow wind instruments. According to *Ajitāgama* and other Āgamas, these four instrument types plus the human voice make up the famous "five great sounds" (*pañcamahāśabda*), and this totality of sound brings pleasure to Śiva (Raghavan 1958).

Rhythms of the drum play a major role throughout the festival. They accompany all processions and tribute-offerings, as well as the raising and lowering of the festival banner. However, in one important rite at the commencement of the festival, the chief drummer (called *bherītāḍaka* or simply *vādyaka*) is singled out. During the drum-beating rite that follows the raising of the festival flag, the chief priest ritually consecrates the *bherī* drum and calls upon the chief drummer to play a series of distinct rhythms (*tāla*), as the Rudragaṇikās dance, at each of the eight directions. The *Mahotsavavidhi* gives the names of the individual rhythms for each location, but it requires the drummer's special expertise to give musical form to these rhythms. During this rite the chief drummer receives the sacrificial thread that marks him as a temporary brahmin, along with sandalpaste, garlands, and other adornments.

At several points during the *mahotsava*, including the festival of Dancing Śiva and the festival of the Goddess, Aghoraśiva recommends that entertainment (*vinoda*) be provided for an audience that would include Śiva and the Goddess (in image forms) along with select human invitees. He does not specify what these entertaining performances might be, but other Āgamas suggest that they be concerts of dance, music, and anything pleasing to the gods. We might postulate that this is the context within which drama performances might be incorporated into the *mahotsava*, as they subsequently were in practice.

Other Festival Personnel

Still other specialists are required to insure the proper conduct of the festival. Among these Aghoraśiva refers to the artisan and the astrologer.

During the festival the work of artisans (*śilpin*) is crucial. They must select and prepare the wooden flagpole, they design and create the festival banner, they construct the altars and fire pits of the sacrificial pavilion, and they prepare the many vehicles and especially the great wooden chariot for processions. The *śilpins* have their own textualized bodies of specialist knowledge in the form of Śilpaśāstras, such as the Chola-period *Mayamata* (5.13–25), which also set forth qualifications for the various categories of artisans. Aghoraśiva refers to the Śilpin in the singular, no doubt referring to a head artisan who acts as supervisor of his own ranked group of artisans, assistants, and laborers. Important as the Śilpin would be to the proper conduct of the festival, Aghoraśiva's prescriptions insure that the master artisan is ritually subordinate to the chief priest, during such rites as the opening of the eyes (*netromilana*) of the Nandin banner.

Aghoraśiva also speaks of a *kartṛ* (literally, agent) who is assigned to fix the proper time for the festival, based on a calculation of *nakṣatras*. The term could refer to the chief priest as *kartṛ* of the entire festival, but it seems more likely that Aghoraśiva here denotes a specialist known elsewhere in the Āgamas as the *daivajña*, "astronomer" or prognosticator. According to Brunner, the *daivajña* is necessary to all occasional and optional Śaiva rituals for determining favorable times to conduct important actions (*SP* 4 pp. x–xi). During the festival, this person must reckon a variety of timings, such as the "auspicious moment" (*muhūrta*) for commencing the chariot procession. Trained astronomers brought to their ritual task a large body of specialized knowledge, in the form of Jyotiḥśāstras.

Beyond the ritual labor requiring specialized knowledge and skill, there are countless additional tasks that need to be accomplished in preparation for and during a nine-day temple festival. During the festival, someone must fetch provisions and paraphernalia, carry poles and pots, transport icons from place to place and lift them onto vehicles and into palanquins, pull and push and carry all sorts of things. For the most part, Aghoraśiva does not mention the categories of menial laborers necessary to the conduct of a festival, since he directs his comments to a chief priest and largely confines his recommendations to those tasks he considers ritually significant. The *Mahotsavavidhi* and other Āgama texts, however, do specify one group of temple workers: the *paricārakas* or temple "attendants." The *paricārakas* assist the priests throughout the festival, through such physical actions as transporting pots, raising images onto vehicles, and carrying tribute offerings during *balidāna*. They play an especially important role during the raising of the festival banner. During this rite the *paricārakas* wear the turban (*uṣṇīṣa*) and upper cloth (*uttarīya*) that signify ritual competence, and they pull the ropes that hoist the flag high onto the pole. They are never called upon to recite mantras, however, or perform any ritual action that requires full priestly competence. Aghoraśiva says nothing about the qualifications or initiatory status of the *paricārakas* in *Mahotsava-vidhi*, but other Āgamas indicate that they should have received at least the first level of common Śaiva initiation (*samayadīkṣā*) (*UKĀ* 24.53–55).

Patron and Ruler

Every festival requires provisions and it needs people to supply those special resources. As in the Vedic sacrificial system, so in Śaiva public rituals one person is designated as *yajamāna*, literally the "sacrificer" or the patron, in the singular. However, while the Yajamāna plays a key ritual role in Vedic sacrifice, Aghoraśiva does not grant this figure a great deal of ceremonial prominence in his prescriptions for the *mahotsava*. The Yajamāna does appear in processions and assemblies, and carries out a few special ritual tasks. During the Trident Ceremony, for example, he performs a set of daily rites along with the priests. His most important ritual role, however, comes at the end of the festival, when he honors the chief priest and other officiants by presenting them with honoraria (*dakṣiṇā*). In that task he represents the community as a whole in recognizing the contributions of priests and others. In the Vedic system the Yajamāna receives the full benefits of the sacrificial performance, but Aghoraśiva makes no mention of this for the Śaiva festival. When Aghoraśiva does include statements about the fruits of festival actions, these generally speak of benefits to the entire community, not just to the patron.

Another shadowy presence in Aghoraśiva's festival guide is the Ruler, referred to as *rājan*, *nṛpa*, and *bhūpa*. Aghoraśiva does not qualify this term any further, so it could refer to the highest level of imperial lordship, such as the Chola king during Aghoraśiva's time, or to some intermediate political authority or local chief. The Ruler is distinct from the Yajamāna; there is no sense here that the Ruler need be the festival patron either directly or symbolically. The king does not appear to have any ritual responsibility in the festival, as far as Aghoraśiva is concerned. However, in processions the Ruler does march with his entourage of attendants (*bhṛtya*) on the left side of the deity, while the chief priest walks with his underlings on the god's right side. In the priest's procession, likewise, both Yajamāna and Ruler acknowledge the pre-eminence of the priest, in the domain of this festival, by walking behind the palanquin in which the priest is carried.

Other Participants

All those who attend the *mahotsava* become participants in a temporary Śaiva world that is enacted and extended throughout the community during festival time. Some, we have seen, are ritual agents and performers who help through their actions to create that world. Others participate simply by being there. Some festival events are relatively restrictive, but the most important ceremonies of the festival—the raising and lowering of the banner, the daily processions, the final bath—are intended to be open affairs accommodating large congregations of people.

Aghoraśiva often signals the comprehensive openness of festival events with terms like *sarvajana* (all people). Just as the priests summon all deities to take part in the festival, so the high-raised festival banner and the resounding clamor of drums and conches broadcast an invitation to all humans in the surrounding area. Elsewhere Aghoraśiva refers broadly to *sarvabhakta* (all devotees) or *bhaktajana* (the full group of devotees). Here *bhakta* refers to an open-ended group, with no limits based on initiation, training, gender, or class status. All devotees, he says, may march along with the deities in procession, or bathe at the *tīrtha*, or receive gifts.

Participation in the festival world is sometimes graded or ranked. Throughout the ceremonies Aghoraśiva calls for actions that single out some participants. For example, at the onset he instructs important festival participants to tie on a special *rakṣasūtra*, a protective wristlet (section 12). First the priest ties a cord around the central Śiva-liṅga, around the ceremonial Trident, and on the wrists of all the processional icons. After protecting the deities, Aghoraśiva continues, the priest ties wristlets on himself, on the assisting priests, on the tribute-carrier (*balivāhaka*), and on the chief drummer. In effect, the rite of *rakṣabandhana* articulates an inner group of deities and important ritual actors at the center of the festival, who require special protection.

Likewise, processions have their own spatial hierarchies, in Aghoraśiva's view. All devotees are encouraged to join the festival processions, and *Ajitāgama* (27.157) specifies that all four *varṇa* classes and all four categories of Śaiva initiates should be included. However, the *Mahotsavavidhi* also sets out a spatial organization for the processors. The deities march in a definite order, of course, with the central Somāskanda icon (Śiva with Umā and Skanda) both preceded and followed by Śiva's family and closest relations: Nandin, Gaṇeśa, Skanda, Devī, and Caṇḍeśa. Humans should likewise arrange themselves around the deities in a certain order. Closest to Śiva on the right hand side is the officiating priest. On Śiva's left is the Ruler, along with his entourage. In front of the deity are musicians, dancers, and singers. Rudragaṇikās dance along both sides of the processing deities. Mahāśaivas should march in front of the parade, and behind come brahmins who recite the Vedas. After them come Maheśvaras. The processional party constitutes a mobile assembly, and proximity to the central Śiva is an index of festival status.

In *Mahotsavavidhi*, Aghoraśiva does mention several special categories of persons who do not carry out any definite ritual action, but who may march in processions, receive things, or simply be present. He assigns a special place at the front of processions to those he calls Mahāśaivas. Other Āgama texts identify Mahāśaivas as brahmins not of the five Ādiśaiva *gotras*, but who have undergone Śaiva initiation. Because they are not Śaiva brāhmaṇas, they are not eligible to undergo *ācāryābhiṣeka* and become temple priests performing services on behalf of others. At least in the processions, however, they are worthy of some distinction within the Śaiva community. Maheśvaras also march in processions, but behind the Mahāśaivas and Vedic brahmins. In Āgama usage, Maheśvara refers to members of any *varṇa* who have undergone at least the first level of Śaiva initiation, *samayadīkṣā* (*SP* 3 p. 416 n. 457). In the *Mahotsavavidhi* they are assigned one optional ritual task: in the gathering of earth (*mṛtsaṅgrahana*) they may carry the pots of earth after it has been collected for the sprouting rite of *aṅkurārpana*.

Within the Śaiva system, the Sādhakas constitute a special category of religious virtuosi who practice a renunciatory discipline centered on mantra recitation. To become a Sādhaka, one must undergo the full sequence of Śaiva initiations, and then a special consecration, the *sādhakābhiṣeka* (Brunner 1975). They are not qualified to perform Śaiva ritual on behalf of others, and Aghoraśiva gives them no ritual assignment during the *mahotsava*. Sādhakas apparently do attend temple festivals, however, and at several moments they receive powder or paste to smear on themselves, as an acknowledgement of their special status in the Śaiva community. For example, in the festival of Dancing Śiva, the priest prepares a black balm and smears it on the images of the deities, then on himself. The black balm is then distributed in order to the *mūrtipas*, to the Sādhakas, and finally to all devotees present.

Aghoraśiva assigns at least one ritual task, optionally, to those he calls *suvāsinīs*, married women of good homes, in the plural. During the rite of illumination (*nīrājana*), either married women or Rudragaṇikās may wave the lamp in front of the deity (section 15). Other Āgamas sometimes give these virtuous women additional festival roles. For example, in the wedding festival (which Aghoraśiva merely mentions without giving any procedural details), married women prepare the image of the goddess and honor her before she is taken to the wedding pavilion.

Finally, some groups are mentioned in *Mahotsavavidhi* only as recipients of festival largesse. So at several points Aghoraśiva directs that gifts of gold, food, and other valuables be given to brahmins, without specifying which brahmins. I assume here that all brahmins, regardless of *gotra* or initiatory status, could partake of these presentations. At the conclusion of the Gaṇeśa festival, which precedes the main nine-day Śiva *mahotsava*, gifts should be given to the wretched (*dīna*), the poor (*krṛpaṇa*), and the blind (*andha*). Giving to these worthy and needy recipients is an inherently auspicious action, appropriate to the world of the festival.

Aghoraśiva's Vision of an Ideal Festival

In the *Mahotsavavidhi*, Aghoraśiva outlines a vision of how an ideal Śaiva temple ought to be conducted, from a priest's point of view. His background and his aim in composing the text naturally entail that he delves into certain topics in considerable depth while leaving other matters tantalizingly unexplored. To place Aghoraśiva's vision of the festival in broader perspective, I would like to conclude this Introduction by juxtaposing the *Mahotsavavidhi* with a differing vision, Cēramāṉ Perumāḷ's poetic rendering of Śiva's own procession at Mount Kailasa, the *Tirukkayilāyañāṉavulā* also called the *Ādiyulā*. Cēramāṉ Perumāḷ, a ruler of the Chera region, composed this Tamil devotional *ulā* or "processional poem" in the eighth century C.E.[10] As part of the Śaiva devotional canon, the *Tirumurai*, the poem would certainly have been known to Aghoraśiva.

Cēramāṉ Perumāṉ's Vision of Śiva's Procession

The procession that Cēramāṉ Perumāḷ sees originates not in any human-built temple in Tamilnad, but rather in Śiva's principal palace in Śivapuram ("Śiva-town") on Mount Kailasa, deep in the Himalayas. According to later tradition, Cēramāṉ traveled there with the Śaiva poet-saint Cuntarar. As related in Cēkkiḻār's twelfth-century *Periya Purāṇam*, Cēramāṉ abandoned his own

[10] I am grateful to Blake Wentworth for sharing his unpublished translation with me. His 2009 University of Chicago dissertation makes a significant contribution to the study of this productive genre of Tamil devotional literature. During Aghoraśiva's own lifetime, as we have seen earlier, the Chola court poet Oṭṭakkūttar composed three *ulās* celebrating the processions of the Chola rulers. Later *ulās* often focused on processional icons of temples, and these poetic compositions in turn were sung by Rudragaṇikās in the course of festivals. See Ceyaraman 1966, Swaminathaiyar 1994, and Thirumavalavan 1991.

kingdom to accompany the saint on the journey to Kailasa, but he was turned away at the gates. Deprived of a direct view of Śiva, Cēramān̲ envisioned Śiva in a divine procession leaving the palace, and composed his *ulā* to celebrate that visionary parade. He opens his poem by pointing to the paradoxes and imponderables of Śiva's nature. When Śiva appeared physically as the Pillar of Fire, he observes, even the gods Viṣṇu and Brahman were unable to fathom the full extent of his being. Yet out of grace Śiva does appear, both to gods and humans, in a great variety of forms.

> his appearance is beyond the understanding of the lofty gods
>   whom he himself created in accordance with his own designs
> but to those who think of him incessantly
>   in whatever guise
> he bestows his grace and appears within their hearts. (6–7)

It is just such a heart's-eye manifestation that Cēramān̲ relates to us. Thanks to his incessant devotional contemplation, we can infer, Śiva appeared to him much as he appears before the gods and sages who throng around the palace at Kailasa. And so he can appear to all those who "think of him" incessantly.

The narrative of the poem begins with Śiva inside his lovely palace and the gods outside in the courtyard clamoring for a glimpse of the Supreme One. Śiva decides to grant their wishes, but before he goes out, Cēramān̲ reports, Śiva's wife Pārvatī must attend to his appearance. She weaves flowers into his hair, festoons him with garlands, powders his chest with cool sandalwood, clothes him in silk, and adorns him with ornaments all over his body. The poet carefully details each one: golden anklets, crown with crest-jewel, gem-studded forehead plate, fish-shaped ruby earrings, several necklaces of diamonds and pearls, upper-arm brassards, shimmering belt, waist-cord, and bracelets (16–21). When Śiva is fully adorned, he stands up and ventures out through the gateway.

As Śiva comes into view, the attending gods honor him. The Ādityas sing his praises, Agastya plays his lute, and Yama recites auspicious words. The deities render services suited to their own natures. The fire-god Agni burns incense, Varuṇa the sea-god carries a jeweled pot of holy water, the wind-god Vāyu sweeps the processional route, and the rains sprinkle the path with water. Amidst the songs, praises, and physical signs of attendance and adoration, Śiva mounts his favored mount Nandin.

> Thus worshiped by the gods,
> our Lord mounted his lofty young bull
>   its body dazzlingly, radiantly white,

and while attentive goblins stood watch
he passed out beyond the seven holy gates. (34–35)

Moving beyond the palace gate, Śiva's procession commences.

In Cēramāṉ Perumāḷ's vision, the other primary gods surround Śiva and form his entourage. Skanda rides on his peacock in front of Śiva, and Indra on his elephant brings up the rear. Brahman escorts Śiva on his right side, and Viṣṇu is on the left. The love-god Kāma also accompanies Śiva's procession, as do Gaṇeśa and Aiyanar. Durgā rides her lion mount, accompanied by the Seven Mothers. Still other deities and divine powers add to this parade of divinity: Vidyādharas, Yakṣas, Asuras, Rākṣasas, the six seasons, the asterisms, the mudrās, mantras, and many more take part in this mobile display of Śiva's manifest powers. Cēramāṉ Perumāḷ also dwells on the many drums and other musical instruments that sound forth in all directions. Royal insignia also appear in the procession: the bull-banner, ensign, parasol, and yak-tail fan. And as Cēramāṉ's vision unfolds, the unblinking celestials praise their leader Śiva in a series of epithets.

And as they praised and praised his form,
a rain of flowers fell
    bewildering the senses
and goodness spread throughout the four directions. (56)

Śiva's procession is an active display of lordship that spreads out and infuses its surroundings with goodness.

Cēramāṉ Perumāḷ's perspective is a broad one. It encompasses not just Śiva both inside and outside his palace, and not only all the gods and other beings who march along with Śiva. The poet also draws back to observe those who await and observe the procession.

beautiful women
    fragrance drifting from their flowered raven braids
feel a newness in their hearts
when the beautiful Lord approaches. (58)

He particularly delights in describing the responses of female observers. It is not only the "newness in their hearts" that he evokes in elaborate poetic detail, but the thrills of sensual excitement throughout their bodies.

From golden child to lady
women flocked together joyfully,
and dazzling ornaments . . .

flashed with gold.
Ascending to the rooftops, they stood and worshiped
heartsick with longing as their passions rose. (67–69)

Females of all ages, from child to matron, respond to the appearance of Śiva in distinct erotic modes suited to their ages. For Cēramāṉ this is not incidental to the poem, but at its heart. Together with the portrayal of Śiva's procession itself, the description of the erotically charged devotional responses of women to the overwhelming visual presence of Śiva forms the second key theme of Cēramāṉ's *ulā*.

After celebrating the turmoil, the exuberant and passionate reactions of the women of Śivapuram when Śiva processes, Cēramāṉ Perumāḷ shifts in his final stanza, to address his audience directly.

So protect your womanhood!
Protect your two lithe arms!
Cinch tight your striking girdle!
the Vagabond, the Lord with the battle axe
    garlanded with the crystal waters of the Ganges
    and cassia flowers born of the rains,
comes riding his bull in procession!

It is an ironic challenge to a female addressee. If the women of Śivapuram cannot resist the Lord's powerful charisma when he comes riding his bull, how can others be expected to do so? Cēramāṉ closes by suggesting that the Vagabond Śiva on his bull ventures far beyond the Himalayas. Śiva's procession brings the god within view of all.

Perspectives of Poet and Priest

If Cēramāṉ Perumāḷ presents us with Śiva's procession as envisioned by an inspired royal devotional poet, Aghoraśiva's priestly vision in the *Mahotsavavidhi* is considerably more mundane and more practical. Cēramāṉ invites his many Tamil auditors to transport themselves imaginatively, to witness Śiva's own procession throught the streets of his Himalayan home. Aghoraśiva instructs his more select audience of initiated Śaiva priests on how they should enable Śiva and his retinue, in the form of mobile bronze icons, to process through the roads surrounding any Śaiva temple. Cēramāṉ focuses his devotional attention on the agency of Śiva, who decides to favor his followers by appearing to them outside his palace, and who acts on the females of Śivapuram with irresistable erotic force. In aiming his advice toward temple priests, Aghoraśiva assumes that their agency is key to the festival. The priests perform the liturgical actions that allow Śiva to show himself to his worshipers outside the temple.

In both works, the god's procession is the center of attention. The procession involves the god's own movement, outward, from a relatively inaccessible location inside his dwelling place to a more accessible setting where multitudes of followers and interested bystanders may catch a glimpse of their lord. Cēramāṉ frames this within a paradox of Śiva's own divine nature: Śiva is ultimately transcendent, but also becomes immanent in a multitude of forms. He demonstrates this through a temporal movement from a private domain to a public one, or in classical Tamil terms from *akam* (the "interior") to *puram* (the "exterior"). For a transcendent god like Śiva, becoming present in a mobile icon, dressing, being ornamented, and riding forth on a bull or other mount are all moments in a process of manifestation or emanation. Śaivas like Aghoraśiva understand this, and enact it, as one phase in a circular or oscillating movement. Śiva's procession is a *pradakṣiṇa*, a circumambulation, that necessarily returns home to the inner temple sanctum after encircling the outer boundaries.

The procession itself is imbued with the signs of Śiva's cosmic lordship. In the *Ādiyulā* the fully adorned Śiva rides out from the palace on his bull Nandin, surrounded by an entourage of other gods on their own mounts, and accompanied by all the insignia of royalty. Likewise, Aghoraśiva recommends that Śiva ride a variety of vehicles in his twice-daily processions, which point to different aspects of Śiva's lordly nature. Here too Śiva processes with a retinue that includes other deities and human attendants as well. Like mobile courts, these entourages are arranged according to a hierarchical etiquette of proximity. Those who stand or march closest to the presiding lord share most closely in his sovereignty.

The appearance of Śiva in visible, tangible form acts like a great magnet, drawing all beings toward his manifestation. In Cēramāṉ's poetic rendering, the gods and sages outside the palace clamor for Śiva to come into view, and when he does the women all rush to their rooftops for a transforming look. Aghoraśiva instructs the temple priests to invite all beings to attend the festival where Śiva will come out from the temple. The drums and conches, the raised flags, and the priestly proclamations all signal the attraction of the festival to all people. Cēramāṉ ironically challenges his audience to resist Śiva's charismatic allure, in confidence that this cannot easily be done. Here and there, Aghoraśiva also reminds his audience of the great benefits that come from seeing Śiva and participating in his festival.

Cēramāṉ Perumal is deeply interested in the emotional responses of those who see Śiva in his procession. He devotes over half of the *ulā* to his exploration of female devotion. Through their excited reactions, the women of Śivapuram act in the poem as models of devotional response for all votaries of Śiva. By contrast, Aghoraśiva does not address the nuances of *bhakti* at all, since it is not a matter of priestly control. Nor does he claim any poetic insight into the emotions of others. Instead he is concerned with the proper liturgical practices that will allow other *bhaktas* to encounter Śiva outside the temple. Moreover, Aghoraśiva locates these divine processions in the broader ritual framework of a nine-day festival.

Cēramāṉ's poetic vision limits itself to a single processional appearance of Śiva as the deity moves through a surrounding throng of devotees. The temple festival that Aghoraśiva outlines, by contrast, draws upon many other ritual forms, as a comprehensive meta-performance. Over the course of the temple festival Śiva appears in a variety of manifestations, and his special presence suffuses the entire festival, not just the moments of procession. Moreover, the temple festival (much like the temple itself) allows for the recognition and honoring of multitudes of other deities.

Every Village as Śivapuram

Cēramāṉ Perumāḷ's *ulā* articulates a heart's eye vision of Śiva's own procession in Śivapuram, in the form of a Tamil devotional song that enables others to reenvision it for themselves. The south Indian temple festival seeks to enact a similar vision in practical terms. Any community may be transformed into Śivapuram through the instrumentality of the festival procession.

Śaiva Siddhānta theology asserts unequivocally that Śiva is the Lord of the Cosmos, the divine paradigm for any earthly ruler. One center of this cosmic empire is Śiva's Himalayan home on Mount Kailasa, where he dwells in a palace in Śivapuram. There he holds court, attended by the numerous subordinate gods and other beings who enact his will throughout the world. But Śiva may take on many worldly manifestations as well, without subtracting from his cosmic plentitude. Hence there is no problem, within the Śaiva perspective, with Śiva being present simultaneously in many Śaiva temples, nor with his presence in multiple icons within a single Śaiva shrine.

It is often pointed out that Hindu temples, with their myriad orderly legions of deities, can be seen as microcosms or replicas of the mountain homes of the gods, such as Mount Meru, Viṣṇu's Vaikuṇṭha, or Śiva's Kailasa. The south Indian temple festival—with its renovations of the surrounding town, its broad invitations and congregations of humans regardless of status, its multiplicity of divine manifestation and its repeated processions of the gods—seeks to extend this replication more broadly. Through the festival, the community surrounding Śiva's temple-palace can become, for a time, Śiva-puram. Aghoraśiva's *Mahotsavavidhi* seeks to set out the liturgical actions by which priests may achieve this transformation.

Translation

CONTENTS

A. Procedures for the Great Festival
1. Determination of Proper *Nakṣatras*
2. The Festival of Gaṇeśa
3. Acquisition of the Pole
4. The Flagpole
5. Collection of the Earth
6. Sprouts
7. Sacrifice to the Bull
8. The Flag-raising Ceremony
   8a. Meditation on the Flagpole
   8b. Measure of the Tribute Balls
   8c. Benefits of the Flag-raising Ceremony
9. The *Brahmatāla* on the *Bherī* Drum
10. Worship in the Sacrificial Hall
11. The Trident Ceremony
   11a. The Sacrificial Fuel-sticks
12. Tying the Protective Cord
13. Presentation of Tribute
   13a. Meditation of Pāśupata
   13b. Special Tribute

14. The Order of Processions
14a. Perambulation
15. The Illumination Ceremony
16. Collection of Holy Water
17. The Festival of Powder
18. Final Bath at the Holy Bathing Place
19. The Bath with Pots
20. The Flag-Lowering Ceremony
21. The Festival of Caṇḍeśa
22. Worship of the Priest
23. Raising the Deity onto the Chariot
24. The Festival of Dancing Śiva
24a. The Black Balm
25. The Wedding Ceremony
26. The Festival of the Goddess
27. The Festival of the Devotees
28. Pacification Rites for the Festival
29. Śiva's Five Activities and the Festival

B. Procedures for Monthly and Other Festivals
30. Principles for Determining Auspicious Times
31. Festival of the New Moon
32. Festival of the Full Moon
33. Procedures for Festivals Related to the Stars
34. The Weekly Festival

A. Procedures for the Great Festival

First comes the ceremony for the Bull Nandin. Second is the hoisting of the flag.
Third is the sounding of the great rhythm. Fourth is raising the sprouts.
Then comes the description of the sacrificial pavilion, and next the rite of the Trident.
Seventh is the giving of tribute. Eighth is the order of vehicles in procession.
Ninth is the entertainment assembly, and tenth the waving of lamps. Eleventh is tying the thread, and twelfth the collection of water for bathing.
Thirteenth is the festival of powder. Fourteenth is going into the water.
Fifteenth is lowering the flag, and sixteenth is the special final bath.
Seventeenth is the ceremony of marriage and the final one is the festival of devotees.

One should know that the festival is divided into these and other divisions.[1] The rules for the nine-day festival will be given here, as this is the best among all types, from the Śaiva through the Daivika categories of festivals.[2]

This is how: One should begin with the preparatory ceremonies on the night prior to the festival.[3]

From the time of raising the flag to that of lowering it, the officiating priest and others performing the festival should eat only one meal a day and they should sleep on the ground. During this time they should abstain from any anointing with oil, from intercourse with women, from eating the food of others, and the like. They should bathe at the three proper times each day. They

[1] This list of eighteen divisions (*bheda*) of the festival corresponds closely to the list attributed to *Kāmikāgama*, quoted in *MĀŚ* (pp. 57–58), but not found in the published *UKĀ*. *MĀŚ* (p. 58) also quotes a list of twenty divisions from *Vīratantra*. See table 1.

[2] Other Āgamas such as *Ajitāgama* (27.3–7) and *Rauravāgama* (18.8–21) categorize *mahotsavas* according to their number of days in length, from one day up to seventeen, and the presence or absence of various rites. See table 2. Bhatt's edition of *Ajitāgama* (1964) cites the nine-day festival as optimum; within the Āgama classification the nine-day festival is called Daivika or Śākta. The Śaiva type is the briefest, a one-day festival. *Rauravāgama* also provides similar lists from *Sūkṣmāgama* and *Kāraṇāgama*. Aghoraśiva here declares the nine-day festival best, calling it *sarvakāmika*, or granter of all desires.

[3] *Adhivāsana* (from *vas*, to dwell) is a general term for preparatory rites, employed in many Indian rituals. In the Śaiva context, *Pauṣkarāgama* defines it simply as "that which one must do first, in view of a ritual occurring the next day" (quoted in *MṛĀV kr* 7.0). Brunner-Lachaux specifies that *adhivāsana*, in a more restricted sense, is "the dwelling near God, during at least one night, of objects and persons who will be central to an important ceremony requiring a ritual preparation" (*SP* 2 p. 36 n. 1). *Adhivāsana* is required for Śaiva rituals of initiation, consecration of icons, and for public festivals.

TABLE 1 Divisions of the Festival According to *Mahotsavavidhi* and Other Sources

Mahotsavavidhi	Section in *MV*	*Kāmikāgama*	*Vīratantra*
Vṛṣayāga	Sacrifice to the Bull (7)	Vṛṣayāga	Vṛṣayāga
Dhvajāroha	Flag-raising Ceremony (8)	Dhvajāroha	Keturohaṇa
Bṛhattāla	*Brahmatāla on the Bherī* (9)	Brahmatāla	Bherīghoṣa
Aṅkurārpana	Sprouts (6)	Aṅkurārpaṇa	Tīrthāṅkura
Yāgaśālā-lakṣaṇa	Sacrificial Hall (10)	Yāgaśālārcana	Yāgaśālā
Astrayāga	Trident Ceremony (11)	Astrayāga	Yāgakarman
Balidāna	Presentation of Tribute (13)	Balidāna	Balidāna
Yānakrama	Order of Processions (14)	Yānakrama	Utsava
Pariveṣa	Perambulation (14a)	Pariveṣa	Pariveṣaṇa
Nīrāñjana	Illumination Ceremony (15)	Nīrāñjanakrama	
Kautuka	Tying Protective Thread (12)	Kautuka	Kautukārambha
Tīrthasamgraha	Collection of Holy Water (16)	Tīrthasamgraha	Tīrthasamgraha
Cūrṇotsava	Festival of Powder (17)	Cūrṇotsava	Cūrṇotsava
Tīrthaka	Final Bath (18)	Tīrthaka	Tīrthakārya
Avaroha	Flag-lowering Ceremony (20)	Avaroha	Dhvajārohaṇa
Snapana	Bath with Pots (19)	Snapana	Ghaṭasnāna
Vaivāhika	Wedding Ceremony (25)	Vaivāhika	
Bhaktotsava	Festival of the Devotees (27)	Bhaktotsava	Ketubhaktotsava
	Raising Deity onto Chariot (23)		Rathāroha
	Hunting Festival		Mṛgayātra
	Worship with Powder		Cūrṇāhuti
	Silent Procession		Maunotsava
	Festival of Caṇḍeśa (21)		Caṇḍayāga

Sources: Kāmikāgama, quoted in *Mahotsavavidhi* of Aghoraśiva, pp. 57–58; *Vīratantra*, quoted in *Mahotsavavidhi* of Aghoraśiva, p. 58.

should begin each day by shaving, and they should put on clean, well-beaten clothes. Starting with a resolution, they should honor their chosen deity, and begin the ceremonies.

On the morning prior to raising the flag, one should shave.

On the first, second, third, fourth, fifth, sixth, seventh, eighth, and ninth days tribute should be offered two times per day.[4] On the day of the final bathing, one should first give the morning tribute, and then begin the ceremony of powder and the bathing.

[4] *Balidāna* the giving of tribute, is a common rite in Śaiva and more generally Indic ritual. In the Vedic tradition, *bali* denotes food offerings to a variety of lesser divinities and semi-divinities, spirits, and beings (*bhūtas*) who do not receive the primary sacrificial offerings. *Bali* is not offered in fire, but put down or strewn on the ground or on a pedestal (Gonda 1980: 417). *Manusmṛti* (3.87–93) provides a list of *bali* recipients that includes dogs, outcasts, Caṇḍālas, lepers, crows, and insects. P. V. Kane sees this as "the outcome of the noble sentiment of universal kindness and charity (1968–74: 2.746)." In Śaiva *mahotsava*, likewise, *balidāna* serves a universalizing or congregative purpose, in line with the overall aims of the festival. Practical specifications for distributing tribute will be given below, in section 13.

TABLE 2 Types and Durations of Mahotsavas According to the Several Āgamas

No. of Days	*Ajitāgama*	*Dīptāgama*	*Sūkṣmāgama*	*Kāraṇāgama*	*Rauravāgama*
1 days	Śaiva	Śaiva	Śaiva	Śaiva	Śāntika
3 days	Gauṇa	Gauṇa	Gauṇa	Gauṇa	Pauṣṭika
5 days	Bhauta	Bhautika	Bhautika	Bhautika	Jayada
7 days	Bhauvana	Bhauvana	Bhauvana	Bhauvana	Dhanada
9 days	Śākta	Daivika	Daivika	Daivika	Sārvakāmika
11 days	Raudra		Paitṛka		
12 days	Saura	Paitka			
13 days		Kaumāra	Kaumāra	Kaumāra	
14 days	Mānava	Sāvitra			
15 days	Pakṣa	Cāndra	Sāvitra	Sāvitra	
17 days			Cāndra	Cāndra	
27 days				Saura	

Sources: Ajitāgama 27.3–7; *Dīptāgama* 83. 8–11, quoted in Bhatt, ed. *Rauravāgama* 1 p. 69; *Sūkṣmāgama* 13.15–17, quoted in Bhatt, ed., *Ajitāgama* 1 p. 312; *Kāraṇāgama, uttarabhāga*, quoted in Bhatt, ed., *Ajitāgama* 1 p. 312; *Rauravāgama* 18. 8–10.

The nine-day festival begins with raising the flag.[5]

1. *Determination of Proper* Nakṣatras

In the month of Mārgaśīrṣa, the festival should end on the Ārdra *nakṣatra*. In Puṣya month, it should end on Puṣya *nakṣatra*. In Māgha, it ends on Māgha. In Phalguna, on Uttaraphalguna. In Caitra month on Citra *nakṣatra*. In Vaiśākha it ends on Viśākha; in Jyeṣṭha on Jyeṣṭha or Mūla. In Āṣāḍha month it should end on Uttarāṣāḍha or Pūrvāṣāḍha. In Śrāvaṇa it ends on Śravaṇa. In Bhādrapada month, the festival ends on Pūrvabhādrapa. In Āśvina on Aśvinī, and on Kārtika it ends on Kṛttika. These are the good *nakṣatras* on which to end the festival.[6]

If the temple is on the ocean shore, the festival may end on the juncture. If it is on a river or the like, it may end either on the juncture or not.[7] In Māgha

[5] *Dhvajārohana*, the ritual of flag-raising, is a necessary feature of a nine-day festival, and of those lasting longer than nine days. Shorter festivals may omit it (*Ajitāgama* 27.23). The flag-raising ceremony, described in section 8, marks the official commencement of the festival.

[6] The timing of the festival, within any given lunar month, is calculated from its completion, that is, the final rite of bathing (*tīrtha* or *avabhṛta*). The starting point of the festival, the rasing of the flag, is then extrapolated from this end point, based on the number of days duration of the festival. Within each lunar month, the texts specify a particular day by its *nakṣatra*, that is, the asterism or constellation through which the moon passes on that day. Here Aghoraśiva's list agrees almost completely with those of *Rauravāgama* (18.1–5) and *Suprebhedāgama* (*RĀ* 1 p. 68 n. 2).

[7] Juncture (*parvan*) here denotes the "joint" between waxing and waning lunar fortnights.

month it may end on the sixth day of the waxing moon, or in Jyeṣṭha on the eighth day of the waning moon.

Alternatively, one may have the final bathing performed on the *nakṣatra* of the chief priest, the king, the patron, the deity, the village, or the like, or on a *nakṣatra* designated by the agent.[8]

One should set the final bathing in the morning if it is to be done in the ocean, in the afternoon if in a tank or the like, and at midday if in a river. One should set the final bathing in the evening if the *nakṣatra* is Aditya.

When there are two lunar mansions (*ṛkṣa*) or two lunar days (*tithi*) in the same month, it should be in the next month. If it is joined on both sides, or if it is connected to the sun's passage (*saṅkrānti*), then it should be set on the previous *nakṣatra*.

It is best if the festival, from the raising of the flag to the final bath, is performed within a single month. One may begin the final bath at the end of the equinox, or the solstice, or an eclipse.

In the Śiva-festival of Śaiva through Āditya types, the final bath may be in the morning or at night, and the flag-raising should be in the morning.[9] Here night denotes evening, and day denotes morning. So one should perform the raising of the flag in the morning.

> On the flag one should place only the Bull emblem, and no other emblem. if one begins the festival with the emblem of others, it will bring great misfortune.[10]

A person should not perform a foundation rite for a village or the like, or a wedding, during the festival of God. If this is done, there will be misfortune for the king and the kingdom.

[8] Other Āgamas like *Ajitāgama* (27.16–17) and *Rauravāgama* (18.5) also allow these alternative methods of fixing the date. The *nakṣatras* of priest, king, or patron would be the *nakṣatras* of their days of birth. The *nakṣatra* of the deity would be calculated from the consecration of the principal Śiva-liṅga of the temple (*liṅga-pratiṣṭhā*), and that of the village would be based on the founding of the community. *Rauravāgama* (18.6) specifies that the choice is made according to the decision of the agent (*kartṛ*), which here could denote the presiding priest (*ācārya*), the patron (*yajamāna*), or more likely the astronomer (*daivajña*). The astronomer elsewhere determines proper timing for festival events.

[9] The reference to *śaivāditya* probably refers here to the different categories of Śaiva *mahotsavas* given in several Āgamas. According to these lists, the Śaiva would be the one-day festival, while the Āditya (or Saura, Sāvitra) would be one of the lengthiest, from thirteen days (according to *Ajitāgama*), fifteen days (*Sukṣmāgama*), and up to twenty-seven days (*Kāraṇāgama*) (quoted in Bhatt, ed., *AĀ* 1 p. 312).

[10] The verse here refers ahead to the design scheme of the festival flag, as described in section 7 below.

2. *The Festival of Gaṇeśa*

Before beginning the festival, one should renovate all the festival conveyances, from the vehicles through the great chariots.[11] One should decorate all festival locations, starting with the homes of the deities and ending with the roads, with stalks of banana and areca trees, with seasonal fruits, sprouts, and flower garlands gathered from the coconut, lime, and other trees, and with mirrors, gateways, canopies, banners, garlands, and the like.[12] The temporary pavilions, the rest pavilions, and other pavilions should also be ornamented.[13] One should have the ground swept and sprinkled with water, and then have the ground purified.[14]

One should have a festival of Gaṇeśa performed lasting nine days, seven days, three days, or one day, at the conclusion of the Bhadrakālī festival.[15]

Here is how it should be done. One should first honor all the icons of Gaṇeśa, Skanda, and Vīraśāsta, and the twenty-five icons of Śiva, Skanda, Caṇḍeśa, Śiva's Trident, and the Devotees with the five cow-products, and then ornament them.[16] At an auspicious moment for the

[11] *Vāhana* (vehicle) generally denotes zoomorphic conveyances of the gods, such as the bull Nandin of Śiva and the eagle Garuḍa of Viṣṇu. Here *vāhanas* are fabricated vehicles of transport, upon which the iconic deities are mounted for transport. In a festival, Śiva may ride a different *vāhana* in each procession. In section 14, Aghoraśiva sets out a schedule of *vāhanas* for each morning and evening procession. (See Smith 1981 for a valuable overview of temple *vāhanas* within the south Indian Pañcarātra Vaiṣṇava tradition, and Waghorne 1991 for an excellent general study of south Indian *vāhanas*.) The chariots (*ratha*) and other conveyances such as palanquins will be discussed below, in sections 14 and 23.

[12] Since the festival involves an expansion of the divine realm beyond the confines of the temple, it is important to repair and beautify both within and outside the temple. In particular, the processional routes should be adorned with auspicious items. Among these general festive decorations, gateways (*toraṇa*) are decorated arches that serve as passageways. See Dagens 1984: 82 on temporary decorative arches.

[13] These are *maṇḍapas* (pavilions), both permanent and temporary, that will be used in the festival. The temporary pavilions (*prapā*) are constructed in light materials, without a base, to serve public ceremonies. See *Mayamata* 25.26–29.

[14] *Bhūśuddhi*, the purification of the ground, here indicates simple acts, such as clearing the ground and drawing auspicious designs in powder, nowadays called *kōlam* in Tamil. The work of Vijaya Nagarajan (2000; forthcoming) examines the contemporary practice of *kōlam* among Tamil women as "a ritual of generosity." The *kōlam*, she notes, "is designed to invite, host, and maintain close relationships with the goddesses Lakṣmī and Bhūdevī, who will in turn prevent harm, illness, and laziness from entering the household" (2000: 455), or here, the expanded terrain of the festival.

[15] The festival of Gaṇeśa is held prior to the main festival, as is appropriate to Gaṇeśa's status as Vighneśa, the remover of obstacles. The reference here to the festival of Bhadrakālī poses more of a problem, since Aghoraśiva gives no further comment on this preliminary festival.

[16] Aghoraśiva prescribes a simple general honoring here of all the portable (*cala*) icons to be used in the festival. The *pañcagavya* (five cow-products) are cow dung, urine, ghee, yogurt, and milk, mixed together with mantras in a ritual manner. See *SP* 2, *prāyaścitta* vv. 105–110, on the preparation of *pañcagavya* in a Śaiva ritual context. Great powers of purification are ascribed to this decoction, and it is employed in many purificatory rites as well as rites of expiation. The use of *pañcagavya* is attested in the later phases of Vedic ritual tradition, but the Śaivas of course infuse the preparation with the mantras of Śiva's powers, not the Vedic hymns. See Gonda 1980: 185 and Kane 1968–74: 2.773–74.

festival, the officiating priest, the assistant priests, the king, and the patron, along with the brahmins and the musicians in attendance should start the worship of Gaṇeśa by declaring this an auspicious day, adding the word "Mahādeva."[17] One should first bathe, then honor the deity, and present to him *modaka* sweets, fried edibles, and other good things to eat.[18] He should then have the brahmins fed. He announces, "May there be no obstructions to this festival! " Then he should have the temple workers, and all the unfortunate, blind, and poor people and others pleased with food and clothing.

He should have the Trident and Caṇḍeśa, preceded by Gaṇeśa, raised into chariots or palanquins.[19] Then, accompanied by mirrors, umbrellas, yak-tail fans, other accouterments, and lots of banners, and accompanied also by sandalwood, flowers, incense, lamps, various musical instruments, and the sounds of the Vedas, they should circumambulate the village.[20] Then they should enter the audience hall.[21]

[17] A group including the significant priests and notable personages gathers to begin the festival ceremonies. For discussion of the personnel of the festival, see the Introduction. Here the term *tauryatrikas* probably refers to performers of the "triple symphony" of vocal music, instrumental music, and dance (bodily music) featured in many festival events (*Amarakośa* 1.1.7.10). Aghoraśiva does not specify how to calculate the "auspicious moment" (*śubha-lagna*) to commence this ceremony; this would probably involve the expertise of the astronomer (*daivajña*). The declaration of an auspicious day (*puṇyāhavācana*) is a frequent feature in the festival. The priest will proclaim, "Let there be well-being! " (*svasty astu*), and others around him agree by repeating the sentiment. The *puṇyāhavācana* is a Vedic practice (Gonda 1980: 262; Kane 1968–74: 2.216–17) that survives in many Indian ritual contexts. See Diehl 1957 for a description of *puṇyāhavācana* as a self-standing ceremony in south India. Aghoraśiva makes the Śaiva transformation of this general ritual procedure explicit by adding the name of Śiva, Mahādeva, to the formula.

[18] Gaṇeśa is partial to *modaka*, similar to the modern *laḍḍu* so often seen in Gaṇeśa's hand or trunk. *Modaka* are balls of steam-cooked rice paste prepared with coconut and molasses (*SP* 4 p. 53 n. 183 and Acharya 2002: 160).

[19] A small procession involving three icons marks the Gaṇeśa festival. Each icon is raised into its own conveyance (*yāna*). *Rathas* (chariots), *śibikas* (palanquins), or other conveyances may be used. Chariots are wheeled carts pulled by ropes (see section 23 for a full description), while palanquins are litters on poles carried on the shoulders of bearers. *Mayamata* 31.2–29 describes several types of *śibikas*.

[20] The procession does a *pradakṣiṇa* (circumambulation) of the village. *Pradakṣiṇa* is the general Indic procedure of circling an object, person, or location, in a clockwise direction so as to keep one's right side always toward the thing being encircled. Circumambulation is common in Vedic ritual, and there its purpose, says the *Taittirīya Āraṇyaka* (2.2) is "to shake off evil. " In Vedic interpretive texts, it is identified with the daily movement of the sun, and related to the greater status of the right side (Gonda 1980: 58–60). In the Śaiva festival context, *pradakṣiṇa* most often denotes the clockwise processional movement of divinities around the temple or surrounding community. The various accouterments of the festival procession will be discussed below.

[21] The *āsthāna-maṇḍapa*, or audience hall, is a rectangular pavilion intended for audiences of gods and kings (Dagens 1984: 109). Here the festival icons are kept between festivals and clothed for processions. See *Mayamata* 25.72–75 for a formal description.

3. *Acquisition of the Pole*

One should then acquire the pole for the flagstaff, following procedures similar to those followed in acquiring a stone for a liṅga.[22]

One should select a tree from one of these species: wood-apple, *khādira*, pine, breadfruit, *arjuna*, *aśoka*, acacia, or bamboo. Examine it from top to bottom.[23] One should honor Śiva, present some tribute, and make a protective encirclement.[24] Then it is cut down with an axe.[25]

If it falls to the east, to the north, or to the northeast, that is auspicious, but otherwise one should abandon the tree.[26]

The tree should be squared, and then together with the *śilpin* the priest should take hold of it, lift it onto a cart, and take it to the temple.[27] There one

[22] The procedures for obtaining a proper stone for a Śiva-liṅga are given in the Āgama treatments of *liṅga-pratiṣṭhā* such as in the *Somaśambhupaddhati* (see *SP* 4 pp. 24–32) and in Aghoraśiva's *Śivapratiṣṭhāvidhi*. See Takashima 2005 for a study of early Śaiva Āgama treatments of *pratiṣṭhā*. The use of similar procedures for acquiring the flagpole indicates the important role it will play in the festival, as another site for the presence of Sadāśiva. The acquisition of the pole is necessarily done prior to the commencement of the festival proper. In modern south Indian festivals, this rite is unnecessary, since the main flagpole is a permanent fixture, not a wooden pole used only for one festival.

[23] *MĀŚ* (p. 59) gives the same list of trees acceptable for use as a flagpole, only adding *candana*, the sandal tree. *MĀŚ* also provides longer lists from *Kāmikāgama* and *Kāraṇāgama*, and other texts likewise give lists of proper flagpole trees. *MĀŚ* adds that the presiding priest should make sure it is firm and straight from root to tip.

[24] The priest offers a brief *pūjā* according to the rules, specifies the *MĀŚ* (p. 59), with sandal, flowers, food-offerings, incense, lamps, and the like, and with offerings of tribute, presumably to conciliate any other spirits inhabiting the tree. *Nirodhana* (protective encirclement) is a ritual act aimed at detaining the presence of the divine in some object. As *Jñānaratnāvali* puts it, "*Nirodhana* is a petition, that the Lord remain always full of grace toward one" (see *KKD*, "Establishment and Other Acts of Recognition, " p. 147). In daily worship, it forms part of the sequence employed during invocation of Śiva within the liṅga. The priest forms the gesture of restraint (*samnirodha-mudrā*) with his hands, and recites the AGHORA mantra.

[25] The cutting of the tree would be the preserve of the *śilpin*, not the *ācārya*. *MĀŚ* specifies that the tree should be chopped down with an axe in the manner stated in the *śilpaśāstras* (*MĀŚ*, p. 59). The south Indian *śilpaśāstra* work, *Mayamata* (15.81–102) provides more detailed instructions for the *śilpin* in the context of its discussion of building materials, including wood for pillars. The *śilpin* should go to the forest at a propitious time, make offerings to the chosen tree (including meat offerings), spend a night next to the tree, and pronounce a mantra before he commences the chopping:

> Let Spirits, Divinities, and Demons disperse! On you, O trees, let Soma bestow power! May it be propitious for you, O sons of Earth! Divinities and Demons, I shall accomplish this act and you must change your dwelling place. (Dagens, tr., *MM* vol. 1 p. 203)

He whets his blade and makes three knocks on the trunk to examine the sap. Then he chops it down.

[26] *Mayamata* (15.94–98) agrees that the north and east directions are the proper ones for the tree to fall, and adds other prognostications. If cries of lions, tigers, or elephants are heard when the tree falls, that is a good omen, while the sound of cries, laughter, shrieks, and whispers augur poorly. A tree falling such that its root is above the top will bring about the death of relatives and servants. If the trunk is broken during the fall it heralds the cutter's death, and so on. The *śilpin* clearly must be an expert woodsman and prognosticator as part of his specialized knowledge.

[27] *MĀŚ* (p. 60) realistically suggests hitching bulls to the two ends of the pole to lift it into the cart. It also makes the transporting of the pole more festive by suggesting that musical instruments accompany the priest and artisan on their return to the temple.

washes it with the five cow-products, ties a protective thread at its top, and announces again an auspicious day.[28] He takes it to the bathing-pavilion, and rubs it with sandal, oil, and the like.[29] Then he has betel-nut and presents given to everyone.

4. *The Flagpole*

The priest prepares a platform there and places the pole in the middle.[30] He should ornament it with cloth and the like, and decorate it with flowers and other decorations. He shows it incense and lamp. On its three portions, square, octagonal, and circular, he should honor the three elements starting with the Śiva-portion, along with their presiding lords.[31] He has the pole raised up while reciting OM, placed in its proper location, and then he should have it installed, following the procedures given for ordinary installations.[32]

[28] The *rakṣasūtra* or *kautuka* (protective cord) is a cord of cotton or more costly threads tied around the wrists of many participants in the festival, including priests, patrons, artisans, musicians, dancers, Śiva-liṅga, portable icons, and chariots. The *rakṣasūtra* has its own ritual preparation, and the tying of the *rakṣasūtra* on the icons forms an important rite within the festival. Aghoraśiva treats this in section 12 below. Tying of the *rakṣasūtra* is also enjoined for other public rituals, such as *liṅga-pratiṣṭhā* (*SP* 4 p. 146 n. 401).

[29] The *snāna-maṇḍapa* (bathing pavilion) is a special building for bathing icons, within the temple grounds either in the courtyard in front of the cloister or incorporated within the cloister (*MM* 23.72–73). *Mayamata* (25.61–69) gives specifications for two types of square pavilion suitable for bathing, the *padmaka* type "lovely as a lotus" and the *bhadraka* type.

[30] *Sthaṇḍila* (platform) denotes a surface, either on the ground or raised above it, prepared for ritual activity. It may be smeared with cow dung to purify it, and a design may be laid out on it with rice powder. Such ritually prepared surfaces are used repeatedly in the *mahotsava*, as in other Śaiva rituals.

[31] The portions here are the three *tattvas* or *tattva*-groups Śiva, Vidyā, and Ātman, with presiding lords Rudra, Viṣṇu, and Brahman. Within these *tattva*-groups are arrayed the thirty-six constituent elements (also called *tattvas*) of the manifest world. Here the three *tattva*-groups correspond to three portions of the flagstaff, as in other ritual contexts they correspond to three portions of the Śiva-liṅga, which also has square, octagonal, and circular portions. See diagram 1, and Janaki 1988, figs.1 and 10.

[32] *MĀŚ* quotes lengthy discussions from *Kāmikāgama* (*UKĀ* 6.32 ff.), *Kāraṇāgama*, and *Uttarasvāyambhuvāgama* on the design of the flagpole and how to set it up. According to the texts, there are several possible locations for the flagpole: at the entrance to the temple, in front of Nandin or behind him, between the entry tower (*gopura*) and the main altar (*mahāpīṭha*), within the first enclosure wall, or within the entry tower (*UKĀ*, quoted in *MĀŚ*, cf. Dagens 1984: 141). It is always aligned along an east-west axis in relation to the principal deity of the temple. In modern practice, says Janaki (1988: 8), the flagpole is usually located between the entry tower and the *balipīṭha* in the outer courtyard of the temple grounds, and always on the temple's eastern axis.

First, directs *Uttarasvāyambhuvāgama* (*MĀŚ* pp. 106–7), dig a hole one cubit deep, and smear it with cowdung. A golden tortoise or bull image may be placed at the bottom of the hole, and then the pole is placed upright in the hole. To support the pole, the *śilpin* must construct an "altar" (*vedikā*), here a square masonry structure with steps forming a belt (*mekhalā*) around it, and a molding in the form of a lotus on top. In the middle of the lotus is a receptacle (*karṇikā*) through which the pole passes. Once this base is constructed, says *Uttarakāmikāgama*, the priest dismisses the *śilpin*, and goes on with a brief consecration of the raised flagpole. The *sāmānya-pratiṣṭhā* (ordinary installation) Aghoraśiva prescribes here may be a simple ceremony, or it may be quite elaborate, as *UKĀ* recommends.

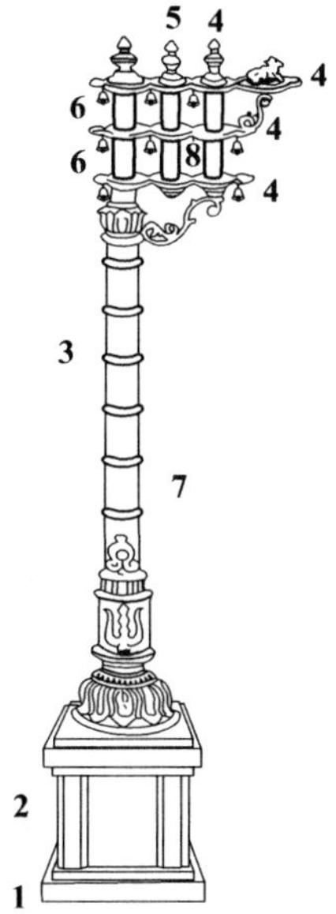

DIAGRAM 1. Flagpole and Deities. Source: S. S. Janaki, *Dhvaja-stambha (Critical Account of Its Structural and Ritualistic Details)* (Madras: Kuppuswami Sastri Research Institute, 1988), fig. 1.

Portions of flagpole	Divine aspects
1. square section	ātmatattva
2. octagonal section	vidyātattva
3. circular section	śivatattva
4. yaṣṭi-phalakas	three Śaktis (Kriyāśakti, Jñānaśakti, Icchāśakti)
5. upadaṇḍas	Sun and Moon
6. small bells	
7. darbhakūrca	
8. iron ring (for hoisting banner)	

In height, the pole should reach the pinnacle (*sthūpī*) of the temple, or the top of the column (*cūlikā*), or the parrot's beak (*śukanāsa*). He should have the flagpole made with three horizontal bars, three planks, and two supporting struts. It should also be fitted with bells and with a bundle of 108 stalks of *darbha* grass. It should have a *darbha*-rope wound around it, and a ring.[33]

These are the procedures for the acquisition of the pole and the installation of the flagpole.

[33] The horizontal bars (*yaṣṭi*) and planks (*phalaka*) are attached near the top of the pole, perpendicular to it, and the two supporting poles (*upadaṇḍa*) intersect them at right angles. Some texts, such as *Ajitāgama* (27.79–80), prescribe lengths of these elements in proportion to the height of the main pole. The small bells are hung from the horizontal bars, at the interstices between the vertical poles. See diagram 1 and Janaki 1988, fig. 1. The bundle of *darbha* grass (*darbhakūrca*) covers the front part of the post. The rope of *darbha* and the iron ring (*valaya*) are for hoisting the flag. See section 8 for the hoisting.

5. *Collection of the Earth*

In a good place such as the bank of a river the priest should collect the earth, according to procedures given previously.[34] He should go to the place together with the icons, starting with Gaṇeśa, and accompanied by various instruments and the sounds of the Vedas, and then gather the earth following previously given procedures.[35] With the earth carried by temple attendants, by Māheśvaras, by Rudragaṇikās, or on elephants or other temple animals, the procession should circumambulate the city, and then enter the temple.[36] There the priest should place it on the altar for the ceremony of the sprouts.[37] He should feed Gaṇeśa with *modaka* sweets, with sweet cake, with sugarcane stalk, and with the seasonal fruits of coconut, bilva, pomegranate, and banana. He offers chick peas, mung beans, betel-nut, and other condiments. Then he worships Gaṇeśa with all the services.

This is the procedure for the Collection of Earth.

6. *Sprouts*

> First are the sprouts for the flag. Second are the sprouts for the festival.

[34] "Whenever *aṅkurārpaṇa* is to be done, one must also perform the collection of earth" (*MĀŚ* p. 74). The collection of earth (*mṛtsaṅgraha*) is required for the subsequent rite of seed-sprouting (*aṅkurārpaṇa*), which is necessary for every public ritual in the Śaiva system. Aghoraśiva here refers to a previous discussion of procedure, perhaps that in *Śivapratiṣṭhāvidhi* (p. 5) attributed to him. The *MĀŚ* (pp. 74–76) quotes an unnamed Āgama that provides helpful additional details. This ceremony, it suggests, should be performed on the night prior to the flag-raising. Good locations for gathering earth include not only river banks, but also tanks, temple grounds, forests, lakes, dams, and other similar places (*MĀŚ* p. 74).

[35] The ceremonial procession to collect the earth features Gaṇeśa. The *MĀŚ* recommends starting with a special *abhiṣeka* of Gaṇeśa and feeding him his favorite sweetmeats, *modaka*, and other edibles. Gaṇeśa rides on a palanquin and circumambulates the town, then proceeds to the place of collection. In this procession, says the *MĀŚ*, the musical instruments are the *bherī* and *paṭaha* drums, the bull-roarer (*vṛṣavādya*), conch, and *dundubhi* drum. There may also be a row of 1,000 lamps attached to the tops of poles. Elephants, horses, and the Rudragaṇikās (temple dancers) accompany the group.

The unspecified text quoted in *MĀŚ* also prescribes the ceremony at the place of collection. Gaṇeśa is brought to the spot, and the priest and brahmins ask his permission to perform the rite. They honor Gaṇeśa, in order to remove any obstacles, and proclaim an auspicious day. The priest sprinkles the surface of the earth, and performs a preparatory sequence of acts from daily worship that consecrates the earth in that location as a divine support. Meanwhile, four brahmins recite the Vedic "Hymn to the Earth" (*bhūsūkta*, from *Taittirīya Samhitā* 1.5.3; see *ŚPV* pp. 10). Finally the ground is broken as the priest recites ASTRA mantra, and the soil collected as he recites MŪLA. They even out the surface of the ground, and return to the temple with the soil.

[36] The personnel carrying the earth may be *paricārakas* (temple attendants), Māheśvaras, or Rudragaṇikās (temple-dancers).

[37] The special altar for the sprout-ceremony (*aṅkurārpaṇa-vedikā*) will be in the northwest corner of the sacrificial pavilion (*yāga-maṇḍapa*). A platform is prepared there with eight buckets (*droṇa*) of unhusked rice, and on it the priest lays out a diagram with sixteen squares, four in the middle for the central pot, and twelve around the perimeter for bowls of three types (*pālikā*, *ghaṭika*, and *śarāva*) (*MĀŚ* p. 90; see also *RĀ* 1, Dagens trans., p. 65 for diagram based on a twenty-five-square *maṇḍala*). In the central four squares a cushion is formed with seven kinds of grain, and a fully dressed pot, called the *somakumbha*, is placed here. Bowls are placed in the other twelve squares, starting in the northeast.

Third would be the sprouts for the bath. One should sprout them as stated previously.[38]

This is the procedure for the raising of sprouts.

7. *Sacrifice to the Bull*

On the day before the hoisting of the flag, at night, one should perform the preparatory rites.[39]

Then the officiating priest should worship Śiva and announce his intention.[40] He covers the place of the Bull Nandin with cloth canopies and the like and has it

[38] The rite of rasing sprouts (*aṅkurārpaṇa*) is always included in lists of constituent rites of the festival, but here Aghoraśiva gives it the briefest treatment, and only refers his reader to an earlier treatment of the topic. Probably that is the treatment in his *Śivapratiṣṭhāvidhi* (pp. 77–86). *Aṅkurārpaṇa* is common to many Śaiva rituals, including installation, consecration, bathing, and other public ceremonies such as festivals (*RĀ* 17.1–2). Several Āgamas have chapters providing general rules applicable to all Śaiva contexts, such as *PKĀ* 63, *AĀ* 35, and *RĀ* 17. *MĀŚ* (pp. 90–93) quotes an unnamed text that gives full procedures in a festival setting, and I summarize that text here.

As Aghoraśiva's verse indicates, *aṅkurārpaṇa* is particularly related to three subsequent parts of the festival: the flag-raising, the festival proper (i.e., processions), and the final bathing. At the prepared *aṅkurārpaṇa-vedikā* (see note 37), with its central Soma-pot and twelve surrounding bowls of gathered soil, the priest performs an initial sequence of acts from daily worship, and ritually constructs a throne in the middle. On that throne he invokes Candra, the Moon, by visualizing Candra's form and reciting the CANDRA-MŪLA mantra. (See *MM* 36.157–59 for a *dhyānaśloka* of Candra's form.) The priest then worships Candra. In the surrounding bowls he invokes a group of twelve Ādityas or Suns, starting with Vaikartana (in *MĀŚ*) or Vaiśvata (according to *Kumāratantra*, quoted in Bhatt, ed., *RĀ* 1 p. 66 n. 6). The twelve Ādityas are also worshiped and honored with food. In another pot the priest prepares the seeds, of fifteen kinds. He soaks and rinses them, then consecrates them and recites mantras over them such that they become *śaiva* (pure). As the conch and other auspicious instruments sound and brahmins recite the Vedic hymns of praise to the plants (*oṣadhi-sūkta*), the priest plants the seeds while reciting the HṚDAYA mantra. After that the seeds are left to germinate. They should be watered daily with water from the Soma-pot.

The shoots are seen as an index, or even as a cause, of the outcome of the festival ceremonies to follow.

> One should consider that, if the sprouts are straight and white, this will bring about the success of the entire ritual. But if they come up crooked and dark colored, this will cause obstacles to all the excellent rites. Recognizing this danger, the true priest should perform a pacification (*śānti*) rite. (*MĀŚ* p. 93)

For a broad discussion of *aṅkurārpana* and related rites in Indic ritual culture, see Biardeau 1986.

[39] *Vṛṣayāga* is classified as a preparatory rite (*adhivāsana*), along with putting up the flagpole and planting the seeds in *aṅkurārpaṇa*. It is best done the night before raising the flag.

The preparatory ritual of *vṛṣayāga* centers around Nandin, Śiva's bull mount. Within the *vṛṣayāga* rite, Nandin has two primary forms: the unmoving stone Nandin that sits permanently outside the sanctum facing the Śiva-liṅga, and the Nandin that is drawn as the principal emblem on the festival flag. During this ritual, the priest and *śilpin* prepare the flag and consecrate it as a divine support for the Bull's presence during the festival. It is called a "sacrifice" because one of the constituent rites is a *homa*, fire-offerings directed towards the Bull. However, the paradigm it follows most closely is that of *pratiṣṭhā*, the installation or establishment of a new icon, in this case the Bull emblem on the flag.

[40] According to *MĀŚ* (p. 121), the *vṛṣayāga* has ten divisions: (1) drawing the Bull, (2) opening its eyes, (3) resting in water, (4) sprinkling, (5) beginning the couch, (6) staying with the pots, (7) imposition of the *kalās*, (8) fire-rite, (9) tying a bracelet, and (10) bathing the flagpole.

decorated.[41] He sits in a steady posture, facing north, and performs the imposition of limbs and other impositions, as previously specified.[42] He prepares reception-water, worships the Lord Nandin, and feeds him rice mixed with mung beans.[43]

He then prepares a platform in front of the Bull, and with his fingers draws the design of a lotus in the middle of it. He strews *kuśa* grass and flowers all around, and sets up nine pots. Onto the middle pot he constructs a sixfold throne and worships the Bull.[44] Then, starting in the east and ending in the northeast direction, he honors the eight forms of the Bull, using the ĀSANA, MŪRTI, and MŪLA mantras for each one.[45]

I honor Ukṣan.
I honor Gopati.
I honor Śṛṅgin.
I honor Nandin.
I honor Vṛṣapati.
I honor Vṛṣāṇin.
I honor Śaṅkukaṇi.
I honor Mahodara.

Or else he may honor the World-guardians.[46]

[41] The fixed image of the Bull Nandin should rest outside the principal temple sanctum, along the east axis, facing the Śiva-liṅga. Nandin should be housed in a simple pavilion (or "kiosk," as Dagens renders it) with four pillars, which is here decorated for the occasion (Dagens 1984:144). On the proper form of Nandin, see *MM* 23. 107–31. His size should be proportional to the primary Śiva-liṅga or the temple door.

[42] That is, the priest performs the imposition (*nyāsa*) of the five *aṅgamantras*, and other sets of mantras, onto his own body, to prepare it as a "body of mantras" capable of carrying out the subsequent ritual actions. The paradigm here is the rite of self-purification in daily worship. See *KKD*, "Purification of the Elements," pp. 94–116, and Davis 1991: 58–60.

[43] The preparation of *arghya* (reception water) is described in *KKD*, "Preparation of Śiva's *Arghya*," pp. 117–18, as part of daily worship. Worship of the Bull here involves the usual offerings, such as sandal, flowers, incense, and lamp, according to *MĀŚ* (p. 121), along with the special food offering of *mudgānna*, rice with mung beans prepared with coconut and butter, similar to modern south Indian *poṅgal* (*SP* 1 p. 214, Acharya 2002: 190–91).

[44] The priest constructs the *ṣaḍutthāsana* (sixfold throne) by reciting six mantras that invoke its six parts or constituent powers: Ananta, Dharma, Jñāna, Vairāgya, Aiśvarya, and Padma. The paradigm here is the construction of Śiva's throne during daily worship (*KKD*, "Worship of Siva's Throne," pp. 127–37; Davis 1991: 122–25), though the procedure here is much abbreviated, as is appropriate to this subsidiary rite. See *SP* 1 p. 128 n. 2 on *ṣaḍutthāsana*.

[45] The priest invokes the eight Nandins, also called the Vṛṣa-vidyeśvaras, into the pots in a circumambulatory order, starting with Ukṣan in the east.

[46] The eight Lokapālas, or World-guardians, constitute a group of eight Vedic deities who appear, in Śaiva ritual contexts, in subordinate roles as agents of Śiva engaged to protect the eight directions. They are arranged in circumambulatory order, starting with Indra in the east. These eight are often joined by two others: Viṣṇu below and Brahman above. Each is associated with a distinctive mount and a weapon.

Direction	Lokapāla	Mount	Weapon
East	Indra	elephant	thunderbolt
Southeast	Agni	ram	spear
South	Yama	buffalo	staff
Southwest	Nirṛti	man	sword
West	Varuṇa	fish	noose

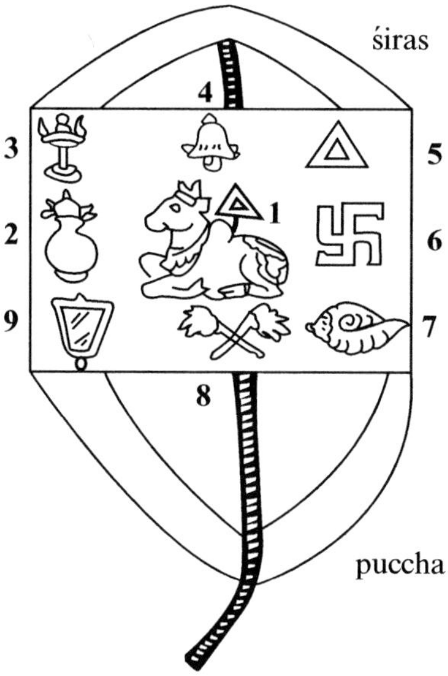

DIAGRAM 2. Design of Nandin Banner. (1) Nandin; (2) full pot; (3) lamp; (4) bell; (5) śrīvatsa; (6) svastika; (7) conch; (8) yak-tail fans; (9) mirror. Source: S. S. Janaki, *Dhvaja-stambha (Critical Account of Its Structural and Ritualistic Details)* (Madras: Kuppuswami Sastri Research Institute, 1988), fig. 5.

The cloth for the flag, as stated previously, should be nine cubits in height or some other amount, and one-fifth that length in width. The tail part should be equal to the height, and the head part should be half that of the tail. It should be made of white, fine, tightly woven cotton cloth, or some other material.[47] One divides it into three parts. In the middle portion, one should have the Bull drawn, in either one or three portions. The Bull should have red

Northwest	Vāyu	deer	flag
North	Kubera	treasure	mace
Northeast	Īśāna	bull	trident
Below	Viṣṇu	Garuḍa	discus
Above	Brahman	swan	lotus

For a comprehensive historical account of the development of the eight World-guardians, see the recent work of Wessels-Mveissen 2001.

[47] *MĀŚ* (pp. 112–20) cites passages from *Kāmikāgama* (*UKĀ* 6.7–32), *Viratantra*, *Sakalāgamasangraha*, and *Kāraṇāgama*, for descriptions of the festival flag (*paṭa* or *dhvaja*). Details differ, but the main features are consistent. The preferred material is fine cotton, though other possibilities also are mentioned, such as *dukūla*, a plant whose inner bark yields a fine cloth. Texts unanimously prescribe white cloth, though *MĀŚ* (p. 117) says color may correspond to the *varṇa* (class), presumably of the patron: white for brahmins, red for *kṣatriyas*, yellow for *vaiśyas*, and black for *śūdras*. The main part of the flag should form a large rectangle, with a cloth tail (*puccha*) below and a head (*śiras*) above, both triangular in form, proportional to the main part of the flag. See diagram 2, and Janaki 1988, figs. 4 and 5. *Vīratantra* (*MĀŚ* p. 116) proposes that the height of the flag be proportional to the temple's main Śiva-liṅga.

horns, ears, and hooves, a yellow tail, and its eyes should be white and black.[48] In front of it one should draw a full pot, and behind it a lamp. A bell, a *śrīvatsa* tuft, a *svastika*, and all the eight auspicious emblems should also be drawn on the flag.[49] Then one may begin the sacrifice to the flag.

Or else one may fix the flag, as before, as the height of the pole, and the width equal to the nose of the pole.[50]

The priest has the auspicious day announced, and sprinkles the flag with the five cow-products and other purifying substances. Then he honors the moving seat for the Bull. In front of the Bull, he prepares a platform, and makes preparations for offering a fire-rite, according to the method previously given in the section on daily fire-rites.[51] Immediately after the purification of the icon, he should prepare two platforms somewhere else, and have the Bull-banner placed in the middle.[52] With a golden needle, he should perform the eye-opening ceremony, reciting either the SŪRYA and SOMA mantras or else the VṚṢA-GĀYATRĪ.[53]

[48] The head *śilpin*, in cooperation with the officiating priest, draws the design on the flag, says *Kāraṇāgama* (*MĀŚ* p. 123). *Uttarakāraṇāgama* also suggests that the astronomer (*daivajña*) should advise them on the auspicious moment (*muhūrta*) to begin the painting, and it should be done in the presence of Śiva (that is, before the liṅga in the main sanctum) and if possible also with the king in attendance. *Kāmikāgama* gives the practical advice to stretch the banner between a pair of reeds to facilitate the painting. The central design on the banner is the Bull Nandin, who may either stand or kneel. Color schemes for the Bull are quite consistent: a white body with colored parts as Aghoraśiva specifies. Nandin should also wear a necklace of small bells.

[49] Auspicious insignia surround the Bull above, below, and on his sides. *Kāmikāgama* (*UKĀ* 6.14–15), for example, prescribes a pair of lamps on the two sides, a pair of yaktail fans and a parasol above the head, and a full-pot and optionally a trident below. Common, as here, is a set of eight auspicious objects, the *aṣṭamaṅgala*: full-pot, lamp, bell, *śrīvatsa*, *svastika*, conch, yaktail fans, and mirror. See diagram 2. The list varies slightly from Śaiva text to text (see *RĀ* 1 p. 79 n. 9 for some examples). The eight auspicious objects are employed in several Śaiva ritual contexts. For instance, gold *aṣṭamaṅgala* are deposited in the foundation of a Śaiva temple during installation rites (*MM* 12.33–35).

[50] Aghoraśiva gives alternative dimensions for the flag, as a long pendant banner hanging the entire length of the flagpole. The "nose" of the pole (*daṇḍanāsa*) indicates the length of extension outward from the central pole made by the horizontal bars (*yaṣṭiphalakā*).

[51] Aghoraśiva's order of presentation is not entirely clear here. The "moving seat" (*calāsana*) for the Bull is not mentioned in other texts. It may simply denote the fluttering flag as a mobile support for Nandin during the festival, in contrast to the unmoving stone Nandin that is a permanent temple support for the Bull. The preparations for the fire-rite (*homa*) to follow involve setting up a fire-pit made of sand (*vāluka*) and kindling a fire in it, using the consecrations starting with *nirīkṣaṇa* (*UKĀ* 6.25). For the procedures of the daily fire-rite that acts as the paradigm here, see *KKD*, "The Daily Fire-Ritual," pp. 178–91. The *homa* will be resumed after the ceremony of opening the eyes and the full invocation of Nandin in the banner.

[52] The purification of the icon (*bera-śuddhi*) here refers to the simple sprinkling of the Bull emblem on the flag. Two-dimensional figures such as the painting here can serve as supports for divine presence just as much as three-dimensional icons. According to the *Kāmikāgama* (*UKĀ* quoted in *MĀŚ* p. 113), a plate (*pātra*) on a three-legged stand should be placed in the center of one *sthaṇḍila*, and the flag deposited there. Also in the center of the *sthaṇḍila* is a pot representing the Bull, surrounded by eight more pots which are the eight Nandins. In the published *UKĀ* (6.19), eight World-guardians substitute for the eight Nandins.

[53] The eye-opening ceremony (*akṣimocana, netronmīlana*) is a key rite in awakening the image. For a manifest icon, says Somaśambhu (*SP* 4 p. 138 v. 177), it is this rite that renders divinity present in it. For a Śiva-liṅga, without parts, the carving of "marks" or *lakṣaṇa* serves the same ritual function.

We honor the one with the sharp horns. We look to the one with four hooves. May that Bull inspire us!

After the eye-opening rite, the priest should show all the auspicious objects to the Bull, starting with a view of a cow.[54] He sprinkles the Bull-banner with earth, with the five cow-products, and with cool water. Then he bathes its mirror reflection with the five cow-products and other liquids, and he has it dwell in water.[55]

The priest takes the Bull-banner out of the water and places it in the sacrificial pavilion. He sprinkles it again with the five cow-products, reciting VṚṢA-GĀYATRĪ, and sets it up on the platform. He honors the six-stage throne on the Bull, then visualizes the form by means of meditation. Then he dresses it with cloth and imposes the five *brahmamantras* on it.[56] He shows it incense and a lamp. He places a sleep-pot nearby, and all around it he imposes the eight forms of the Bull, starting with Ukṣan, and honors them.[57]

The main act involves tracing the eyes on the Bull with a golden needle, while reciting mantras of the Sun and Moon, since the two eyes are identified with these celestials, or the VṚṢA-GĀYATRĪ mantra. One Āgama compilation quoted by Janaki (1988: 33), raises an interesting ambiguity concerning who performs the rite. In Aghoraśiva's *MV* and in the Āgama texts quoted by *MĀŚ*, there is no mention of the *śilpin*, which leads one to assume the act is done entirely by the priest. According to this text, however, the *netronmīlana* of the Bull is first performed by the *śilpin*. The *ācārya* then dismisses the *śilpin*, and reperforms the eye-opening with honey and ghee, reciting the appropriate mantras. This suggests a division of ritual labor similar to that in *netronmīlana* rites in the installation of bronze Śiva images (*pratimā-pratiṣṭhā*), as in *Pūrvakāmikāgama* 68.35–40 (Davis 1997: 35).

[54] No text quoted provides a full list of auspicious sights for the newly-enlivened Bull in the flag to gaze upon. For a manifest image of Śiva, these might include: ghee, a pot of honey, a calf, a pile of grain, a brahmin, an unmarried girl (*kanyā*), and the assembled devotees (*PKĀ* 65.48–51). The priest recites an appropriate mantra for each sight.

[55] The other substances here would be various liquids used in bathing images (*snāpana*), such as the five nectars (*pañcāmṛta*). *Jalādhivāsa*, dwelling in water, is a standard part of any Śaiva installation of stone or metal icon, where after having its eyes opened (or marks carved, in the case of a liṅga), it stays for some length of time in a tank or other body of water. Here, on account of the more perishable quality of the painted image, it is the mirror bearing its reflection that actually resides in the water.

[56] Here begins the construction of the divine body (*divyadeha*) or body of mantras (*vidyādeha*), leading up to the *jīvanyāsa* or imposition of the living spirit. The installation of a Śiva-liṅga serves as the paradigm here, with some modifications. For the sixfold throne, as Nandin's seat, see note 44 above. The priest visualizes the form of Nandin according to a *dhyānaśloka*, such as:

> One should visualize the Bull as white, with all red hooves. His two eyes are white and black, and his two horns are red. His pair of ears is red in color, and he is adorned with a yellow tail. He wears a beautiful colored garland of bells. He may either stand or sit. (Janaki 1988: 32; cf. *MĀŚ* pp. 117–18)

The priest's visualization here corresponds closely to the *śilpin's* painting. The imposition of the five *brahmamantras*, corresponding to the five faces of Sadāśiva, completes the initial ritual construction of the Bull's *āsana* (throne) and *mūrti* (embodiment). After this, three sets of impositions will infuse this embodiment with divine energies, transforming it into a *vidyādeha*.

[57] The *nidrākumbha* (sleep-pot) is placed here, presumably, to assure that the Bull sleeps well during the festival to come. (On the use of *nidrākumbha* in *liṅgapratiṣṭhā*, see *SP* 4 p. 150 n. 423.) The eight forms of the Bull are as above, in the pots placed in the eight directions in the *sthaṇḍila*.

Standing at the base of the Bull, the priest imposes the thirty-four *tattvas*, from the head down to the feet, along with their presiding lords, in the following manner.[58] Starting with the mantras:

> I bow to the Sadāśiva-tattva.
> I bow to Brahman, lord of the Sadāśiva-tattva.

he honors each *tattva*, ending with:

> I bow to the Earth tattva.
> I bow to Śrīkaṇṭha, lord of the Earth tattva.

He divides them into three portions, and presents a wreath of flower garlands.[59] Then, meditating on the three divisions as before, he honors the eight forms, in order starting in the east, as follows:

> Earth, Fire, the patron, Sun, Water, Wind, Moon, and Ether.

The priest imposes Ukṣan, Gopati, Śṛṅgin, Nandin, Vṛṣapati, Vṛṣāṇin, Śaṅkukaṇi, and Mahodara as the presiding lords of the eight forms.[60] Then he performs the imposition of the living spirit, reciting the Bull's MŪLA mantra.[61] He honors the Bull with all the services, starting with establishment,

[58] The *tattvas* here are the constituent units of the manifest world. According to the Śaiva Siddhānta theology that Aghoraśiva espouses, there are thirty-six *tattvas*, divided into "pure" and "impure" domains (*śuddhādhvan* and *aśuddhādhvan*). (On the emission and reabsorption of the thirty-six *tattvas*, see Davis 1991: 44–46.) Each *tattva* has a presiding lord (*adhipa*). Here the priest imposes thirty-four of these *tattvas* along with their lords—omitting the two highest *tattvas*, *śivatattva* and *śaktitattva*—according to the order of emission onto the Bull. Each imposition (*nyāsa*) is done with an appropriate hand gesture and the recitation of its mantra. The two highest *tattvas* are excluded here because Nandin extends only up to the (beginning of the) *śakti-tattva* (see *SP* 4 p. 166 v. 219). Only Śiva extends up to the full thirty-six tattvas.

[59] The three *khaṇḍas* (portions) here are the three groups of *tattvas*: Śiva, Vidyā, and Ātman (see note 31 above). The Bull is divided into three portions above the neck, knee to neck, and foot to knee, and the priest imposes the three *tattva*-groups along with their presiding lords Rudra, Viṣṇu, and Brahman onto the Bull. Janaki (1988: 35) gives the mantras for each of these impositions.

[60] The *aṣṭamūrti* (eight forms) is another tabulation of units making up the world: the five material elements (*bhūtas*), Sun, Moon, and soul (*ātman*) or patron-sacrificer (*yajamāna*). In an old Śaiva formulation, a form of Śiva serves as lord over each: Śarva over Earth, Bhava over Water, and so on (*SP* 1 p. xi). In some Śaiva Siddhānta texts, the eight units here are interpreted as forms that Śiva's Śakti takes on: Vāmā takes on the form of Earth, Jyeṣṭhā as Water, and so on (*SP* 1 p. 168 n). Here, since the presiding deity of the ritual is Nandin, the eight Nandins instantiated in the eight surrounding pots serve as presiding lords of these eight forms. Janaki (1988: 37) gives examples of the mantras, which follow the form (for Ukṣan as lord of Earth in the east):

> OM HĀM KṢMĀMŪRTAYE NAMAḤ
> OM HĀM KṢMĀMŪRTYADHIPATAYE UKṢĀYA NAMAḤ

[61] The act of *jīvanyāsa*, or imposition of the living spirit, brings the spirit (*jīva*) or soul (*ātman*) into the body of mantras now imposed onto the Bull emblem. The procedure here corresponds to that used in the rite of *āvāhana* (invocation) in daily worship, as well as that in *śivaliṅgapratiṣṭhā*. See *KKD*, "Invocation of Śiva," pp. 144–47 for Aghoraśiva's explication of the procedure in *nityapūjā*; Davis (1991: 122–34) outlines the procedures.

and then constructs three enclosures on the outside around it, with ashes, *darbha* grass, and sesame.[62]

Calling for the World-guardians, he honors them in the fire, and recites the mantra:

I honor Ādhāraśakti in the fire-pit.

He makes three oblations, and honors the three *tattva* groups:

I honor Brahman in the *ātma-tattva*.
I honor Viṣṇu in the *vidyā-tattva*.
I honor Śiva in the *śiva-tattva*.

For each one, he gives three ladles of ghee.[63] Then he honors the eight forms starting with Earth, giving three oblations for each:

I honor the lords of each form.

Then he gives 100 or 50 oblations, individually, with the MŪLA mantra, the *brahmamantras*, and the *aṅgamantras*. Finally, he makes a complete oblation.[64]

The officiating priest takes the pot of pacifying water in hand and approaches the Bull. He sprinkles the Bull with the pacifying water from the pot, and then while reciting its MŪLA mantra he touches it three times with the base,

---

Briefly, this involves the ascending pronunciation (*uccāraṇa*) of the root-mantra (MŪLA), in this case the MŪLA mantra of the Bull:

OM HĀM VṚM HĀM VṚṢABHĀYA NAMAḤ

The process unites the Bull with his mantra, whereby the Bull may be led into the divine body constructed for him.

62 For the *upacāras* (services) immediately following the invocation of the deity, the priest uses the *mudrās* of establishment (*sthāpana*), presence (*sannidhāna*), and restraint (*sannirodha*) along with appropriate mantras to maintain the presence of the deity. See *KKD*, "Establishment and Other Acts of Recognition," pp. 147–48 on the invocation sequence, with Nirmalamaṇi's brief explanation of the significance of these acts. Compare *SP* 1 pp. 190–92 vv. 66–70 for another explication. The three enclosures (*prakāra*), formed by circling the object with three materials and reciting ASTRA, protect the newly installed divine presence. Three are required, Brunner-Lachaux postulates, because threats may come from three regions: earth, atmosphere, and sky.

63 The priest now returns to the fire-pit that has already been set up, to take up the fire-rites (*agnikārya*) again. (This is the eighth division of *vṛṣayāga* in the *MĀŚ* list, given in note 40.) This is intended to purify, reiterate, or enhance the life of the newly present Nandin. According to *Kāmikāgama* (quoted in *MĀŚ* p. 114), the priest first invokes the Bull in the midst of the fire, along with his limbs, and refreshes him with fire-offerings of sticks (*samidh*), ghee (*ājya*), and cooked rice (*caru*). Oblations are then offered to the three *tattva* groups and their presiding lords in the fire, and to the set of eight forms and their lords (note 60 above), just as they have been imposed on the flag emblem. For the equivalent procedure in *liṅga-pratiṣṭhā*, see *SP* 4 p. 172 vv. 231–32.

64 The *pūrṇāhuti* (complete oblation) brings about the completion of the fire ceremony. Standing rather than sitting, the priest makes an oblation with a full ladle of ghee. For detailed instructions in the context of daily fire-rites, see *SP* 1 p. 262 vv. 52–56.

middle, and tip of *kuśa* grass, visualizing the tripartite division of *tattvas*.[65] He does repetitions of the VṚṢA mantra, offers an oblation, encircles it with the KAVACA mantra, restrains it, and then announces Śiva's command to the presiding lords of the *tattvas*.[66] He imposes Jñānaśakti and restrains her.

They should then pass the remainder of the night with fire-oblations accompanied by the sounds of the Vedas and other auspicious hymns, or with dance, song, and other festivities, according to their devotion.

When he has completed the preparatory rite of the Bull, offered tribute in the directions, and made food offerings, the priest should sleep, as before.

These are the procedures for the preparatory rites of the Bull.

8. *The Flag-raising Ceremony*

On the following morning, the officiating priest should perform his morning bath and other daily ablutions, and after completing them he should impose mantras on himself, prepare ordinary reception-water, and perform all the rites of worship of the self, as he does daily.[67] Then he honors the banner and the

[65] The *śāntikumbha*, a pot of pacifying water kept near the fire, contains water specially prepared through the invocation of Śiva's Pāśupata weapon. Aghoraśiva sets out the procedures for its preparation in his *Śivapratiṣṭhāvidhi* (pp. 251–56) (cited by Brunner-Lachaux in *SP* 4 p. 176 n. 518). The priest invokes the *pāśupatāstra* into the pot, following the usual method of invocation, offers the usual services, and recites the PĀŚUPATĀSTRA mantra one hundred times. Imbued with Śiva's most potent weapon, the water has great powers to subdue threatening forces. The three portions of *kuśa* grass touch the portions of the enlivened Bull-emblem corresponding to the *tattva* groups: the base of the *kuśa* grass touches the lower part of the Bull from foot to knee, where is located the *ātma-tattva* presided over by Brahman, the middle touches the middle of the Bull's body where is the *vidyā-tattva* and lord Viṣṇu, and the tip touches the Bull above the neck where Rudra presides over the *śiva-tattva*. According to Janaki (1988: 38–39), this procedure completes the unification of the divine Bull, who has now been honored in three locations: the flag, the pot, and the fire.

[66] *Avakuṇṭhana* (encirclement) with the KAVACA (or armor) mantra and *nirodhana* (restraint) are ritual gestures intended to protect and assure the continued presence of the deity during the course of the ritual. Śiva's *ājñā* (command) here likewise is that the presiding lords of the *tattva* groups should remain present for the duration of the festival.

[67] The raising of the flag is the central rite of inauguration for the festival, and Aghoraśiva emphasizes its great benefits by including *phalaśruti* verses below (section 8c). Janaki (1988: 19–20) cites a Tamil poem by the thirteenth-century Śaiva teacher Umāpati, *Koṭikkavi*, composed on the occasion of a festival flag-raising at Chidambaram, which stresses its theological implications and salvific aims: "I hoist the flag with the sincere prayer that the Lord may confer His grace on the bound souls. In fact the flag and the post stand before us only to bring out significantly these latent ideas."

The priest must prepare himself for the ceremony by performing his ordinary daily rites (*nityakarman*), such as Aghoraśiva outlines in the first section of *KKD* (pp. 9–68). Aghoraśiva here emphasizes the morning bath (*prātasnāna*), the imposition of mantras onto his body (*sakalīkaraṇa*), and the preparation of ordinary reception-water (*sāmānyārghya*). In *sakalīkarana*, the Śaiva initiate recites mantras (especially the *brahmamantras* and the *aṅgamantras*) and touches different parts of his body, in order to purify and empower it as a *vidyādeha* or body of mantras, and so make it capable for subsequent ritual activity (*KKD*, "Imposition of Mantras on the Hands and Body," pp. 39–45).

pots, in proper order. He also offers 108 oblations in the fire, using sticks, ghee, and cooked rice, and then offers a complete oblation. He restrains it, and then constructs three circles around the pavilion.[68] He summons the attendants and sprinkles them with water, reciting ASTRA, and has each of them put on a turban and an upper cloth.[69] They lift the banner and the primary pot along with the others, and together with the icons starting with the Trident and ending with Caṇḍeśa, they circumambulate the village, accompanied by all the musical instruments, by the sounds of the conch and drum, and also by the sounds of the Vedas and other auspicious hymns.[70]

They reenter the temple, and on three platforms the priest places the banner on one, the King of Weapons on another, and the pot on the third.[71] The priest declares an auspicious day, and sprinkles them with the five cow-products and reception-water. He sprinkles the Bull on the banner with the water from the central pot, and performs an *abhiṣeka* with the eight subsidiary pots, starting with the pot of Ukṣan.[72] Then he adorns the banner with

[68] The *maṇḍala-traya* (three circles) here are no doubt similar to the three *prakāra* (enclosures) of ashes, *darbha* grass, and sesame that the priest constructed around the banner previously (note 62).

[69] "In rites of bathing, special purifications (*prokṣaṇa*), public ceremonies (*yāga*), fire-rites, and mantra-repetitions, the initiated Śaiva should wear a turban (*uṣṇīṣa*) and an upper cloth (*uttarīya*)," says *Dīptāgama*, quoted by Nirmalamaṇi in his commentary on Aghoraśiva's discussion of *dīkṣā*. These two items of ceremonial clothing indicate participation and ritual competance at several points within the festival, as well as in other public Śaiva rituals. *Dīptāgama* goes on: "The *uṣṇīṣa* is white, fine, soft cloth with a fringe, then cubits in length and one-fifth or one-seventh that amount in width. The experienced Śaiva will wrap it one, two, or three times around the head and tuck the end above the right ear." However, Nirmalamaṇi observes that *uṣṇīṣa* may also mean crown (*makuṭa*). As Brunner-Lachaux notes (*SP* 3 p. 27 n. 48), Śaiva texts elsewhere speak of crowns to be worn by priests in public ceremonies. As for the *uttarīya*, it is a long piece of cloth that, recommends *Dīptāgama*, should be tied and worn in the manner of a sacrificial thread (*yajñopavīta*) over the left shoulder and tied under the right.

[70] The preliminary procession before raising the flag features the flag and the pot, both supports for Nandin. They are placed on palanquins or on shield-like platforms (*kheṭaka*), says *MĀŚ* (p. 136). Accompanying these two are several icons, led by the *triśula* (Trident), also called the *astrarāja* or King of Weapons. The *triśula* is identified with Śiva's famous *pāśupata* weapon. In Śaiva temples, says *Rauravāgama* (33.11–12), a trident should be set up in the temple courtyard in front of the Nandin image, and it should be the same height as Nandin. In festival processions a portable trident is used.

Aghoraśiva never specifies what he means by *sarvatodya* ("all the instruments"). See below, note 98, for a list given in the *MĀŚ*, for the procession during *bherītāḍaṇa*.

[71] The three *sthaṇḍilas*, one cubit in diameter, are to the south of the flagpole. *MĀŚ* (pp. 135–36) prescribes five *sthaṇḍilas*, adding platforms for Caṇḍeśa and the *bherī* drum to the three for banner, Trident, and Bull-pot. In addition to the primary pot, the pots of the eight Nandins are set up around the Bull-pot.

MĀŚ goes on: the presiding priest (*guru*, called here the *sampanna-karaka* or "complete agent") along with brahmins and astronomers (*daivajña*) sit on pleasant seats, facing north. First they should honor Gaṇeśa, Lord of Obstacles, and then declare an auspicious day (p. 136).

[72] *Abhiṣeka* here, and throughout the Śaiva ritual system (and more broadly in Indic ritual as well) refers to a rite of affusion, often translated as "consecration." Pots of water or other liquids, into which various substances may have been added, are ritually infused with the powers of mantras or deities. These empowered liquids are then poured over a recipient, and transmit their powers to that recipient. The recipient might be a human (as in *ācāryābhiṣeka*, the consecration of a priest), a deity in icon form (as in the daily *abhiṣeka* of the Śiva-liṅga), or here a banner that serves as a two-dimensional icon of Nandin the bull.

sandalpaste, and offers it food such as oblation food and chick peas.[73] Next he performs an *abhiṣeka* of the Trident also with the water from that pot, adorns it, feeds it, and honors it with all the services ending with mantra-recitations. He presents indigo-powder to the Trident, puts some of the powder on himself, and then has the indigo-powder given to the king, the devotees, the temple assistants, and everyone present.[74]

The priest has the flag-pole decorated. He honors the Bull in the main pot with its GĀYATRĪ mantra.[75]

He has the god placed in a chariot or other vehicle. The Trident is in front, and the officiating priest is in front of that. Behind comes the patron along with all the devotees. Accompanied by all the instruments, by the auspicious sprouts and full pots, by various kinds of parasols, yak-tail fans, and lamps, by the ten gifts for a trip, and by song, dance, and offerings of tribute in the directions and sub-directions, they circumambulate the city.[76] Returning to the temple, they approach the flag and announce an auspicious day.

The priest sprinkles the altar, and honors it starting with Śakti and ending with Śakti.[77] He meditates on the flagpole.

[73] *Havis* (oblation food) denotes food prepared for offering in fire as a sacrificial oblation. In this context, it is rice cooked in a ritual manner (*caru*), over a Śiva-fire, with mantra recititations. See *KKD*, in Surdam 1984: 81–86, and *SP* 3 pp. 64–93 for detailed instructions on the ritual preparation of rice for initiation ceremonies.

[74] *Rajanīcūrṇa*, a powder made of indigo (L. *Indigofera tinctoria*) or curcuma (L. *Curcuma longa*), is moistened to form a paste, and distributed here to all participants.

[75] The Bull's VṚṢA-GĀYATRĪ mantra is as given above, in the section on "Sacrifice to the Bull." *MĀŚ* (pp. 137–38) gives a more complete outline of the honoring here of the Bull-pot and all the eight surrounding pots. This includes the construction of a sixfold throne, *āsana, mūrti*, invocation, and offering all services. At this point, according to *MĀŚ*, the priest also offers worship to the flag (following the same paradigm of worship as with the Bull-pot), and to the Trident. The *MĀŚ* prescribes that the priest perform the rites of the Trident and the *bherī* drum at this point as well; in *MV*, Aghoraśiva discusses these in section 9, on "The *Brahmatāla* on the *Bherī* Drum."

[76] Aghoraśiva prescribes a second procession prior to the raising of the flag. The presiding god here is Nandin present in the Bull-banner. In this procession, the auspicious sprouts (*mangalāṅkura*) planted during the earlier *aṅkurārpaṇa* ceremony are also carried.

Aghoraśiva also specifies that the processors carry the *yātrādāna*, a set of gifts presented to a traveler at the outset of a trip. Brunner-Lachaux gives the traditional list of ten gifts: cow, land, sesame, gold, ghee, cloth, grain, sugar-cane, silver, and salt (*SP* 4 pp. 228–30 n. 117). This gift is a normal part of the preliminary rites for a festival, comments Brunner-Lachaux, meant to cover (at least symbolically) the costs of the God's procession around the temple, viewed as a pilgrimage (*yātrā*).

[77] Here the priest continues the process, begun with the initial acquisition and setting up of the pole, to reconstruct the flagpole ritually as a primary site for Śiva's presence during the festival. The key act here is the imposition of Sadāśiva onto the pole. The paradigm for this is the invocation of Sadāśiva in the Śiva-liṅga during daily worship. As Janaki points out in her study of *Dhvaja-stambha*, the festival flagpole parallels the central temple liṅga in important respects, and many Āgamas call it the *kāraṇa-liṅga* (instrumental liṅga), as distinct from the *sūkṣma-liṅga* (subtle liṅga) inside the sanctum and the *sthūla-liṅga* (gross liṅga) which is the temple tower (*vimāna*) itself (Janaki 1988: 6–8).

The first act in the invocation process is to construct a throne for Sadāśiva. The masonry base of the pole, called the *vedikā* or altar, is reconstructed as a divine throne of five stages, much as the *pīṭha* (pedestal) of the Śiva-liṅga is reconstructed during daily worship. For Aghoraśiva's account of that process, see *KKD*, "Worship of Śiva's Throne," pp. 127–37. Davis (1991:123–37) provides a general overview of the process, and *SP* 1, Plate 5,

8A. MEDITATION ON THE FLAGPOLE.

> With one foot, two arms, and three eyes, he has a cord of *darbha* grass
> that adorns him like the hair above the navel.
> With his white body form, he reaches up to the temple's parrot-nose
> standing straight as the stalk of a lotus.[78]

The officiating priest invokes Sadāśiva onto the pole.[79] He honors in order the three Śaktis on the three cross-bars, Sun and Moon on the two supporting struts, the divine snake Takṣa on the rope, the wind god Vāyu on the banner cloth, and the Bull on the flag-design.[80] He feeds mung-rice or payasam to the Bull and presents incense and lamp.[81] He gives gold and other presents to brahmins.

---

offers a chart of throne stages. This divine throne, the Āgamas often say, reaches "from Śakti to Śakti," that is, from Ādhāraśakti, the "Supporting Śakti" at the base, up to Paraśakti, the "Highest Śakti" located in the middle of the highest stage of the throne.

[78] This *dhyānaśloka* for the *dhvajastambha*, which anthropomorphizes the pole, is common to many Āgamas. Janaki observes (1988: 17) that it is recited in practice in present-day temples. Janaki quotes a parallel passage from *Kāraṇāgama* (*UKārĀ* 24.148–49): the tip of the pole is the crown, the cross-bars form the face, the two ropes are like arms, the *darbha* bundle is the matted hair, the cloth banner resembles skin, and the pedestal base is the seat.

[79] Aghoraśiva's terse statement about invoking Sadāśiva here refers to a complex ritual procedure in which the priest first constructs a divine body of mantras (*vidyādeha*) that constitutes Sadāśiva, and then invokes Śiva himself to inhabit this mantra-body. *MĀŚ* (p. 140) spells out some of this. After meditating on the flagpole according to the method previously described, the *MĀŚ* directs, the priest imposes the *brahmamantras* onto it, starting with the head and ending with the feet. He then imposes thirty-eight *kalāmantras*, following several different methods of imposition, and unties these mantra powers with the VIDYĀDEHA mantra into a single divine body. Then the priest should invoke Śiva into it by reciting the MŪLA mantra and displaying the *netra-mudrā* (eye gesture). For the paradigm procedures in daily worship, see *KKD*, "Imposition of Śiva's Embodiment," pp. 138–47. Davis 1991: 125–33 gives an overview of the process.

[80] In addition to Sadāśiva on the main pole, other parts of the flagpole assembly becomes divine supports. The three Śaktis on the cross-bar are Kriyāśakti, Jñānaśakti, and Icchāśakti. See diagram 1.

[81] Aghoraśiva points to a worship of the Bull in the banner here, with food offerings (*naivedya*). Payasam (*pāyasa*) is the familiar south Indian rice pudding made by cooking rice in milk, with sugar and legumes (cf. *SP* 1 p. 212 n. 3; Acharya 2002: 180). *MĀŚ* (p. 141) prescribes a full worship of the flagpole into which Sadāśiva has just been invoked, presenting all sixteen *upacāras* (services). One list of sixteen common services, from *Kāraṇāgama* includes:

invocation (*āvāhana*)
establishment (*sthāpana*)
offering of water for feet (*pādya*)
sipping water (*ācamana*)
reception water (*arghya*)
bathing or affusion (*abhiṣeka*)
clothing and sandal perfume (*vastra-gandha*)
flowers (*puṣpa*)
incense and lamp (*dhūpa-dīpa*)
food-offering (*naivedya*)
tribute (*bali*)
fire-offerings (*homa*)

Raising up the flag cloth and tying it with the rope, the presiding priest announces to Śiva, "The festival that is to be done is now taking place."[82] With the sound of the *brahmatāla* rhythm, he makes tribute offerings consisting of numerous coconuts in order to expel any obstacles to the festival. And at an auspicious moment, to the accompaniment of many instruments, the officiating priest stands at the base of the flagpole, sprinkles the assistants who have carried the flag with reception water, touches himself and others, and together with the image-keepers he quickly has the flag hoisted.[83] One should circle with the rope round the flagpole in a left-hand direction and then tie it to the base of the pole.

From now until the final *tīrtha* bath, one should worship the Bull three times or two times each day.

Next the priest goes near the pot and offers expiatory oblations, and he dismisses the Bull from the sacrificial fire.[84] In the cardinal and intermediate directions he should have pure dance performed.[85]

---

procession (*śrībali*)
song and music (*geya-vādya*)
dance (*nṛtta*)
dismissal (*udvāsana*)

(*SP* 1 App. VII, "Upacāra du culte de Śiva.")

[82] The priest's verbal formula here signals the official start of the nine-day festival. *MĀŚ* adds that the priest should receive permission (*anujñā*) from Śiva before beginning.

[83] Participants here, according to the *MĀŚ*, are the *deśika* (chief priest), the *mūrtipas* (image-keepers), the temple assistants who physically carry the flag (*aropita-paricāraka*), as well as *sādhakas* (Śaiva adepts) and *bodhakas* (scholars) (p. 142).

Uttarasvāyambhuvāgama lists some of the auspicious sounds that should accompany the raising of the flag: recitations of the four Vedas in all four directions, dance, song, and instrumental music, fanfares played on conches and *kāhalī*-horns, shouts of victory, sounds of the Vedas (*brahmaghoṣa*), blasts of the bull-pipe (*vṛṣanāla*), and the ringing of bells (*MĀŚ*, p. 110). It is worth noting that the defining festival instrument in modern south Indian festivals, the *nātasvaram* or *nākasvaram*, is not listed or elsewhere in the *MV*. It appears to have been introduced to the south around the thirteenth century (Rangaramanuja Ayyangar 1981). In general, important public rites of the festival feature a tumult of sound. Drums and conches broadcast the festival. A Vaikhānasa text cited by G. Colas (1996: 321) provides an interesting perspective on the festival embrace of noise: "Neither piśāca or rakṣas, demons nor ghosts enter into a place filled by the sounds of conches, *bherī* drums, and *paṭaha* drums, the musical instruments employed in the festival."

[84] Other texts recommend additional rites after raising the flag. *Uttarasvāyambhuvāgama* calls for a complete daily worship (*MĀŚ* p. 111). *MĀŚ* suggests that the priest give an *abhiṣeka* with the primary Bull-pot to the base of the flagpole, and with the eight surrounding pots in the eight directions around the base (*MĀŚ*, p. 143). Then he should offer food to the primary Bull and the eight surrounding Nandins.

With the completion of this major ceremony, Aghoraśiva prescribes a *prāyaścitta*, a rite of expiation. As *Uttarasvāyambhuvāgama* puts it, "To remove what has been severed, broken, or worn out, O Skanda, the priest should perform a rite of expiation at once, and then a purifying oblation (*śāntihoma*)" (*MĀŚ* p. 111). The wear and tear here denote all ritual errors that may have been committed during the ceremony. The expiation consists in offering 108 oblations while reciting MŪLA, followed by a complete oblation (*pūrṇāhuti*), then by offerings of food, sipping water, sandalpaste, betel, and the like (*SP* 2 p. 124 n. 3). The rite of pacification (*śānti*) similarly consists of 108 oblations into the fire while reciting the ASTRA mantra (*SP* 2 p. 132 n. 2). Fuller discussion of final pacification rites for the festival is given in section 28 below. The *visarjana* (dismissal) of the Bull from the fire concludes the fire-rites, as it does during the daily fire ritual.

[85] *Śuddhanṛtta* (pure dance) denotes a style of dance employed in several public rituals. *Rauravāgama*, which devotes a brief chapter to the topic, states that *śuddhanṛtta* should be performed for bathing ceremonies, daily festivals, great festivals, *abhiṣekas*, installations, and sprinkling rites (*RĀ* 19.1–2). It appears to have been the

These are the procedures for raising the flag.

8B. MEASURE OF THE TRIBUTE BALLS.

Twenty-five balls of food, each big as a coconut,
Should be thrown at the base of the flagpole.
The childless woman who eats that ball of food will obtain a son,
For the Bull's leftovers destroy all disease and all faults, O Skanda.[86]

8C. BENEFITS OF THE FLAG-RAISING CEREMONY.

In the land where the flag is fixed to the pole
There will be no untimely death and no poverty, even among sinners.
One need not fear snakes, nor eclipses, nor other disturbances,
Nor wrong views, moreover, even among yogins.
Clouds give rain at the right time, food is plentiful, the king victorious,
All creatures are at peace, and the clouds are full of water.
The ungrateful person, the brahmin-killer, the killer of cowsũ
If they view the fixing of the flag, they are liberated from their sins.
How much more the sponsor's offspring for three generations!
When the great flag is raised,
the benefits are multiplied ten-million times.[87]

9. *The* Brahmatāla *on the* Bherī *Drum*

The festival guides say it brings pleasure to all the gods
When the *bherī* drum is beaten at the time of evening worship.
In front of Śiva or the flag, it begins to summon the gods.[88]

---

special preserve of the class of temple women known in *MV* and other Āgamas as Rudragaṇikās. According to Janaki (1988: 52–53), the temple dance traditions of *śuddhanṛtta* continued in temples into the twentieth century, especially in the Tanjavur region. See Kersenboom 1987 on the continuing traditions of female temple dancers in Tamilnad.

Here Aghoraśiva's statement that *śuddhanṛtta* is to be performed in all the eight directions suggests links to the directional music-and-dance performances described in section 9, "The *Brahmatāla* on the *Bherī* Drum."

86 This brief inset subsection appears to refer to the *bali* offerings made just prior to raising the flag.

87 The same *phalaśrutis* are given in *MĀŚ* (p. 144). That text inserts a penultimate line:

> for they shake off a multitude of sins
> And become liberated along with their kinsmen.

The fourth line here (starting "nor wrong views") appears corrupt and I have made a guess at the translation.

88 The ceremony here called *bherī-brahmatāla* (the *brahman* rhythm on the *bherī* drum) may also be called *bherītāḍaṇa* (beating the *bherī*), *navasandhinṛtta* (dance at the nine junctures), or *sandhyāvāhana* (invocations at the junctures). It features, as these names indicate, the chief drummer (*vādyaka*) playing distinct rhythms at each

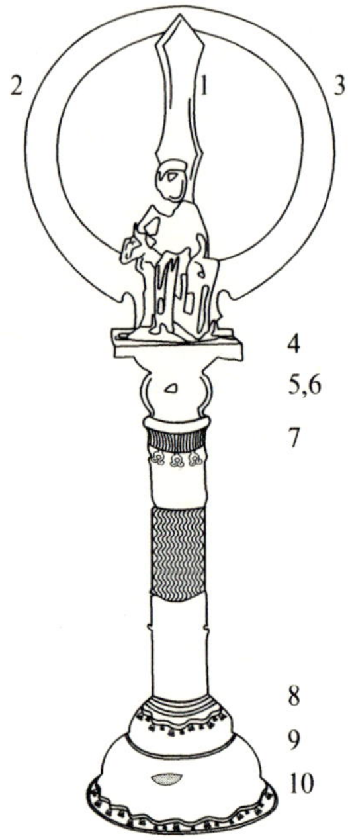

DIAGRAM 3. Trident and Deities. Source: Stella Kramrisch, *Manifestations of Shiva* (Philadelphia: Philadelphia Museum of Art, 1981), no. 128, p. 154 (Chola period bronze trident, from Eilenberg Collection). Compare: S. S. Janaki, *Dhvaja-stambha (Critical Account of Its Structural and Ritualistic Details)* (Madras: Kuppuswami Sastri Research Institute, 1988), figs. 13 and 14.

Portion of Trident	Deities
1. middle prong	*śivatattva*
2. left prong	*vidyātattva*
3. right prong	*ātmatattva*
4. plank	Pārvatī
5. pot	Skanda
6. face of pot	Ganeśa

of nine locations (*sandhi*, that is, junctures or boundaries of the festival terrain) in the temple or in the surrounding community, accompanied by appropriate dances at each location. These performances invoke and honor the deity at the center (Brahman) and the eight protectors of the quarters, the World-guardians (*lokapālas*). See Janaki 1988: 42–54 for a general discussion of this important rite within the *mahotsava*.

As these lines of verse suggest, the ceremony generally takes place on the evening after the morning flag-raising. "The day when one has raised the flag, on that very night one should beat the *bherī* drum," says *Rauravāgama* (18.59). However, some texts such as the *MĀŚ* suggest that some parts of this ritual—the impositions onto Trident and drum—be done as part of the flag-raising ceremony itself. Aghoraśiva's own prescription in the next line, for three *sthaṇḍilas* including one for the flag, also seems to imply a time before the flag has been raised.

The priest should make three platforms there, and place the Trident on one of them, the flag in front of that, and the *bherī* drum in front of that. He should put the drumstick to the right of the drum.

Then, on the Trident he should impose the *tattvas*, the worlds, the letters, the words, the mantras, and the *kalās*.[89]

In the same manner, on the prongs, the priest should invoke the *tattva* groups and their presiding lords.[90] On the middle prong he recites:

> I honor the *śiva-tattva*.
> I honor Rudra, presiding lord of the *śiva-tattva*.

On the left prong:

> I honor the *vidyā-tattva*.
> I honor Viṣṇu, presiding lord of the *vidyā-tattva*.

On the right prong:

> I honor the *ātma-tattva*.
> I honor Brahman, presiding lord of the *ātma-tattva*.

On the plank:

> I honor Pārvatī.

[89] This set of six impositions, called the *ṣaḍadhvan* or "six paths," constitutes a complete set of realities, a "total conceptualization," as Janaki puts it, of the divisions of material reality in the Śaiva Siddhānta cosmology. They are:

thirty-six *tattvas*, or basic constituents of material being (see Davis 1991: 44–45)
two hundred twenty-four *bhuvanas* or worlds (see *SP* 3, Pl. VII A-E)
fifty-one *varṇas* or letters of the alphabet
eighty-one *pādas* or words in the VYOMAVYĀPIN mantra (see Bhatt, ed., *MPĀ* pp. xi-xvi, and *SP* 3 p. 240 n. 192 and Pl. VIII)
eleven *mantras* of the mantra collection (*samhitāmantra*) made up of the five *brahmamantras* and the six *aṅgamantras*
and five *kalās*, or divisions of reality (*śāntyatīta, śānti, vidyā, pratiṣṭhā*, and *nivṛtti*) (Davis 1991: 95–98)

As Brunner-Lachaux points out, these sets are not successive, but parallel, and they encompass one another, with the five *kalās* forming the most encompassing set. See *SP* 1 pp. xiii-xxii for a general overview of the six paths, and Pl. V, "Englobement des réalités de l'Univers par les cinq *kalās*," for a comprehensive chart of the six paths as embedded in the five *kalās*.

[90] The Trident is Śiva's familiar three-pronged implement, but in its mobile iconic form the three prongs sit atop a complex base: a horizontal plank (*phalakā*) at the base of the prongs, a thickened pot-like shape beneath that (which might also feature small figures of Śiva, Pārvatī, and the Bull), a short cylindrical pole (*daṇḍa*), and eight-petal lotus, and beneath that a square base. See diagram 3. Now that the priest has constructed the Trident as a comprehensive support through impositions of the six paths, he imposes a host of deities onto the various parts. *MĀŚ* (pp. 138–39) agrees closely with *MV* here. See also Janaki 1988: 43–44 and her Figs. 13 and 14.

On the pot-like place:

I honor Skanda.

On its face:

I honor Gaṇeśa, Lord of Obstacles.

On the tip of the pole:

I honor Kāma.
I honor the Sun.

On the base of the pole:

I honor Caṇḍeśa.

On the seven petals, starting in the southeast direction:

I honor Brahmāṇī.
I honor Māheśvarī.
I honor Kaumaurī.
I honor Vaiṣṇavī.
I honor Vārāhī.
I honor Māhendrī.
I honor Cāmuṇḍī.[91]

In the middle of the western petal:

I honor Jyeṣṭhā.[92]

In the middle of the northern petal:

I honor Kātyāyanī.[93]

At the base of the Trident he should invoke the eleven Rudras, the twelve Ādityas, the eight Vasus, the two Aśvins, and the eighteen members of Śiva's retinue, the Gaṇas.[94] He honors them all, has invitations and blessings called out to them, and has the *bherī* drum beaten.

[91] The familiar *saptamātṛkās* (Seven Mothers) appear on the petals of the lotus, omitting the eastern petal. For the forms of the Mothers in a south Indian Śaiva context, see *MM* 36.211–34.

[92] Jyeṣṭhā appears here independently as the elder sister of Lakṣmī. *MM* 36.268–73 gives an iconographic description.

[93] Ten-armed Kātyāyanī, more commonly referred to as Durgā Mahiṣāsuramardinī, stands in the act of cutting off the buffalo demon's head. See *MM* 36.258–64, where Durga is described separately in four-armed and eight-armed forms.

[94] At the base of the Trident are located divinity-groups. The Rudras, Ādityas, Vasus, and Aśvins together make up the conventional cohort of thirty-three (Vedic) gods in Śaiva texts. The group of eleven Rudras appears

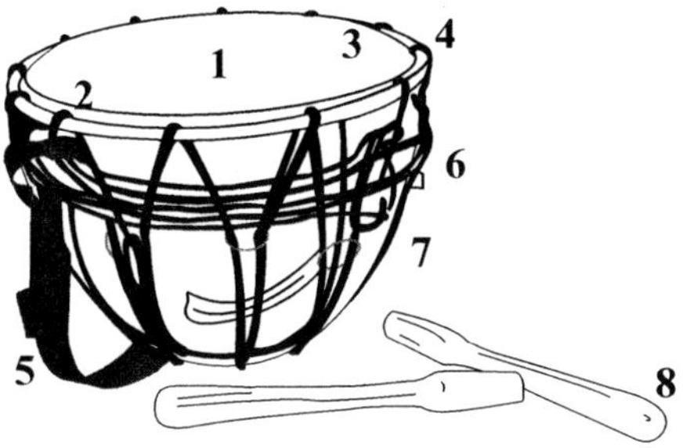

DIAGRAM 4: *Bherī* Drum and Deities. Source: Modern Nagara drum; see P. Sambamoorthi, "Catalogue of the Musical Instruments Exhibited in the Government Museum, Madras." *Bulletin of the Madras Government Museum* n.s. 2, no. 3 (1931), Pl. VI; C. R. Day, *The Music and Musical Instruments of Southern India and the Deccan*, 2d ed. ([1891] Delhi: B. R. Publishing, 1974, Pl. XI. See also *Mahotsavavidhi* of Aghoraśiva; *Rauravāgama* 18.49-52.

Parts of Drum	Deities (*MV*)	Deities (RĀ)
1. center of drum-head	Rudra	
2. left part of drum-head		Candra
3. right part of drum-head		Sūrya
4. seven hooks	Seven Mothers	Seven Mothers
5. handle/strap	Nine Planets	Mahāpadma
6. body of drum		Viṣṇu
7. strings	Vāsukī	Eight Nāgas
8. drumsticks	Skanda	Skanda

Then the priest covers the drum with a colored cloth and worships Rudra at its center, the seven Mothers on its seven hooks, the nine planets on its handle, the snake Vāsukī on its strings, and Skanda on its drumstick.[95] Then he decorates it with sandalpaste and the like, and proceeds to the rite of beating the drum.

in Epic and Puranic texts, either as forms of Rudra or as distinct beings subject to Śiva's command. In addition, Śiva's own retinue of Gaṇas, usually numbered as eighteen, appear as an undifferentiated group of followers (not to be confused with the individuated group of Śiva's household, the Gaṇeśvaras).

[95] In *bherīpūjā* (worship of the drum) the principal drum is also seen as a support for multiple divinities. The contemporary south Indian temple drum is the *tavil*, but here the *bherī* drum is a larger kettledrum also known as the *nāgara* or sometimes as *dundubhi*. As Sambamoorthy (1931: 20) describes, it is a "large hemispherical kettle-drum covered with hide and used in temples. The shell is of copper, brass or sheet-iron rivetted together. The diameter of the head is about 2 1/2 to 3 feet. The skin is strained upon hoops of metal and stretched by leather thongs passing around the underside of the shell." He goes on to explain that the *nāgara* is "placed on a two-wheeled carriage, and drawn by a person who follows the procession of the Deity. The player sits on the carriage and beats the drum with two curved sticks." (See also Day 1974, Pl. XI.)

The priest first purifies the drum, according to *MĀŚ* (p. 139) with the *catussamskāra* (fourfold consecration) that is commonly employed to consecrate implements for ritual use. On *catussamskāra*, see *KKD*, "Gathering the Paraphernalia of Worship," pp. 92–93. Then he meditates or invokes or honors deities within the drum and its parts, in due order. Aghoraśiva's arrangement of deities agrees closely with *MĀŚ* (p. 139), but other lists vary

The officiating priest meditates that the drumstick has the form of *bindu*, and hits the drum three times with *darbha* grass.[96]

Those who are in range to hear that sound are delivered from sin.

The priest next summons the chief drummer, and has him put on a sacrificial thread, an upper garment, sandalpaste, garlands, and other adornments. Then he places a flower in the drummer's hand. At the priest's command, the drummer throws the flower on the drum. Taking the instrument on his shoulder, he beats it in the *Nanditāla* rhythm.

The priest then announces the festival and invites all the deities, starting with Śiva, including the eighteen members of Śiva's retinue, the World-guardians beginning with Indra, the oceans, mountains, underground regions, and all beings.[97]

In order to invite the divinities starting in the center, the priest first goes to the place of the Bull, accompanied by the Trident and the processional icons including Somāskanda, Devī, Gaṇeśa, Skanda, Nandin, Caṇḍeśa,

---

somewhat. According to *Rauravāgama* (18.49–52), for example, Candra and Sūrya should be on the right and left drumfaces, and Viṣṇu inhabits its body. The hooks (*kīla*) are the seven Mothers, and on the leather straps are not just Vāsukī, but a group of eight Nāgas. The carrying strap is Mahāpadma (another Nāga), and the stick is Skanda. See diagram 4; also cf. Janaki 1988, Fig. 12.

[96] *Bindu* (literally, "point") denotes, within the Śaiva Siddhānta system, the point of origin or material cause of the pure domain (*śuddhādhvan*). *Māyā*, by contrast, is the material cause of the impure domain (*śuddhādhvan*). But as Brunner-Lachaux points out, *bindu* also pervades all the pure realities that emerge from it. See *SP* 1 Introduction, pp. xvi-xx, for a discussion of the Śaiva Siddhānta cosmology. Here the priest's meditation suggests the connection between *bindu* and *nāda*, primordial sound. *Nāda* is the subtle source of all more audible, differentiated sounds. *Bindu*, say the texts, is "made of *nāda*." Perhaps striking the drum with *darbha* ritually creates this subtle sound, from which all the subsequent sounds made by the drummer, musicians, and singers will emerge. Aghoraśiva's next statement, concerning those fortunate enough to hear the subtle sound (*nāda*) made by grass on drum, reinforces this connection.

Rauravāgama states that ASTRA mantra should be recited as the priest strikes the drum. *MĀŚ*, instead, proposes that three Vedic mantras be recited: *brahmajajñāna* (*Taittirīya Samhitā* 4.2.8.2), *idam viṣṇuh* (*RV* 1.22.17), and *tryambaka* (*RV* 7.59.12) (p. 141). "By hearing these sounds," it concludes, "the worlds are freed from all faults." In another section, *MĀŚ* (pp. 389–90) adds announcements that the priest may make while striking the drum:

> I hereby strike the *bherī* drum, to urge on all those who live in the heavens, in the sky, and on earth to come to this festival, and to pacify those denizens of hell who may be hostile to our well-being. By order of Pārvatī, excellent daughter of Himālaya, I firmly strike the *bherī* drum that begins the festival every day, first to declare well-being for all the worlds, and then to protect all living creatures, animals, and birds.

[97] These invitations (*āhvāna*) to all gods and all beings to attend the festival take the form of *gadya-padya*, prose and verse compositions that praise the deities. *MĀŚ* (p. 61) specifies that drums, musical instruments, and dance should accompany the invitations. The chief priest, along with the image-protectors, adepts, and scholars, should stand to the south of the pole, grasp its base with their hands, and issue invitations to all the deities, with the best prose and verse recitations (*gadya-padya*). Janaki (1988: 45–48) discusses these recitations as *cūrṇikā*. After these comprehensive invitations, the priest and others honor and invite the deities of the eight directions, in *sandhyāvāhana* (evening invocation).

and the Devotees, and also by all the auspicious objects.[98] He presents worship and tribute, and pleases the Bull with dance, song, and music.[99]

He goes to the *brahmasthāna*.[100] In that circle he performs all the acts starting with the announcement of an auspicious day and sprinkling, meditates, and offers worship. He presents tribute in order to feed the spirits. After that, he has the lord of the *brahmasthāna* pleased: the rhythm (*tāla*) is the *brahmatāla*, the melody (*rāga*) is *vaṅkula*, the dance (*nṛtta*) is *samapāda*, the mode (*paṇ*) is *pañcama*, and the instrument (*vādya*) is *gucchapuṭa*.[101]

Then he goes to Indra's direction, and in that circle he performs the acts of worship, as before, from making a seat through the offering of tribute.[102] Here

[98] The *sandhyāvāhana* procession begins at the *nandisthāna*, the location of the fixed Nandin. The Trident figures in this ceremony as the key processional icon. *MĀŚ* (p. 62) provides a more elaborate inventory of the processional party here. The parade should be led by lamps (*dīpikā*), this being an evening ceremony. In addition to the Trident and the processional icons, *MĀŚ* specifies that an *annaliṅga* (Śiva-liṅga made of rice) and the auspicious sprouts from *aṅkurārpaṇa* should be present. Elephants, horses, and Rudragaṇikās (temple dancers) should be on the two sides of the procession. Auspicious objects include the usual: umbrellas, yak-tail fans, banners, flags, coverings, and arches. Finally, *MĀŚ* lists the instruments for this musical procession: *bherī* drum, *paṭaha*, *tāla* (cymbals), *svastika*, *vīṇā* (lute), *veṇu* (flute), *mṛdaṅga* (two-headed drum), *vṛṣavādya*, *devadundubhi* (large kettle drum), *śaṅkha* (conch), *kāhalī* (horn), and *jhallarī* (tambourine).

Ajitāgama (27.128–31) suggests that the four categories of instruments be used. These categories, familiar from the classical text *Nāṭyaśāstra* (17.1–2), are: (1) skin percussion instruments (*ātodya*, "struck") such as the *mṛdaṅga* drum, (2) stringed instruments (*vitata*, "stretched") like the *vīṇā*, (3) metal percussion instruments (*ghana*, "hard") like gongs and cymbals, and (4) hollow wind instruments (*suṣira*, "tubular") such as the reed-flute. These four instrument families plus the human singing voice make up the famous *pañcamahāśabda* (five great sounds), according to *Ajitāgama*, and this totality of musical sound brings Śiva pleasure. See Raghavan 1958 for further references to the *pañcamahāśabda*.

[99] The worship offered Nandin here should be a full *pūjā* sequence, according to *MĀŚ* (pp. 62–63): construction of a sixfold throne, worship of the Bull's throne and form, invocation of the Bull with the VṚṢA-MŪLA mantra, then offering of all services, including feeding, incense, lamps, and illumination (*nīrājana*). After this the priest offers tribute (*bali*), and then follows the musical interlude, which pleases (*santoṣana*) the deity.

This forms the pattern for each subsequent location in the *sandhyāvāhana*. At each place, the presiding deity is worshiped, tribute offered, and then the deity is pleased by appropriate music and dance.

[100] The *brahmasthāna* denotes the center of a site or building, and the presiding World-guardian of the center is Brahman. Here the *brahmasthāna* refers to the central *balipīṭha* (tribute-pedestal) near the fixed image of Nandin.

[101] Most Āgama accounts specify distinct rhythms (*tāla*) to be played at each of the nine directions during the *navasandhi* ceremony. The *tāla* names are reasonably consistent from text to text, with some variation. Similar *tālas* are employed in the daily *nityotsava*. See table 3. Aghoraśiva's account here is more complete in providing not only the specific rhythm, but also the melody (*rāga*), mode (*paṇ*), dance (*nṛtta*), and instrument (*vādya*), for each direction. See table 4. Without the specialized understanding of the musicians involved, however, it is difficult to know what these terms mean. As Janaki notes (1988: 50–52) in her erudite discussion, both *rāga* and *paṇ* refer to names of melodic forms, since *paṇ* is basically the old Tamil equivalent for *rāga*. The "instruments" listed here give names of *tālas*, not of recognizable musical instruments. The dance here, Janaki observes, was mostly *śuddhanṛtta*, with rhythmic phrases but not mimetic gestures.

Janaki adds some interesting observations on the continuation of the *navasandhi* performative traditions into the early twentieth century, in the form of *kavuttuvam*, and calls for a critical interdisciplinary study of the *navasandhi* tradition (1988: 52–54).

[102] Each of the eight directional World-guardians are now worshiped and serenaded, in circumambulatory order starting with Indra in the east. These take place at the eight *balipīṭhas* around the temple courtyard, or

TABLE 3 Tālas in Nityotsava and Mahotsava

Direction	Lokapāla	Tāla (nityotsava)	Tāla (mahotsava)
Brahmasthāna	Brahman		brahman
East	Indra	sama	sama
Southeast	Agni	baddhāvaṇa	mattavaraṇa
South	Yama	bhṛṅginī	bhṛṅginī
Southwest	Nirṛtti	malli	matta
West	Varuṇa	nava	naga
Northwest	Vāyu	bali	bali
North	Soma	koṭiśikhara	gauli
Northwest	Īśāna	taṇkari	dakkari

Sources: *Ajitāgama* 27.29–31 (*nityotsava*); *Mahotsavavidhi*. Compare: *Uttarakāmikāgama* ch. 5; Saskia C. Kersenboom, *Nityasumaṅgalī: Devadasi Tradition in South India* (Delhi: Motilal Banarsidass, 1987), p. 117.

the rhythm is *samatāla*, the dance is *bhujaṅga*, the mode is *kaumeśī*, and the instrument is *sācapata*.

In the southeast corner he performs rites from worship through tribute to Agni. The melody is *varāṭi*, the rhythm is *mattāvaraṇa*, the dance is *maṇḍala*, the mode is *kolli*, the instrument is *udghaṭita*. He has the deity pleased with these.

In the south corner he performs the acts from worship through tribute for Yama, and he pleases the deity with the following: the melody is *rāmagiri*, the rhythm is *bhṛṅgiṇītāla*, the dance is *daṇḍapāda*, the mode is *kauśika*, and the rhythm is *militamaṭṭaya*.

In the southwest he gives worship and tribute to Nirṛti, and has the following performed: *bhairavī* melody, *mattatāla* rhythm, *bhujaṅgatrāsa* dance, *naṭṭabhāṣā* mode, and *lambaka* instrument.

In the west he gives tribute as previously to Varuṇa, and has the following performed: *kuñjari* melody, *nāgatāla* rhythm, *ākuñcika* dance, *śrīkāmara* mode, and *simhanāda* instrument.

In the northwest he gives tribute as before to Vāyu, and has the following performed: *deśagiri* melody, *balitāla* rhythm, *bhujaṅgalamita* dance, *takkeśi* mode, and *jhampaṭa* instrument.

In the north he meditates on Kubera and presents tribute as before, and pleases him with the following: the *gauḍhika* melody, *gaulitāla* rhythm, *ākuñcita* dance, *kauśika* mode, and the *pañcama* instrument.

In the northeast, he meditates on Īśāna, worships him, and offers tribute, as before, and pleases him with these: *tuṇḍīra* melody, *ṭhakkarī* rhythm, *urdhvapāda* dance, *śālāpaṇi* mode, and *kumbha* instrument.

beyond the temple walls. Aghoraśiva's reference to the "circle" (*maṇala*) here suggests that the priest outlines ritual circles with rice-flour or some similar powder at each location.

TABLE 4 Elements of *Bherītādana* According to the *Mahotsavavidhi*

Location (deity)	*Rāga*	*Tāla*	*Nṛtta*	*Paṇ*	*Vādya*
Brahmasthāna (Brahman)	*vaṅkula*	*brahma*	*samapāda*	*pañcama*	*gucchapuṭa*
East (Indra)		*sama*	*bhujaṅga*	*kaumeśī*	*sācapata*
Southeast (Agni)	*varāṭi*	*mattāvaraṇa*	*maṇḍala*	*kolli*	*udghaṭita*
South (Yama)	*rāmagiri*	*bhṛṅgiṇī*	*daṇḍapāda*	*kauśika*	*militamaṭṭaya*
Southwest (Nirṛti)	*bhairavī*	*mallatāla*	*bhujaṅgatrāṣa*	*naṭṭabhāṣā*	*lambaka*
West (Varuṇa)	*kuñjari*	*nāga*	*ākuñcika*	*śrīkāmara*	*simhanāda*
Northwest (Vāyu)	*deśagiri*	*bali*	*bhujangalamita*	*takkeśi*	*jhampaṭa*
North (Kubera)	*gauḍhika*	*gauli*	*ākuñcita*	*kauśika*	*pañcama*
Northeast (Īśāna)	*tuṇḍīra*	*ṭhakkarī*	*ūrdhvapāda*	*śālāpāṇi*	*kumbha*

Rāga refers to melody or scale.
Tāla refers to the rhythmic pattern.
Nṛtta indicates the dance step.
Paṇ also refers to melody, based on Tamil tradition.
Vādya generally indicates instrument, though here it is not clear what this means. Here the terms seem to refer to *tālas*.
Compare: S. S. Janaki, *Dhvaja-stambha (Critical Account of Its Structural and Ritualistic Details)*. (Madras: Kuppuswami Sastri Research Institute, 1988), p. 51; Saskia C. Kersenboom, *Nityasumaṅgalī: Devadasi Tradition in South India* (Delhi: Motilal Banarsidass, 1987), pp. 127–28.

When he has circumambulated in this order, starting in the east, he enters the temple and throws some special tribute at the base of the flagstaff or on the tribute-pedestal.[103]

These are the procedures for the great rhythm ceremony.

10. *Worship in the Sacrificial Hall*

After removing the auspicious sprouts in the manner described previously, the priest next worships in the sacrificial hall.[104]

[103] *MĀŚ* (pp. 63–64 and 146–47) again provides a more elaborate procedure for the conclusion of this ceremony. After the *navasandhi*, the group should circumambulate the town, so as to invite humans as well as gods to the festival. Before reentering the temple, rites of *nīrājana* (illumination) and *pariveṣa* (circling of light) are performed at the gateway door. The procession then enters the temple, proceeds to the base of the flagpole, and gives *viśeṣabali* (special tribute) there. Other items are to be disposed of. The rice-liṅga is thrown into water, and the auspicious sprouts poured out onto the *balipīṭha*. With the temple-dancers still holding lamps, the festival icons are returned to their own places. The head priest and his assistants rinse their feet, sip water, smear themselves with ashes, and go into the sanctum for a final session of mantra-recitations. Then they may sleep.

[104] Aghoraśiva uses the term "worship" (*arcana*) here, though this section actually gives a description (*lakṣaṇa*) of the sacrificial hall and its preparation for subsequent acts of worship. The preparation should take place prior to the flag-raising ceremony, as Aghoraśiva notes later in this section.

One of the three sets of sprouts from the earlier *aṅkurārpaṇa*, called the *mangalāṅkura* (auspicious sprouts), is removed since the flag-raising ceremony for which that set was intended has now been completed. Aghoraśiva alludes to a previous account of the method of removal. *MĀŚ* prescribes that they should be poured out on the *balipīṭha* at the conclusion of the *navasandhi* rite (p. 147).

The pavilion should be five cubits or more, located in front of the deity or in the northeast, southeast, north, or west part of the temple grounds.[105] There should be a door in the west. In the middle of the pavilion an altar should be constructed, as described previously, smooth as a mirror, together with a socle.[106]

Outside of the altar he should have fire-pits placed, in order, from the east to the northeast. The firepits are half-moon, triangular, circular, hexagonal, lotus, and octagonal in form. In between the east and northeast, the firepit should be either circular or square.[107]

Or else, in the case of five firepits, the principal one will be circular in the northeast, and in the four cardinal directions the firepits will be square.

Or there may be one firepit, either circular or square.

[105] The *yāgaśālā* or *yāgamaṇapa* is an open pavilion constructed for special ritual occasions, including ceremonies of installation, initiation, and festivals (*MĀŚ* p. 148). Prescriptions for the location of the *yāgaśālā* in relation to the central shrine vary from text to text (cf. Dagens 1984: 110). *MĀŚ* suggests different locations according to the particular occasion: for *pratiṣṭhā* ceremonies the pavilion should be in front of the temple (that is, to the east), while for *utsavas* it may be either to the northeast or southeast.

The layout of the *yāgaśālā* is square, ranging from five up to twelve cubits (*hasta*) on each side. The pavilion has either twelve or sixteen pillars. *MĀŚ* lists thirty-two types of trees that give poles suitable for use as pavilion pillars.

As a constructed place of habitation (*vāstu*), the *yāgaśālā* sits on a site that must be transformed ritually. This requires a worship of the site (*vāstupūjā*) or pacification of the site (*vāstuśānti*). *MĀŚ* (pp. 77–83) quotes an unnamed source that describes the procedures. A geometric design (*vāstumaṇḍala*) is laid out on the surface, which then serves as the underlying ritual ground plan for the pavilion. For the festival *yāgaśālā*, the proper *maṇḍala* is called *paramaśāyin*, containing eighty-one squares. Onto the squares are invoked and honored a host of fifty-three deities (*devatās*), starting with Brahman, the Vāstunātha or Lord of the Site, in the innermost nine squares. See diagram 5. Many other texts, both Āgamas and Śilpaśāstras, relate similar procedures of *vāstuśānti*, with slight variations in design. See, for examples, *Ajitāgama* ch. 8, *Mayamata* 7.33–40 (and Fig. 7), and *Mānasāra* ch. 7. Stella Kramrisch also discusses the procedures in *The Hindu Temple*. The *vāstumaṇḍala* described in *MĀŚ* corresponds most closely to the diagram in *SP* 4, Pl. 6.

MĀŚ goes on to explain the procedures for honoring each divinity. The priest invokes each one with a mantra and worships with a series of offerings. He gives food offerings (*bali*) to each. Other texts like *Somaśambhupaddhati* prescribe that one offer different foods to each deity (*SP* 4, pp. 50–54).

[106] The *vedikā* (altar) is a simple raised platform, square, with its sides one-third the width of the *yāgaśālā*. It occupies the nine central squares of the underlying *paramaśāyin* diagram, equivalent to the domain of Brahman. Flat and smooth on top, the *vedikā* will subsequently support the pots established there during the Trident ceremony to follow. The *vedikā* is elevated by a small *upavedikā*, a projecting socle two digits (*aṅgula*) high. See Dagens 1984: 111.

[107] Normally, says *Ajitāgama*, there will be nine *kuṇḍas* (firepits) in the *yāgaśāla* for major ceremonies, five for lesser ones, and one for small rituals such as *pavitrotsava* (Dagens 1984: 111). In the case of nine *kuṇḍas*, which would be the ideal case for a *mahotsava*, they should be located in the eight directions, plus a ninth one in between the northeast and east ones. Using the underlying eighty-one-square *paramaśāyin* diagram, the *kuṇḍas* are placed in the middle of the three rows of squares surrounding the *vedikā* (*MM* 25.42).

Aghoraśiva's specification of seven *kuṇḍas* is problematic. However, his sequence of *kuṇḍas* agrees with that of *Mayamata* (25.42), only omitting the first two listed there, which are square and vulva-shaped. Descriptions of the various *kuṇḍa* shapes are provided in *Mayamata* 25.43–54 and *Rauravāgama* ch. 14. See also the diagrams in Bhatt, ed., *RĀ* 1 pp. 54–55.

He smears the floor with cowdung, and then decorates the pavilion with cloth-banners, flags, parasols, garlands of *darbha* grass, and the like, and door-arches.[108] He gathers the eight auspicious objects:

> Mirror, full pot, bell, and a pair of yak-tail fans,
> *Śrīvatsa*, *svastika*, conch, and lamp:
> These are eight auspicious objects of the gods.

together with the ten Weapons:

> Thunderbolt, spear, club, sword, and noose,
> Flag, mace, trident, lotus, and discus—

the *sruk* and the *sruva* ladles, and other paraphernalia for the ritual.[109] He should do this on the evening prior to the start of the festival.

This is the description of the sacrificial hall.

11. *The Trident Ceremony*

The officiating priest together with the assisting priests first complete an evening *sandhyā* ceremony and a special *sandhyā*, and enter the temple.[110] He prepares a platform in front of the deity and sprinkles it reciting ASTRA. Then he takes smooth, solid, unblemished new pots made of one of the substances from gold to clay. They are adorned with bundles of grass, with covers, with cloth, fruit, sprouts, and strings, and with gold, jewels and the like inside, and with all the characteristics explained elsewhere.[111] He cleans

[108] *MĀŚ* prescribes a more elaborate decorative scheme for the *yāgaśāla*: *toraṇas* (decorative archways), banners, mirrors, parasols, garlands of fruit, fruits such as breadfruit, betel tree branches, sugar-cane stalks, garlands of *darbha* grass, banana stalks, and coconuts.

[109] According to *Cintyāgama*, the eight auspicious objects are placed on the *upavedikā* (socle) of the central *vedikā*, two in each cardinal direction (*SP* 2 App. 1 p. 331 n. 2). The *āyudhas* (Weapons) here are those belonging to the World-guardians, starting with Indra's thunderbolt in the east, and including the lotus of Brahman and the discus of Viṣṇu. For descriptions of the ladles, see *MṛĀ kr* 6.33–43 and illustrations in Bhatt, ed., *MṛĀ* opp. pp. 66–68.

[110] *Sandhyā* rites are performed at the junctures (*sandhi*) of the day: at dawn, noon, sunset, and midnight. Aghoraśiva prescribes these as part of the daily ritual activities (*nityakarman*) of initiated Śaivas. Procedures for *sāya-sandhyā* (evening *sandhyā* rites) largely follow those for morning rites, as spelled out in *KKD*, "Meditation on the *Sandhyā* with Attributes" and the following sections, pp. 49–67. The worshiper first visualizes and honors the *sandhyā* itself, either as a form of Śiva's Śakti (in the evening, as Raudrī) or in a formless state, depending on one's initiatory status, and then offers a series of water ablutions while reciting mantras that evoke Śiva and his mantra-powers, as well as various categories of beings. The *viśeṣa-sandhyā* (special *sandhyā* rite) is a set of additional ablutions for special occasions. One example would be the additional libations Aghoraśiva describes in *KKD*, "Salutation of the *Sandhyā*" (pp. 63–67), to honor eight groups of deities (Ādityas, Vasus, Rudras, and so on). The recognition and honoring of a still greater community of divine beings accords well with the general incorporative intent of the festival.

[111] The priests here prepare pots that will serve as supports for Śiva, Śakti, and the eight Vidyeśvaras in the *yāgaśālā* during the festival. The technique of pot-preparation briefly described here is common to many Śaiva rituals. The pots may be made of gold, silver, brass, or clay, in order of preference. They are wrapped with a lattice

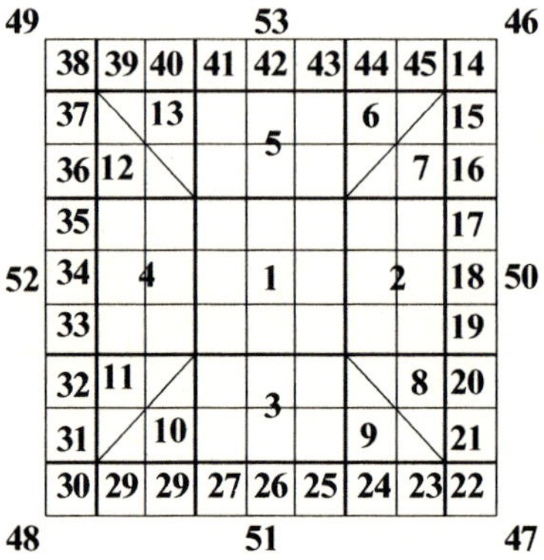

DIAGRAM 5. Vāstumaṇḍala Paramaśāyin type (Eighty-one squares) According to *Mahotsavavidhikrama Āgamaśekhara* (*MĀŚ*). Source: *Mahotsavavidhikrama Āgamaśekhara*, pp. 78–80. Compare: Hélène. Brunner-Lachaux, tr., *Somaśambhupaddhati* (Pondicherry: Institut Français d'Indologie 1963–98), vol. 4, Pl. VI; Bruno Dagens, tr., *Mayamatam: Treatise of Housing, Architecture and Iconography* (New Delhi: Indira Gandhi National Centre for the Arts, 1994), vol. 1, fig. 7; Stella Kramrisch, *The Hindu Temple* (Delhi: Motilal Banarsidass, 1946) fig. 7; Gérard Colas, *Le temple selon Marīci*, (Pondicherry: Institut Français d'Indologie, 1986), Pl. 5.

1. Brahman
2. Marīci
3. Vivasvat
4. Mitra
5. Dharādhara
6. Āpa
7. Āpavatsa
8. Savitṛ
9. Savitra
10. Indra
11. Indrajita
12. Rudra
13. Rudradāsa
14. Īśāna
15. Parjanya
16. Jayanta
17. Mahendra
18. Ravi
19. Satya
20. Bhṛśa
21. Antarikṣa
22. Agni
23. Pūṣan
24. Vitatha
25. Gṛhakṣata
26. Yamarāja
27. Gandharva
28. Bhṛṅga
29. Mṛga
30. Nirṛti
31. Dauvārika
32. Sugrīva
33. Puṣpadanta
34. Varuṇa
35. Asura
36. Śoṣa
37. Roga
38. Vāyu
39. Nāga
40. Mukhya
41. Bhallāṭa
42. Soma
43. Argala
44. Aditi
45. Diti
46. Carakī
47. Vidarī
48. Putanā
49. Pāparākṣasī
50. Skanda
51. Aryaman
52. Jṛmbhaka
53. Pilpiccha

of strings, and dressed with white cloth. In the mouths of the pots are a bundle of grass (*kūrca*), shoots or leaves, and fruit (such as coconut). Another grass bundle is suspended over the coconut. See the photograph in Bhatt, ed., *MṛĀ* opp. p. 93. The pots are filled with water that is enhanced by various valuable substances. In the view of *Mṛgendrāgama*, these may include all the jewels, herbs, metals, juices, perfumes, and *kuśa* grass, along with seeds (*MṛĀ kr* 7.21).

them with water, reciting ASTRA. He shows them incense, and fills them with sandal-water, reciting HṚDAYA. Then he places the Śiva-pot in the middle atop the platform, the Śakti-pot to its north, and the eight other pots surrounding them. He honors the Śiva-pot with the MŪLA mantra, the Śakti-pot with ŚAKTI, and the other pots with the mantras of the Vidyeśvaras, starting with Ananta and ending with Śikhaṇḍin. Surrounding them are the Gaṇeśvaras, starting with Nandin, and the Weapons.[112]

He summons the temple attendants and has them carry the Śiva-pot and Śakti-pot, in the proper manner, and the Weapons starting with the thunderbolt and ending with the discus.[113] Accompanied by the tumult of conches and *dundubhi* drums and by the sounds of the Vedas and other hymns, they circumambulate the temple and enter the sacrificial hall.

On the middle of the altar, the priest spreads eight bushels of paddy along with *darbha* grass and husked rice, half of that amount of sesame-rice and the seven types of dal. In the middle of that he places the Śiva-pot and Śakti-pot, and the eight pots of the Vidyeśvaras.[114] He sets up additional deities, starting with Dharma and ending with Sūrya, all in their proper places.[115]

[112] The eight Vidyeśvaras are Ananta, Sūkṣma, Śivottama, Ekanetra, Ekarudra, Trīmūrti, Śrīkaṇṭha, and Śikhaṇḍin, starting from the east in circumambulatory order. Within Śaiva theology, these are eight agents that Śiva assigns to exercise dominion over the impure domain (*aśuddhādhvan*) (see Davis 1991: 118–19). The Gaṇeśvaras are a group of eight deities that, in a sense, constitute Śiva's household: Nandin, Mahākāla, Bhṛṅgin, Gaṇeśa, Vṛṣabha, Skanda, Ambikā, and Caṇḍeśa. The Weapons are those belonging to the World-guardians.

[113] The *paricārakas* (attendants) carry the Śiva and Śakti pots, in the proper manner, on their heads. They must also carry the eight pots of the Vidyeśvaras, as well as the Weapons, atop their heads.

[114] On the flat surface of the *vedikā*, priests prepare a bed of grains for the pots to rest upon during the festival. Then, according to the *MĀŚ* (p. 157), one outlines a lotus in the middle and strews *kuśa* grass and flowers over it. The *śiva-kumbha* (Śiva pot) and *vardhanī* (Śakti-pot) are first placed in the central position, and then the eight pots of the Vidyeśvaras are also set on top of the *vedikā*, clockwise, starting with Ananta in the east and ending with Śikhaṇḍin in the northeast.

[115] Aghoraśiva's brief direction here to set up pots in "places starting with Dharma and ending with Sūrya" (*dharmādisūryāntasthāne*) points to a more elaborate preparation of the *yāgaśāla*. *MĀŚ* gives a fuller explication of the process (p. 158). At the *upavedikā* (socle) of the altar the priest should set up pots at the corners in the intermediate directions, from the southeast clockwise to the northeast, for the four powers: Dharma, Jñāna, Vairāgya, and Aiśvarya. To the northeast of the *vedikā* he sets up a pot for Yāgeśvara, Śiva as Lord of the Sacrifice, and another for Yāgeśvara's consort, Yāgeśvarī. Finally, continues the *MĀŚ*, the priest sets up twenty-seven more pots, starting with Īśāna and ending with the Preceptors. The twenty-seven are to be located around the outer perimeter of the *yāgaśāla*. In other texts including *KKD* (*pavitrotsava*), this set of twenty-seven begins with Sūrya rather than Īśāna, and includes:

Sūrya
four *kalās* (*śānti*, *vidyā*, *nivṛtti*, and *pratiṣṭhā*)
eight Gaṇeśvaras, identified as Door-guardians
Vāstunātha, namely, Brahman as the Lord of the Site
Lakṣmī
ten World-guardians (Indra and the others, including Brahman and Viṣṇu)
Gaṇapati, and
the Preceptors

(See *SP* 2 App. 1 p. 334, and Bhatt, ed., *MṛĀ*, diagram between pp. 128–29.)

The priest together with the assisting priests and the patron then perform an initial worship of Gaṇeśa and proclaim an auspicious day. The priest performs a Sun worship, according to daily procedures, up through the rite of dismissal. He sips water, performs *sakalīkaraṇa*, and prepares common reception water. He honors the four doors, starting in the east, and at each door, two by two, he honors the Gaṇeśvaras, from Nandin through Caṇḍeśa, as previously described. In the west he propitiates the door-guardians, as in daily worship, and then worships the Lord of the Site in the southwest.[116] He sits down to the south of the central altar, facing north, and performs the purification of the elements and other rites of self-purification, and prepares special reception water.[117] He adorns himself and the assisting priests with sandal-paste, turbans, and the like. Then he prepares the five cow-products, according to the proper procedures, and purifies the pavilion by sprinkling the cow-products, reception water, and water. He honors the Śiva-pot and Śakti-pot, as before, ending with mantra-recitation. Then he visualizes and honors the World-guardians along with their vehicles and weapons.[118] He worships

[116] With the pots set up in the *yāgaśālā*, worship may begin. The procedures Aghoraśiva prescribes here follow the paradigm of *nityakarman*, daily ritual activities. *MĀŚ* (pp. 158–60) largely accords with Aghoraśiva's account, but adds useful details. Chief priest (*deśikottama*), assisting priests (*ṛtvig*), and patron (*yajamāna*) sit to the south of the *vedikā*, facing north. The chief priest first performs several acts of self-purification by imposing mantras on his hands and body (*karaśuddhi, dehanyāsa*), then meditates on Śiva and receives Śiva's permission to proceed with the rite. He mentally visualizes Gaṇeśa and worships him, and has the auspicious day proclaimed, adding the word "Mahādeva." The pavilion is sprinkled with water. Then he performs Sun worship, as in *nityakarman*, up through the dismissal of Sūrya (*KKD*, "Worship of the Sun," p. 69–85). In addition to sipping water, he covers his body with ashes, then performs the rite of *sakalīkaraṇa* and the preparation of *sāmānyārghya*. The priest leaves the pavilion, says *MĀŚ*, with a pot of *arghya*, in order to perform *dvārapūjā*. Since the *yāgaśālā* has four entries, the priest visualizes and honors the four doors and the eight Gaṇeśvaras who flank the doors, left and right of each door. Here he follows procedures Aghoraśiva has described previously in the context of *pavitrotsava* (see *SP* 2 pp. 42–47). Before reentering the pavilion through the western entry, the priest visualizes and worships a group of seven Door-guardians arrayed around the doorway: Gaṇeśa, Sarasvatī, Mahālakṣmī, Nandikeśvara, Gaṅgā, Mahākāla, and Yamunā. The procedures, as specified for *nityapūjā*, are given in *KKD*, "Worship of the Door as Part of Śiva Worship," pp. 87–90. Finally, in the southwest corner, the priest should mentally visualize and honor Brahman, the *vāstunātha* or Lord of the Site, following *nityapūjā* procedures, as in *KKD*, "Entry into Śiva's Sanctum," p. 92.

[117] The priest continues the sequence of actions modeled on *nityakarman*. Here he performs *ātmaśuddhi* (self-purification), also called *bhūtaśuddhi* (purification of the elements) since one of the main acts of *ātmaśuddhi* is to reabsorb and thus purify all the material constituents of the body. Self-purification transforms the worshiper's body into a *vidyādeha*, a mantra-body capable of worshiping Śiva (see *KKD*, "Purification of the Elements," pp. 94–113, and Davis 1991: 51–60). *Ātmaśuddhi* concludes with an *antaryāga*, interior worship of the worshiper's body as itself a site of Śiva's presence. *Viśeṣārghya* (special reception water), which can only be prepared by one who has become suitably pure, is necessary for the worship of Śiva. See *KKD*, "Preparation of Śiva's Arghya," pp. 117–18 for Aghoraśiva's method of preparing *viśeṣārghya*.

[118] The Lokapālas or World-guardians are visualized according to their *dhyānaślokas*, such as those in *Pūrvakāmikāgama* (4.480–86) or more elaborately in *Mayamata* (36.136–62). The Lokapālas with their *vāhanas* (mounts) and *āyudhas* (weapons) are listed in note 46 above.

Mahālakṣmī, Gaṇeśa, and the line of preceptors. He announces Śiva's order to all.[119]

The priest then sits to the south of the platform and constructs for the Śiva-pot a throne beginning with Śakti and reaching up to Śakti. He imposes mantra powers on it, following the stick method, the bald head method, and the *kalā* method.[120] He meditates that Śiva is endowed with all the six paths, as previously, and invokes Śiva's presence.[121]

The priest then performs the imposition of Śrīkaṇṭha on the Śakti-pot.[122] He visualizes the Goddess:

> Two arms and pleasing looks, youthful with nice breasts,
> Garbed in silk clothes, peaceful, with smiling face,
> Wearing all her ornaments, sitting in the same posture as Śiva,
> And wearing a basket-shaped crown—
> So one should envision the Goddess.

[119] In *nityapūjā* the worshiper honors Gaṇeśa, Lakṣmī, and the line of seven Preceptors (*gurupaṅkti*) before turning his attention to the Śiva-liṅga. Here too the worship of these deities immediately precedes the invocation of Śiva in the Śiva-pot. The priest visualizes them according to *dhyānaślokas*, invokes them with their own mantras, and honors them with several offerings. See *KKD*, "Worship of Gaṇeśa, Lakṣmī, and the Line of Preceptors," pp. 126–27, for the procedures from *nityapūjā*. The *gurupaṅkti* (consisting of Sadāśiva, Ananta, Śrīkaṇṭha, Ambikā, Skanda, Viṣṇu, and Brahman) are envisioned according to a common ascetic pattern:

> They have matted locks, pale white limbs, wear yoga-cords and sacrificial threads. Their hands display the gesture of yoga above their navels. They have two arms and gentle eyes.

In *nityapūjā* the worshiper requests and receives permission from these divinities to worship Śiva. Here, by contrast, the priest announces Śiva's command (*anujñā*) to each of the ten World-guardians. "O Indra," he begins in the east, "by Śiva's command, you should stay at attention here until the completion of the ceremony, to quell all obstacles in your own direction (*SP* 2 p. 68 v. 42)." And so he goes in each direction, inserting the appropriate name of the World-guardian at each one.

[120] The priest begins the process of invoking Śiva into the *śivakumbha* here by constructing an *āsana* (throne) from Ādhāraśakti up to Paraśakti, as in *nityapūjā* (see note 77 above). Next the material pot must be transformed into a suitable *mūrti* (embodiment) for Śiva through the imposition of mantras. Aghoraśiva prescribes three methods for this imposition. Following the *daṇḍa-bhaṅgi* (stick method), the five *brahmamantras* are imposed in a vertical manner, starting with ĪŚĀNA at the head and proceeding downward. Following the *muṇḍa-bhaṅgi* (bald-head method), the priest imposes the five *brahmamantras* as the five faces of Sadāśiva, with ĪŚĀNA as the upraised face, TATPURUṢA as the eastern face, and so on (see Brunner-Lachaux, *SP* 1, p. xxxiii). The *kalā-bhaṅgi* follows a similar pattern, employing the five *kalās*: *śāntyatītā-kalā* is imposed on the top of the head, *śānti-kalā* on the eastern face, and so on.

[121] On the *ṣaḍadhvan* or six paths, see above, note 89. The invocation of Śiva's presence in the pot would follow the paradigmatic procedures of invoking Śiva as Sadāśiva in the Śiva-liṅga during *nityapūjā*. See above, note 79, on invoking Śiva in the flagpole.

[122] As with the Śiva-pot, the *vardhanī* or Śakti-pot must also have a *mūrti* imposed and the presence of the Goddess invoked. The priest performs a *śrīkaṇṭha-nyāsa*, elsewhere termed *akṣara-nyāsa*. This set of mantra impositions (as specified in Kumarasvami Gurukkal 1994: 230–35) involves placing the letters of the alphabet onto different parts of the body, along with male and female divine powers. So the priest imposes the letter *a* on the topmost portion, and recites a mantra invoking Śrīkaṇṭha and Pūrṇodari, and so on with each of fifty-one letters.

He then invokes the Goddess with her MŪLA mantra.

The priest worships Śiva and Śakti, and their five entourages with the five services, and feeds them.[123] He honors them with mantra-recitations, offers them to Śiva, and makes a request.[124] Then he honors the four powers, Dharma and the others, in the intermediate directions, starting in the southeast. He announces the command of Śiva, and then he should go up to the principal fire pit.

The officiating priest should perform the fire rites there, starting with consecration of the fire pit and ending with a complete oblation.[125] He has the fire divided into nine or five parts, and has them deposited them in the various fire pits, starting in the east. The priests honor Śiva together with his limbs in each one. Then, along with the image-protectors, the officiating priest offers oblations of milk-rice, and makes an expiation-offering with its parts.[126]

They honor Śiva individually in each fire pit.

IIA. THE SACRIFICIAL FUEL-STICKS.

In the cardinal directions starting with east are ficus, *udumbara*,
fig, and banyan.

[123] The honoring of the *pañcāvaraṇa* or five entourages also follows the paradigm of *nityapūjā*. The priest envisions Śiva and Śakti as seated at the center of a royal court, surrounded by five concentric groups of divinities: (1) the *brahmamantras* and *aṅgamantras*, (2) the Vidyeśvaras, (3) the Gaṇeśvaras, (4) the World-guardians, and (5) the Weapons of the World-guardians (see Davis 1991: 67–68 and *SP* 1 App. VIII). In *KKD*, Aghoraśiva prescribes worship of only one entourage, in the case of *ātmārthapūjā* (*KKD*, "Worship of One Entourage," pp. 154–62). Each deity is visualized, invoked with a mantra into the mentally constructed embodiment, and then honored with *upacāras*. The five *upacāras* (services) here would be offerings of *pādya* (foot-water), *ācamana* (sipping water), *arghya* (reception water), *puṣpa* (flowers), and *dhūpa* (incense).

[124] In *nityapūjā*, as here, the priest or worshiper performs a *japa* (mantra recitation) of the MŪLA mantra, substantializes that *japa* in a flower, offers it to Śiva in the Śiva-liṅga or (here) in the Śiva-pot, and then makes his request of Śiva. In *nityapūjā* he does so in these three verses:

O Protector of the secret and the very secret, accept these mantra recitations I have made.
When these recitations remain with you, may success come to me through your grace.
O Lord, consume and destroy all my *karman*, both good and bad. I am at your feet, beneficent one.
Śiva is the donor. Śiva is the consumer. Śiva is this entire world. A Śiva worships everywhere. I am indeed that Śiva. (*KKD*, "Presentation of Mantra Recitations," pp. 165–67)

[125] At the principal *kuṇḍa* the main priest performs fire rites drawn from *nityahoma*, the daily fire ritual, as Aghoraśiva outlines it in *KKD*, "The Daily Fire Ritual," pp. 178–85). This begins with a *catussamskāra* of the fire pit itself. The fire is then kindled or brought from elsewhere, and it is also consecrated. The priest identifies the fire as Śiva-Agni, Śiva who is Fire, and then invokes Śiva into the fire. The sequence ends here with a *pūrṇāhuti*, prior to the fire being divided.

[126] The officiating priest makes offerings at the principal *kuṇḍa*, while *mūrtipas* carry out the same actions at the other *kuṇḍas*. The *prāyaścitta* (expiation) here would be 108 oblations with the MŪLA mantra (as in *KKD*, cited in *SP* 2 p. 125).

At intermediate directions starting with southeast are *śāmī*, acacia,
māyūra, and bilva.
Palāśa is the best of all, and may be used in all directions.[127]

The priests offer oblations of milk rice, puffed rice, mustard-seed, wheat, sesame, mung bean, black dal, legume, *āḍhaka*, chick-pea, and *kulattha*. After offering these substances, they make offerings with the *vyāhṛtis*. Then they offer 108 oblations along with recitations of MŪLA, or one thousand, or half that amount, accompanied by a complete oblation.[128]

The priests offer ear-picks, sandalpaste, and so on. They maintain the fires.[129] The presiding priest has the rice balls to protect the sacrificial fire given to the central liṅga and the other icons, and puts it on himself along with the assisting priests.[130] Then he takes the Trident to the northeast or northwest, and has it set up there.

He should have fire-oblations performed in this way daily, in the evening and morning.

These are the procedures for the Trident ceremony.

[127] The lines of verse here envision different species of fire-sticks being used in the various fire pits in the *yāgaśālā*.

[128] This section seems to reiterate and expand the previous prescription. The more extensive offering of substances here is followed by a *vyāhṛti-homa*. The *vyāhṛtis* are the familiar Vedic utterances BHŪḤ, BHUVA, and SVAR. Within the Vedic liturgical tradition the brahmin recites the three *vyāhṛtis* at the start of all prayers. In Śaiva ritual they are incorporated occasionally into Veda-derived rites such as *agnikārya*. Here the priests offer four oblations with the mantras:

OM BHŪḤ SVĀHĀ
OM BHUVAḤ SVĀHĀ
OM SVAḤ SVĀHĀ
OM BHŪR BHUVAḤ SVAḤ SVĀHĀ

The multiple oblations along with recitations of MŪLA constitute a *prāyaścitta-homa*, an expiation to repair any ritual errors or omissions in this ceremony. Finally, a *pūrṇāhuti* completes this set of acts.

[129] The term *śotra* is obscure. If one reads *śrotra*, it could refer to *śrotra-śodhana*, ear-cleaning sticks, which are offered into the fire during *pavitrotsava* (*SP* 2 p. 98 n. 8).

The important point here is that the priests do not perform the rite of *visarjana* (dismissal), which usually concludes the *agnikārya*. Instead, Aghoraśiva calls for the *nirodhana* (restraint, maintenance) of the Śiva-fire, to prevent Śiva from departing. The fires of the *yāgaśālā* will be maintained throughout the festival, and rekindled periodically for further *homas*.

[130] *Homarakṣā* (fire-protection) may denote a substance such as a rice-ball used to cover the sacrificial fire, to protect the embers until it is rekindled for the next fire-rite. This would be a normal step when the sacrificial fire is to be maintained for subsequent rites, as here (See *SP* 2 p. 126 n. 2). However, here the distribution and putting on of the *homarakṣā* by the priests suggests it may indicate ash from the sacrificial fire, which has special protective powers. The priest prepares a paste by mixing the ashes with ghee, and applies the paste to icons and priests participating in the festival.

12. *Tying the Protective Cord*

The protective cord made of either gold, silver, or cotton, and woven of fifteen, eleven, or nine threads.[131] It should be sixteen fingers in length for the Śiva-liṅga. The cord for the pedestal should be equal to its circumference, and the ones for the pots equal to their spouts.

The priest should spread a platform with rice, puffed rice, and flowers, and draw a lotus design in the middle of it. He places the cord atop the platform, and presents offerings to it such as ashes, saffron, *durva* grass, sandal, flowers, fruit, gold, and betel.[132] He purifies the cord with ashes, reciting the TRYAMBAKA mantra, and has an auspicious day proclaimed.[133] He constructs a sixfold throne and presents incense and lamp.[134] They make a procession around the temple, and go into the sanctum. The priest honors Śiva and presents incense and lamp. Meditating on the snake Vāsuki, he ties a cord around the base of the liṅga, reciting MŪLA, and then ties one at the pedestal spout, reciting

[131] In this ceremony the *rakṣāsūtra* (*kautuka, pratisara*) is ritually prepared and tied around the wrists of festival icons, as well as on several of the human participants. *Ajitāgama* states the principle that one should tie the *rakṣāsūtra* on all images employed in the festival (27.206–7). The wristlet offers protection against possible threats that may occur during the festival, particularly during processions beyond the temple terrain. The rite of *rakṣābandhana* is also generally enjoined for rituals of installation (*pratiṣṭhā*) (*SP* 4, p. xxxiv).

The *rakṣāsūtra* may be woven of gold, silver, or cotton threads. *MĀŚ* places the materials in a hierarchy, with gold best and cotton least desirable (p. 167). Aghoraśiva simply provides several options for the number of strands making up the wristlet, but *MĀŚ* suggests that different recipients require different numbers of strands: for the Śiva-liṅga, the Naṭarāja image, and the presiding priest, the *rakṣāsūtra* should have sixteen threads, for the Somāskanda processional icon twelve threads, for the Skanda icon six threads, and so on.

[132] *MĀŚ* envisions more elaborate preparations. The priest and his assisting priests (*ṛtvig*) first perform the usual rites of *nityakarman*, from *sūryapūjā* (Sun worship) through *nityahoma*. The *sthaṇḍila* for *rakṣābandhana* is then prepared in front of the deity. Atop the *sthaṇḍila* the priest has a three-footed platter set down, and he places substances on the platter in a definite order. In the center he puts the *rakṣā*, as well as an ash-container (*bhasmadhara*), betel, and coconut. Around the sides he places salt in the east, dry cowdung to the south, saffron (*rajanī*) to the west, and rice to the north (p. 163).

[133] The TRYAMBAKA is a well-known Vedic mantra, *Ṛgveda* 7.59.12, addressed to Rudra as the "Three-eyed One."

> We sacrifice to the sweet-smelling Three-eyed One, who increases our well-being. As a ripe cucumber is released from its stem, may he release me from death.

[134] In mentioning the construction of a *ṣaḍutthāsana* (sixfold throne), Aghoraśiva indicates that the *rakṣāsūtra* may be seen not simply as a cord but as a divine support in itself. *MĀŚ* elaborates this possibility by recommending that the priest honor a host of deities within this ritual construction. He honors the *sthaṇḍila* as Ādhāraśakti, the supporting Śakti. The three feet of the platter are honored as the three *tattva* groups, *śiva*, *ātman*, and *vidyā*. The platter itself is the sixfold throne. Lakulīśa is worshiped in the ash, Viṣṇu in the betel, Rudra and Gaṇeśa in the coconut, and the endless snake Ananta in the *rakṣāsūtra*. Finally, the five *brahmamantras* identical with the five faces of Sadāśiva are invoked: TATPURUṢA on the salt in the east, AGHORA on the dried cowdung in the south, SADYOJĀTA on the saffron in the west, VĀMADEVA on the rice in the north, and ĪŚĀNA on the *rakṣāsūtra* in the center (pp. 163–64). All these deities should be worshiped, the *MĀŚ* continues, with offerings such as sandalpaste and flowers, and with mantra recitations.

its root-mantra, ŚAKTI.[135] He sprinkles ashes on them, reciting TRYAMBAKA, and puts saffron over that. He honors them with offerings such as sandalpaste. He ties a cord on the middle prong of the Trident, and then ties cords around the right wrists of all the processional icons, from Trident through the Devotees, reciting TRYAMBAKA along with HṚDAYA.

For female icons, such as Gaurī and the others, the priest should tie the cord around the left wrist, reciting their own MŪLA mantras.

Then the priest should tie cords on himself, the assisting priests, the tribute-carrier, the *bherī* drummer, and the ten Weapons.[136] He sprinkles ash and saffron over them. He places a cord around the middle of the flagpole, and ties it very tight, with flowers and saffron on the knots.

He should have presentations of saffron-powder, gold, fruit, betel, and the like given to everyone.

These are the procedures for tying the protective cord.

13. *Presentation of Tribute*

Next tribute is presented. During the great festival, one should offer tribute in the evening and morning, either starting at the central pedestal and ending at the flagpole, or starting at the Bull and ending at the tribute-pedestal.

The priest should do as follows: He should have pedestals constructed at the proper locations, beginning with the central location. Each pedestal should be one cubit in width and height, or half that in width, or twelve digits or eight

[135] In Śaiva Āgamas, Vāsuki is one of a group of eight Nāgas who form the entourage of Mahānāga or Nāgeśa, the King of Snakes, much as the eight Vidyeśvaras act as Śiva's entourage. *Rauravāgama* provides a *dhyānaśloka* for meditating on Vāsuki: "Vāsuki is red in color. He has three faces and four arms. With two hands he displays the gestures of security and generosity, and in the other two he holds a rosary and a pot" (*RĀ* 57.68). (See *RĀ* ch. 57 on the installation of Mahānāga and his eight assistants.) As with the hoisting rope of the flagpole (identified with Takṣa, another of the eight Nāgas), the cords of the *bherī* drum (identified with Vāsuki), and later in the *MV* the ropes used to pull the great processional chariot, strings and ropes are identified with snake-deities.

The location of the ceremony here is significant. In Āgamas such as *Ajitāgama* (ch. 27) and *Dīptāgama* (cited in Bhatt, ed., *AĀ* p. 333), the *rakṣābandhana* takes place in the *āsthānamaṇḍapa*, the audience pavilion, rather than the sanctum, and the ceremony focuses on the Trident and the processional icons. But in *MV* (and likewise in *MĀŚ*), the scene is shifted to the sanctum, and the principal temple Śiva-liṅga and its pedestal are the first recipients of the *rakṣāsūtra*.

[136] Important human actors in the festival also wear *rakṣāsūtras*: the *ācārya*, his assisting *ṛtviks*, the *balivāhaka* (tribute carrier), and the *bherītāḍaka* (chief drummer). The ten *āyudha* (Weapons) here are those belonging to the ten World-guardians, previously placed in the *yāgaśālā* (see note 46).

MĀŚ introduces an interesting variation here. After the priest has tied *rakṣāsūtras* around the Śiva-liṅga, pedestal, processional icons of the male and female deities, and Trident in the sanctum, and a cord around the flagpole, suggests *MĀŚ*, he should go to the shrine of Caṇḍeśa located to the northwest of the main shrine. There the priest places *rakṣāsūtras* on the wrists of the *bhaktaberas*, the icons of the Devotees, starting with Caṇḍeśa, Śiva's foremost devotee. At Caṇḍeśa's shrine he also places the cords on the ten *āyudhas* and on the human actors (the same ones as in *MV*) (*MĀŚ* pp. 165–66).

TABLE 5 Daily Presiding Deities (*Dinādhipas*)

One-day Festival (*Ajitāgama*)			
1.	Śiva		
Three-day Festival (*Ajitāgama*)			
1.	Brahman		
2.	Viṣṇu		
3.	Maheśvara		
Five-day Festival (*Ajitāgama*)			
	pañcamūrtis		
Nine-day Festival			
	Mahotsavavidhi	*Suprabhedāgama*	*Rauravāgama*
1.	Gaṇeśa	Gaṇeśa	Brahman
2.	Bhūtas	Bhūtas	Bhūtas
3.	Ṛṣis	Ṛṣis	Gaṇeśvaras
4.	Indra	Indra	Gandharvas
5.	Brahman	Brahman	Ṛṣis
6.	Viṣṇu	Viṣṇu	Indra
7.	Rudra	Rudra	Dānavas
8.	Īśvara	Īśvara	Rakṣaseśvaras
9.	Sadāśiva	Sadāśiva	Īśvara
Twelve-day Festival			
	Kāraṇāgama	*Kāmikāgama*	
1.	Gaṇeśa	Gaṇeśa	
2.	Paiśācas	Paiśācas	
3.	Brahman	Brahman	
4.	Gandharvas	Gandharvas	
5.	Bhūtas	Bhūtas	
6.	Skanda	Skanda	
7.	Ṛṣis	Ṛṣis	
8.	Nāgas	Nāgas	
9.	Candra	Aindra	
10.	Viṣṇu	Viṣṇu	
11.	Rākṣasas	Rākṣasas	
12.	Śiva	Śiva	
Thirteen-day Festival (*MĀŚ*)			
1.	Gaṇeśa		
2.	Bhūtas		
3.	Ṛṣis		
4.	Indra		
5.	Brahman		
6.	Viṣṇu		
7.	Rudra		
8.	Īśvara		
9.	Sadāśiva		
10.	Skanda		
11.	Śrī		
12.	Caṇḍeśa		
13.	Kṣetrapāla		

Sources: *Ajitāgama* 27.232; *Mahotsavavidhi* p. 26; *Suprebhedāgama*, quoted in Bhatt, ed., *Rauravāgama* 1, p. 81; *Rauravāgama* 18.91–95; *Kāraṇāgama*, quoted in Bhatt, ed., *Rauravāgama* 1, p. 82; *Uttarakāmikāgama* 6.219–32; *Mahotsavavidhikrama Āgamaśekhara* pp. 169–70.

digits. They are solid, with three steps around them, and each has a lotus-form on top with eight petals and a receptacle in the center. They are made of stone, brick, or hard wood, and should have all the auspicious marks.[137] He smears them, and then ornaments in each direction with five kinds of powder.

He has one bucket of rice cooked, or half that amount. He has the rice placed on a tribute-plate, and sprinkles water on it reciting ASTRA. Then he puts half that amount on another plate, and forms a rice-liṅga, with all the characteristic features.

The rice-liṅga should be twelve digits in height and four digits in circumference, and it should have a pedestal. The priest smears it with yogurt, and then he performs an installation ceremony according to the usual procedures.[138] He meditates.

13A. MEDITATION ON PAŚUPATI.

The god has three eyes and four arms,
And wears a crown of matted hair.
His hands make signs of generosity and security,
And in his other left hand is a rosary,
In his right a trident.
He is endowed with fierce eyes, and a snake is his ornament.
His hair goes up, and his glance down.

So one should honor the divine Lord of Creatures in the middle of the liṅga.[139]

Or else one may honor Śiva as described previously.

[137] *Balipīṭhas* (tribute pedestals) are located either around the courtyard within the temple complex, or outside the temple in the surrounding community, or both. The principal *balipīṭha* should be placed at the *brahmasthāna*, the central location, and others at the eight directions. Aghoraśiva's specifications for the *pīṭhas* roughly correspond to those in other texts, though there are several varieties of *balipīṭhas* (see *MM* 23.74–81 and Dagens 1984: 143). In the square type described by Aghoraśiva, the three degrees of steps (*mekhala*, literally "belts") make it look like a "small pyramid," as Dagens puts it, with a lotus on top. The inner part of the lotus, the *karṇikā* (pericarp), serves as the receptacle for tribute offerings.

[138] The *annaliṅga* or rice-liṅga will serve as a temporary, mobile support for Śiva, visualized here in the form of Pāśupata, Śiva as Lord of Creatures. The priest forms the *annaliṅga* from rice mixed with ghee and yogurt to make it malleable. As with any liṅga, it should be in the shape of a rounded cylinder, and it should have a *pīṭha*, a pedestal that supports it. Since it acts as the mobile support of Śiva during the tribute ceremony, the *annaliṅga* must undergo a *pratiṣṭhā*, or installation ceremony, to transform the material form into a suitable embodiment for the deity. Aghoraśiva does not indicate what procedures he has in mind here, but it would have to be a highly abbreviated form of the *liṅga-pratiṣṭhā* ceremony as elaborated in texts like *SP* vol. 4 and Aghoraśiva's *ŚPV*.

[139] This *dhyānaśloka* is also found in *Pūrvakāraṇāgama* 11.194. A full consideration of forms of Paśupati, based on numerous Āgama sources, may be found in Adicéam 1971. This particular visualized form would be classified as a "fierce" Paśupati. The alternative here is to visualize another form of Śiva, presumably Sadāśiva, on the rice-liṅga.

The officiating priest and the assisting priests, who are carrying the ten Weapons and the Trident, are ornamented with the proper adornments, from ashes to turbans. Accompanied by the attendants, who carry colored flags, parasols, yak-tail fans, and the like, and by musical instruments, bells, and Vedic recitations, and by female and male dancers and singers, they present tribute.[140]

For a nine-day festival, the deities receiving special tribute are said to be as follows:[141]

On the first day, the priest recites:

To Gaṇeśa, Lord of Obstacles, SVĀHĀ.

On the second:

To the Creatures, SVĀHĀ.

On the third:

To the Sages, SVĀHĀ.

On the fourth:

To Indra, SVĀHĀ.

On the fifth:

To Brahman, SVĀHĀ.

On the sixth:

To Viṣṇu, SVĀHĀ.

[140] The daily processions to present tribute to deities at the various *balipīṭhas* involve many participants. Human processors are suitably adorned for the ceremony. As *Kāraṇāgama* specifies, "The priest should summon the *paricārakas*, who have bathed and wear white clothes. The pure priest wears turban, upper cloth, and a *pavitra*-ring" (Bhatt, ed., *AĀ* p. 334). In addition to the persons and items Aghoraśiva lists, there must also be persons carrying the *bali* offerings (elsewhere called *balivāhakas*) and someone holding the *annaliṅga*. *MĀŚ* adds still other items to the procession: incense and lamps, conch and *dundubhi* drum, flute and lute, and all the auspicious emblems (*sarvamaṅgala*, that is, the eight auspicious objects) (p. 168). Significantly, *MĀŚ* also recommends including in the procession the deities, that is, the *utsavamūrtis*, decorated with canopies, raised onto palanquins or shield-like platforms (*kheṭaka*), or carried on the heads of *paricārakas*.

[141] Within the festival calendar, each day has a presiding deity, a *dinādhipa*, who should receive special tribute offerings on that day, both in the morning and the evening (*RĀ* 18.93–94). The Āgamas give different lists of *dinādhipas*. See table 5 for a tabulation from several texts, for one-, three-, nine-, twelve-, and thirteen-day festivals. Aghoraśiva's list corresponds most closely to that of *Suprabhedāgama* (in Bhatt, ed., *RĀ* p. 81) and to the first nine days in the *MĀŚ* list, which continues up to thirteen days (pp. 169–70). It is appropriate, naturally, to begin with Gaṇeśa, the deity responsible for removing obstacles at the start of all undertakings. After that, the *dinādhipas* are arranged in an ascending hierarchical order, culminating on the ninth day with Sadāśiva, Śiva's most complete manifest form.

On the seventh:

To Rudra, SVĀHĀ.

On the eighth:

To Īśvara, SVĀHĀ.

On the ninth:

To Sadāśiva, SVĀHĀ.

On these days the offering is to be done at the end of the daily worship of the Śiva-liṅga.

One should put out plain rice sprinkled with ghee and covered with yogurt, the size of a chicken egg.[142]

13B. SPECIAL TRIBUTE.

Tribute should also be given in the evening and morning, with mantras ending in SVĀHĀ, in the following locations: to Rudra Kumbhodara in the cowpen, to Laṅkā at the *kuśa* grass storehouse, to Gaṅgā in the rivers, to Kṣetramūrti in the tanks, to Sarasvatī and Durgā at the assembly hall, to Mahālakṣmī in the treasury, and to Bhīma at the gateway towers.[143]

[142] Aghoraśiva gives the default recipe for tribute offerings here. But many Āgamas suggest a more varied menu of tribute preparations, with daily specials designed to bring pleasure (*priya*) to the palate of the various *dinādhipas* (*RĀ* 18.95–99, *AĀ* 27.241–47, *UKĀ* 6.219–32, and others.) Here is the menu from *MĀŚ* for the first nine *dinādhipas*, largely the same as that of *Suprabhedāgama*.

1. Gaṇeśa	rice with yogurt, laddu-cake, fruit and sugar candy (*guḍa*)
2. Bhūtas	ghee-rice mixed with yogurt and saffron-powder, known as *kṛsara*
3. Ṛṣis	lotus-roots and tips of *kuśa* grass, white rice with ghee, banana
4. Indra	Cucumis plant (*indravallī*), turmeric mixed with *priyaṅgu* and ghee
5. Brahman	lotus flower, milk-payasa with saffron, and fried rice
6. Viṣṇu	sweet rice with ghee, breadfruit
7. Rudra	sesame rice with ghee and coconut
8. Īśvara	bamboo rice with yogurt and banana
9. Sadāśiva	white rice mixed with yogurt and sugar, and citron fruit

"Or else," concludes *Suprabhedāgama*, "the priest may have white rice mixed with ghee and covered with yogurt given to all the deities, while reciting the mantras of each one."

[143] The overall aim of *viśeṣabali* (special tribute) here is clear, but some of the details are obscure. As part of the festival ceremonies, the temple priests extend the distribution of *bali* beyond the temple, to various locations in the surrounding community. The locations *MV* specifies are: *gosthāna* (cowpen), *kuśa* (grass storehouse), *nadī* (rivers), *taṭāka* (tank), *sabhāsthāna* (assembly place), *kośa* (treasury), and *gopura* (gateway tower). Of the deities honored at these locations, Rudra Kumbhodara ("pot-belly") is a member of Śiva's troops (*gaṇa*). Laṅkā is generally an island, but here seems to be personified as a deity, much as rivers like Gaṅgā are. Kṣetramūrti, the lord of the place, may be the same as Kṣetrapāla, who acts elsewhere as a guardian of Śiva's sanctuaries. Bhīma, one of the eight Mūrtīśvaras, is presiding Lord of Ether.

Ajitāgama (27.229–31) prescribes a similar procedure, though with different locations and deities:

at four-road crossings, to Piśācas;
at three-road crossings, to Rākṣasas;

Setting out from the central tribute pedestal and ending at the tribute-pedestal or at the flagpole, they reenter the temple. The priest places the remaining offerings on the tribute-pedestal. He should throw the rice-liṅga into water. Then he washes his feet, sips water, sprinkles pure ashes on his body, and reenters the temple.[144]

This is the procedure for the measurement of tribute.

14. *The Order of Processions*

The streets should be decorated as described previously.[145] The priest should have the icon of the god Śiva together with Śakti adorned with various ornaments, flowers, and a nimbus. The icon is carried on a chariot, cart, shield-like platform, palanquin, or other conveyance to the place of the principal liṅga.[146]

---

at assembly-places, to Sarasvatī;
at water-reservoirs and tanks, to Jyeṣṭhā;
at banyan trees, to Kṣetrapāla;
at pippala trees, to Gaṇeśa;
at fig trees, to Skanda;
at wells, to Kumbhodara;
at cowpens, to Caṇḍa Rudra; and
at gateway towers, to Bhīma Rudra

[144] After the priest has disposed of the remaining tribute-preparations and the rice-liṅga, and repurified himself, he returns to the presence of Śiva (*śiva-samīpa*) and recites mantras, according to the *MĀŚ* (p. 172). The priest should also recite two *ślokas* of prayer, requesting Śiva's favor for any ritual errors that may have been committed.

> Whatever actions I have done, either good or bad, O eternal God, consume them for me, who bows at the feet of Śiva. Destroy them, O beneficent one. May all that I have done either insufficiently or in excess, out of ignorance, be made complete for me, O highest Lord.

Compare this with similar prayers at the conclusion of *nityapūjā*, such as in Davis 1991: 153.

[145] Here Aghoraśiva begins his directions for the twice-daily processions (*yāna*), the central and most conspicuous ritual actions of the great festival. Decoration of the temple and the surrounding community for the festival has been described in section 2, "The Festival of Gaṇeśa." Another protocol for general festival preparations is given in *MĀŚ*. Before the start of the festival, it says, one must have the vehicles, the temple, the gateway towers, the pavilions, the rest-pavilions, the streets, and the surrounding town renovated (*navīkaraṇa*). The festival locations are then decorated with red ornamental gateways, mango sprouts, coconuts, branches of the betel tree, sugar-cane stalks, colored cloths, vessels of water (for thirsty festival goers), flower garlands, full pots, lamps, auspicious objects, mirrors, and multicolored banners (pp. 173–74).

[146] The principal processional icon of the Śaiva *mahotsava* is Somāskanda, here called "Śiva together with Śakti." In this benign and auspicious manifestation, Śiva sits comfortably on a semicircular throne, his wife Umā or Pārvatī to his left, and their child Skanda stands between them. In this form, adds *Mayamata* (36.62), Śiva fulfills all wishes and desires. See *MM* 36.59–62, Adicéam 1973, and L'Hernault 1978: 49–92 for more extensive discussions of this iconographic form of Śiva in southern India. As L'Hernault notes, the prevalence of Somāskanda forms among the bronze icons of Tamilnad temples reflects its central role in *mahotsava* processions. This *utsavamūrti* has already undergone a *pratiṣṭhā* ceremony transforming it into a suitable support for the divine presence, but before going forth in procession it must also have the special presence of Śiva invoked into it. Aghoraśiva specifies that this invocation be performed in the sanctum, in the presence of the primary temple Śiva-liṅga.

There the priest performs invocation, presents incense and lamp, and worships Śiva with flowers in his cupped hands.[147] He may then begin the procession of Śiva, accompanied by mobile icons starting with Śakti and ending with the Devotees.

In the front of the procession should be Śailādi, adorned with many ornaments, accompanied by musical instruments led by the *bherī* drum. After that comes Nandin along with Gaṇeśa and Skanda. In the middle will be Somāskanda together with the Goddess. Either in front or back of them are the icons of the Devotees. At the rear is Caṇḍeśa.[148]

Aghoraśiva suggests that the icon be brought into the sanctum on its processional conveyance, whether that be a *ratha* (chariot), *raṅga* (cart), *kheṭaka* (shield-like platform), *śibikā* (palanquin), or some other vehicle. The *ratha* will be described below, in section 23, "Raising the Deity onto the Chariot." The *raṅga*, says *Mayamata*, is a "canopy-shaped chariot" or a chariot of which the superstructure is without walls and without roof (*MM* 31.56–57 and *Īśānaśivagurudevapaddhati* quoted in Dagens, trans., *MM* p. 727 n. 39). The term *kheṭaka* denotes a shield. The shield's use as a processional vehicle remains obscure. I suggest it refers to a simple flat platform supported by bamboo poles used for carrying. On the *śibikā*, see note 19 above.

Proper adornment (*alamkāra*) of the icons is crucial. *Ajitāgama* states that an icon raised onto its conveyance should have a protective cord (*kautuka*) tied to its wrist. It should be adorned with a full panoply of ornaments, and covered with lovely colored cloth. It is then endowed with garlands, flowers, a nimbus (*prabhā*), and all the other ornaments. It is further surrounded by its lordly accouterments, such as parasol, yak-tail fans, peacock fans, and banners (*AĀ* 27.252–54). for an important perspective on the Indian metaphysics of adornment, see Coomaraswamy 1977, and on its cultural extensions, Ali 2004: 175–82. Waghorne 1992 and Venkatesan 2004 examine ornamentation in modern south Indian temple settings. Also see the catalog of South Indian ornaments for temple images in Filliozat and Pattabiraman 1966.

147 This invocation of Śiva and Śakti in a mobile icon follows the paradigm of the *āvāhana* sequence in *nityapūjā*. This would include worship of the throne (*āsanapūjā*), construction of the embodiment (*mūrti*), and then *āvāhana* proper. See *KKD*, "Worship of Śiva's Throne," and the following sections, pp. 127–47. Following invocation, Aghoraśiva recommends a simple set of worship services (*upacāra*). The offering of flowers in cupped hands (*puṣpāñjali*) is also termed *paramīkaraṇa*, "rendering the deity supreme." See *KKD*, "Flower Offerings," pp. 162.

148 Aghoraśiva here sets out the normal order of deities in procession, with some additions. The processional group consists of Śiva (in Somāskanda form) with his family and closest relations: his wife Devī, two sons Skanda and Gaṇeśa, his Bull-mount Nandin, and his favorite Devotees, including Caṇḍeśa. The group corresponds roughly to the entourage of Gaṇeśvaras. Each deity will ride in his or her own conveyance, except the Goddess Devī, who occupies the same conveyance as Somāskanda.

The leading icon in Aghoraśiva's list, Śailādi, poses a problem. Śailādi could be a patronymic for Nandin, Śiva's bull, as it is used in texts like *Vāmanapurāṇa*. However, the separate mention of Nandin here seems to preclude that. Most likely it denotes Nandikeśvara. According to the *Liṅgapurāṇa*, Śilada was a *ṛṣi* who received as a boon a child who looked exactly like Śiva. He was known as Nandikeśvara, or Adhikāra-Nandin. What would account for his prominent role at the front of the procession?

The others are well-known divine figures. *Mayamata* gives iconographic directions for Gaṇeśa (36.122–26), Skanda (36.119–21), and the goddess Pārvatī (36.276–78). Aghoraśiva does not specify the identity of the *bhaktabera*, the icons of the Devotees, but leaves it as an open group. So too the *Uttarakāmikāgama*, in its chapter on the installation of Devotee icons, chooses an open-ended definition: "*Brāhmaṇas*, *kṣatriyas*, *vaiśyas*, and *śūdras*, members of intermediate classes, women, preceptors, and kings initiated by them—all those, both living and dead, who are filled with devotion to Śiva (66.1–3)." In practice, this category came to be identified with the sixty-three Śaiva *nāyaṉmār*, the devotional saints of Tamil tradition. On the canonizing and iconizing of the *nāyaṉmār* during the Chola period, see Prentiss 1999: 105–9. For a list of the sixty-three *nāyaṉmār*, see Gopinatha Rao 1999: 2. 475–78.

TABLE 6A Processional Vehicles and Events (Nine-day Festival) According to *Mahotsavavidhi* and Other Āgamas

Day and Time	*Mahotsavavidhi*	*Kāmikāgama*	*Kāraṇāgama*
1st Morning	*Raṅga* (cart)	*Raṅga*	*Śibikā*
1st Evening	*Simha* (lion)	*Hamsa*	*Hamsa*
2nd Morning	*Sūrya* (Sun)	*Sūrya*	*Sūrya*
2nd Evening	*Soma* (Moon)	*Candra*	*Candra*
3rd Morning	*Bhūta*	*Bhūta*	*Simha*
3rd Evening	*Hamsa* (Swan)	*Simha*	*Bhūta*
4th Morning	*Nāga* (Snake)	*Nāga*	*Vāsuki*
4th Evening	*Vṛṣabha* (Bull), *Pariveṣaṇa* (Perambulation)	*Vṛṣabha*	*Makara*
5th Morning	*Āndolikā* (Swing)	*Nandin*	*Prātamañca*
5th Evening	*Śikhariyukta-rāvana* (Rāvana)	*Rāvana*	*Vṛṣabha*
6th Morning	*Śibikā* (Palanquin) or *Kheṭaka* (Platform)	*Śibikā*	*Kheṭaka*
	Cūrnotsava (Powder Festival)	*Cūrnotsava*	
6th Evening	*Gaja* (Elephant)	*Gaja*	*Gaja*
7th Morning	*Ratha* (Chariot)	*Ratha*	*Ratha*
7th Evening	*Kalpataru* (Tree of Plenty)	*Prāyascitta*	*Śeṣa*
8th Morning	*Āndolikā* (Swing)	*Bhikṣātana*	*Puruṣāmrga*
8th Evening	*Aśva* (Horse)	*Aśva*	*Aśva*
	Mrgayātrā (Hunting Expedition)	*Mrgayātrā*	
9th Morning	*Puruṣayantrayukta-Āndolikā* (Swing Held by Man)	*Nara-Śibika*	*Pīṭhā*
9th Evening	*Kheṭaka* (Platform)	*Kalpavṛkṣa*	*Vyāghra*
	Kṛṣṇagandha (Black-balm Ceremony)	*Kṛṣṇagandha*	*Kṛṣṇagandha*
10th Morning	*Ratnasimhāsana* (Jeweled Lion-Throne) or *Śibikā* (Palanquin)	*Simhāsana*	*Simhāsana*
10th Evening		*Vṛṣabha*	*Rāvana*
11th Morning			*Vimāna*
11th Evening		*Vimāna* *Śakti-yātrā*	*Devī*

Sources: Mahotsavavidhi, pp. 27–29; *Kāmikāgama*, from *MĀŚ*, pp. 183–84 (not in published *UKĀ*); *Kāraṇāgama*, from *MĀŚ*, pp. 184–85.

The officiating priest will be on the right side of the icons, and he should recite the MŪLA or AGHORA mantra countless times. On the left side is the king, with his attendants following behind him. In front of the god are dancers and flutists, singers and drummers. On both sides are the Rudra-gaṇikās and others engaged in dance. In front come the Mahāśaivas, and behind come brahmins intoning the sounds of the Veda and other sacred

Caṇḍa or Caṇḍeśa, one of the *nāyaṉmār*, has his own distinctive place in Śaiva iconography and liturgy, including a special festival rite, as Śiva's foremost devotee. He also serves as semidivine administrator of the temple. See section 21 below, and for further discussion, Davis 1991: 156–57 and Edholm 1984.

hymns. After them come the Māheśvaras belonging to all four classes.[149] Those who follow the divine procession obtain the fruit of performing a horse-sacrifice.

Pleasing God in this way, on the first day in the morning, Śiva rides on a cart, and at night on a lion.[150] On the second day he rides on supports of Sun and Moon. On the third day he is on a Bhūta support, and at night on a swan, on the fourth morning on the Snake, and on that night on the Bull. During the procession of the Bull, one should also hold the ceremony of perambulation.

[149] Aghoraśiva outlines the arrangement of human participants in the procession. Most significant are the officiating priest on one side of the procession and the king on the other. As the king is followed by his *bhṛtyas* (attendants, dependents), the priest is also followed by his *śiṣyas* (pupils), adds *Ajitāgama* (27.165). The Mahāśaivas are initiated brahmins not of the five Ādiśaiva *gotras* (and therefore not eligible to become *ācāryas*), and the Māheśvaras are initiates of any *varṇa*. *Ajitāgama* also adds the "many other devotees who are assigned there to perform services (*sevārtha*)," such as the palanquin bearers and rope pullers (27.158). The emphasis here is on inclusive participation or representation of all segments of the Śaiva community. All four *varṇas* should be included, and all four categories of Śaiva initiates as well, says *Ajitāgama* (27.157). The *Vijayottarāgama* observes that persons of different categories of Śiva worshipers, such as those who follow the Vedas, Pāśupatas, Mahāvratins, Kāpālikas, Kaulas, and Bhairavas, may sing hymns to Śiva from their own traditions (Ganesan 2005: 4).

[150] In each procession during the festival, the principal deity appears on a different conveyance. In addition to the palanquin and chariot, these include "elaborately crafted shoulder-borne conveyances" in the shapes of animals, other beings, and natural phenomena, known generally as *vāhana* (vehicles) or *yantra* (supports) (Smith 1981: 13). In modern south Indian temples, as Daniel Smith describes them, these *vāhanas* are made of wood, often plated with metal, decorated with colorful semiprecious gems, wrought with elaborate decorative motifs, and mounted on long poles for carrying (1981: 17–18). See Smith for line drawings of lion, swan, and horse *vāhanas*, as well as others specific to Vaiṣṇava temples.

Śaiva Āgamas set out schedules for festival processions and other ancillary celebrations, listing the particular *vāhana* the deity will ride during each morning and evening procession. *MĀŚ* provides lists from six Āgama texts. See table 6A, on processional *vāhanas* in the nine-day festival. Although no two lists agree exactly, they all draw on the same set of *vāhanas*, and certain parts of the schedule are shared by all or almost all texts. So, for example, almost all authorities prescribe Sun and Moon vehicles for the second-day processions, all agree on the Snake (identified with Vāsuki) for the fourth morning, and all place the great chariot procession, *rathayātra*, for the seventh morning.

The default form of Śiva for mahotsava processions is Somāskanda. However, one Āgama quoted by *MĀŚ* (pp. 244–45, from *Mākutāgama*) specifies an alternative, in which different mobile forms of Śiva may be taken out for each procession:

day	morning	evening
1	Umāsahita	Candraśekhara
2	Sukhāsana	Harihara
3	Ardhanarī	Gangādhara
4	Kalyānasundara	Vṛṣabhavāhana
5	Nandikeśa	Mahāruḍha
6	Bhairava	Tripurāntaka
7	Kāladāha, Kāmāri	Gajasamhara
8 or 9	Naṭarāja	

Mākutāgama goes on to list five types of Naṭarāja forms that may be used: *bhujaṅgatrāsa*, *bhujaṅgalalita*, *bhujaṅgabhairava*, *bhujaṅgavalaya*, and *bhujaṅgakuñcita*.

14A. PERAMBULATION. The perambulation is as follows: In the garden or some other pleasant place, at each corner, the god should be entertained at every step with offerings of fruit and other edibles and with betelnut and other condiments, along with Vedic praises and hymns, with the music of lute and flute, with singers and dancers and Rudragaṇikās.[151] Then the deity is brought back to the temple.

On the fifth day the god is seated on a swing, and at night on a vehicle depicting Rāvaṇa holding up the mountain. On the sixth day he should be mounted on a palanquin or on a shield-like platform, and the festival of powders should be performed, as will be described below.[152] The gods are sprinkled with waters mixed with vermillion, saffron, turmeric, and other substances, and then the gods are smeared with vermillion paste. Then everyone is sprinkled.

That night the deity is mounted on an elephant vehicle. On the seventh day he processes in the chariot, and at night on the tree of plenty.[153] On the eighth day in the morning he goes on a swing.[154] That evening Śiva is mounted on a horse vehicle, and at the time of procession all around him the Rudragaṇikās, wearing all their ornaments, also ride horses, and carry weapons such as spears, bows, and shields.[155]

[151] The term *pariveṣaṇa* indicates service or attendance, and may be used to denote ceremonies of attendance in royal courts. But the *pariveṣaṇa* ceremony here, as Aghoraśiva describes it, involves the deity perambulating through parks and woods. *MĀŚ* calls it a "circumambulation in gardens and forests." (By contrast, some other Āgamas like *Rauravāgama* and *Dīptāgama* place the *pariveṣaṇa* rite in the temple's assembly hall, as a concert or divertissement for the divine lord and his human courtiers. See Dagens and Barazer-Billoret, trans., *RĀ* 1 p. 78 and n. 55.) The emphasis in the perambulation is on giving pleasure (*saṃtoṣaṇa*) to the deity, through delightful offerings and entertaining performances.

Expanding on the *MV* account, *MĀŚ* describes *pariveṣaṇa* as a special extension of the evening procession on the fourth night. Śiva on his Bull-mount and the Goddess on her lion, both full adorned, go forth from the temple accompanied by elephants, horses, Rudragaṇikās, and a full complement of musicians and singers. They process around the town, as usual, and then go wandering off (*bhramaṇa*) in a southwesterly direction, through parks and forests. Their followers please them with offerings of fruit and flowers, and with delightful sounds. At each step of the way, says *MĀŚ*, the deity should be pleased by showers of holy basil (*devavṛnda*) and by heaps of flowers. Then they return to the temple (*MĀŚ* pp. 176 and 192–93).

[152] The *cūrṇotsava* (festival of powders) on the sixth day of the festival is discussed in section 17 below. It may also be performed on the morning of the ninth day.

[153] The preparations for the chariot procession, the most dramatic of all processions, on the seventh morning are described in detail in section 23 below.

[154] According to *Kāmikāgama*, *Śiva* sets forth in the form of Bhikṣāṭana, the beggar, instead of Somāskanda, on the eighth morning (*MĀŚ* p. 183). *MĀŚ* prescribes a separate midday procession of Bhikṣāṭana on the eighth day (p. 177). On the form of Bhikṣātana, see Adicéam 1965.

[155] *MĀŚ* calls this the *mrgayātra*, the hunting procession, and supplements Aghoraśiva's description here with further details. The Rudragaṇikās (here called Rudradāsīs), wearing their ornaments and carrying weapons such as swords, shields, bows, arrows, and spears, ride on horses surrounding Śiva. They are accompanied by the auspicious sounds of *bherī* drum, *paṭaha* drum, singing, and other instruments. In this procession, *MĀŚ* adds, they wander particularly in a westerly direction.

At this time the priest heals what has gone bad and protects what remains good, and announces all that is proper and improper. Then he returns to the temple.

On the ninth day the god is mounted on a swing with a man holding it, and at night, for the ceremony of black balm, he is on a shield-like platform.[156] On the tenth day, the priest should have the god raised on a jeweled lion-throne, a palanquin, or some other conveyance, and they circumambulate the city or village. Then, in front of the temple or the flagpole, he has the leftover food revolved and thrown out at a crossroads.[157]

After the procession the ceremony of illumination should be performed by the officiating priest along with respectable married women or the Rudra-gaṇikās.[158] In front of the entry tower or flagpole, a pot-lamp is presented to the deity, and immediately the Rudragaṇikās circumambulate, carrying pot-lamps, night-lamps, and camphor in their hands, accompanied by dance, song, and all the musical instruments.

In the morning the god accompanied by the icons starting with Śailādi, then Nandin, Gaṇeśa, Skanda, the Goddess, the Devotees, and Caṇḍeśa make a circumambulation and then return to the temple. Then the priest has Somā-skanda brought into the temple, accompanied by auspicious songs and all the musical instruments, and placed in the audience pavilion. A screen for privacy is set up, and the priest feeds the god his principal offering and then worships him with all the services. To remove his fatigue, the priest gives him coconut, sugar-cane juice, mung beans, and fruits that are in season. Then he has the brahmins adorned with sandal and flowers and has them fed.

Other Āgama texts give different accounts of the *mṛgayātra*. For example, *Kāraṇāgama* recommends that Śiva present himself for this ceremony in the form of Kirāta, a mountain huntsman, or Tripurāntaka, conqueror of the three cities. Soldiers accompany him on the procession carrying a variety of weapons, along with all the local people. They should capture elephants, deer, boars, monkeys, and various birds like peacock and cuckoo on this hunting expedition (Bhatt, ed., *RĀ* p. 84 n. 16).

MĀŚ suggests that the *mṛgayātra* can emulate a hunting expedition, as in *Kāraṇāgama*, or a battle (pp. 225–28). Riding on horses and elephants, participants carry various weapons and enact a battle with the demons. Some engage in the battle, others become frightened and quickly flee the situation. After this pantomime, *MĀŚ* continues, one should conduct the procession, with Śiva mounted on a horse, accompanied by the Rudragaṇikās.

[156] The ceremony of *kṛṣṇagandha* (black balm) is a significant part of the Festival of Dancing Śiva (*nṛttamūrtyutsava*). The Dancing Śiva procession takes place on the tenth day of the *mahotsava*, that is, after its official conclusion. Aghoraśiva gives directions for this ceremony below, in section 24.

[157] The *vikṛtānna* (leftover food offering) is piled onto a plate, and this is revolved (*paribhrāmaṇa*) in both directions, to remove its bad qualities. It is then disposed of at a *catuṣpatha*, where four roads converge.

[158] Aghoraśiva describes the procedures of *nīrājana*, the illumination ceremony, to be followed at the conclusion of each procession. In the next section, he describes a special *nīrājana* ceremony. Here he specifies that it may be performed either by *suvāsinīs* (lit., "women of good homes," that is, respectable married women) or the temple women known as Rudragaṇikās. However, he calls for Rudragaṇikās to perform the circumambulation carrying lamps.

He should have the devotees of Śiva and the poor and blind fed without hesitation.

Alternatively one may perform the processions in some other way.

These are the procedures for the festival processions.

15. *The Illumination Ceremony*

For the illumination ceremony, the priest should collect five plates, made of gold, silver, copper, brass, or some other substance.[159] They should be one span in diameter, and have lips of one digit. He places them on a circular diagram and honors them with sandalpaste, flowers, and the like, reciting the set of *brahmamantras* with the seed-syllable of the AGNI mantra, HṚM.[160] He should consecrate them with the fourfold consecration, and display before them the trident gesture and cow gesture.[161] While hymns of well-being and auspicious verses are proclaimed, he places a lamp, surrounded by the plates filled with dough.[162] Carrying these on their heads, they should circumambulate the village. Then they should place them on a diagram in front of the god. The lamp is waved in circles three times before the deity, starting from the head and ending with the feet, while the

[159] *Nīrājana* (from the root *nis-rāj*, to cause to shine upon) denotes the ceremony of illumination, whose central action is the waving or circling of lamps before the deity. The term *ārātrika* is used more or less interchangeably. According to *Kāraṇāgama*, this rite destroys all that is unnatural (*kṛtrima*) and brings benefits to all people (Bhatt, ed., *AĀ* 1 p. 291).

Kāraṇāgama also notes that this ritual has two forms, regular (*nitya*) and occasional (*naimittika*). As a *nitya* rite, it is one of the *upacāras* in *nityapūjā*. "That which is called *nitya* should be done at night, after the dance, for the Śiva-liṅga," says *Kāraṇāgama*. Aghoraśiva described the *nitya-nīrājana* procedures briefly in *KKD*, "Night Offerings," pp. 164–65. As a *naimittika* rite, it appears in various larger ritual complexes, including the festival. "That which is called *naimittika* should be performed at night, at the end of an auspicious ritual, or during a festival, for a mobile icon (*bimba*)." In both cases it is a rite of closure that has a protective or purificatory quality. During the festival it should be performed after each procession.

[160] Aghoraśiva does not specify the location for this *maṇḍala*, and other texts provide various recommendations. *Kāraṇāgama* specifies a square pavilion set up in front of the sanctum (Bhatt, ed., *AĀ* 1 p. 291), while *Kāmikāgama* recommends it be in the sanctum, in the *ardhamaṇḍapa*, or some other location (*UKĀ* 7.3).

[161] In the *triśula-mudrā* (trident gesture), one holds the fingers of the two hands interlaced, with thumbs, middle fingers, and little fingers extended vertically, and index and ring fingers crossed. The gesture thus resembles the three-pronged *triśula* (Janaki 1986: 14–15). For the *dhenu-mudrā* (cow gesture), evoking the udders of the cow, one interlaces the thumbs, and joins the index finger of each hand with the middle finger of the other, and the ring finger of each with the little finger of the other. See *SP* 1 Pl. 1, "Mudrā"

[162] The *svasti-sūktas* (hymns of well-being) refer to Vedic hymns, while the *maṅgala-vācakas* (auspicious verses) refer more generally to any *ślokas* considered to be appropriately auspicious for the occasion.

The dough (*piṣṭa*) on the plates is made from the flour or meal of several grains. *Ajitāgama* calls for a mixture of *kuṣṭha*, sandal, rice, wheat, barley, and beans (24.3–4). Some other texts recommend placing different substances on each plate. For example, *Kāraṇāgama* calls for sandal on a plate to the southeast of the lamp, *arghya* to the southwest, flowers to the northwest, and ashes to the northeast (Bhatt, ed., *AĀ* 1 p. 292).

brahmamantras are recited.[163] The priest should present mirror, parasol, yak-tail fan, fan, ashes, and the like, and flowers in his cupped hands to Śiva, while reciting the MŪLA mantra. He bows. With the Rudragaṇikās carrying them as before, they are placed before the pedestal or the Bull, along with foot-water and other offerings.

The priest washes his feet, and does other purifying acts, and reenters the temple.

These are the procedures for the ceremony of illumination.

16. *Collection of Holy Water*

The priest should collect holy water on the day before the ceremony of bathing at a holy bathing place.[164]

He should tie protective cords as previously, have blessings proclaimed, and then place a water vessel for Manonmanī, and eight water vessels surrounding it in the middle of the pavilion.[165] In the center he envisions Manonmanī.[166]

[163] The deity here is a festival icon of Śiva, most often Somāskanda, and not the principal Śiva-liṅga in the sanctum. The most likely lamp-wavers are the Rudragaṇikās, though Aghoraśiva also gives the option of allowing married women of good homes (*suvāsinī*) to have the honor. *Kāraṇāgama* suggests either Rudragaṇikās or brahmins wave the lamps.

The lamps are revolved in front of the deity three times for the three *tattva*-groups: *śiva-tattva, ātman-tattva,* and *vidyā-tattva.*

[164] *Tīrtha* has three distinct meanings here: (1) holy bathing places, (2) sanctified water, and (3) the final ceremonial bath, also called *avabhṛta*, at the conclusion of the festival. The *tīrtha-saṅgrahaṇa* (collection of holy water) here acts as a preparation for the *tīrthasnāna*, the final bath, which is described in section 18. It should be done on the day before the *tīrthasnāna*, either during the day or night. *Tīrtha-saṅgrahaṇa* involves a set of nine water-vessels, and centers not around collecting holy water but rather around deifying the water in the pots as the holy rivers of India. In some other texts, the Trident figures as an important participant in the *tīrtha-saṅgrahaṇa*.

[165] For the location of this rite, Aghoraśiva simply says a *maṇḍapa*, without further specification. *MĀŚ* prescribes that it be performed in the *yāgaśālā* or in front of the sanctum (p. 298). *MĀŚ* also sets out the usual preparatory procedures that Aghoraśiva here takes for granted. One should construct a *sthaṇḍila*, draw an eight-petal lotus design on it, and strew it with *kuśa* grass and flowers. The water vessels (*karaka*) for Manonmanī and the eight Rivers are fully adorned, as a matter of course, with strings, cover, cloth, grass-bundle, sprouts, and fruit, and are filled with water that has precious substances like gold and jewels added to it (pp. 298–99).

MĀŚ goes on to recommend that the priest perform all the preliminary acts of *nityapūjā* starting with *sakalīkaraṇa*, through the purifications of self, materials, and mantras, as a preparation for invoking the goddesses into the pots.

[166] In Śaiva ritual Manonmanī appears most often as the consort or Śakti of Sadāśiva, Śiva's most complete manifest form. She is, as Brunner-Lachaux puts it, the "non-specialized Śakti of Sadāśiva," in the sense that she is not associated with a particular form of power, as are other Śaktis such as Kriyāśakti or Jñānaśakti (*SP* I p. 168). During *nityapūjā* Manonmanī is envisioned on the central pericarp of Śiva's lotus-throne, presiding over eight Śaktis, Vāmā and the rest, who in turn preside over the eight Vidyeśvaras. Here she appears independently, as the presiding goddess of the holy waters.

Aghoraśiva cites the *dhyānaśloka* of Manonmanī, while *MĀŚ* indicates that this visualization should be part of an invocation sequence (p. 300). The priest should construct a throne (from Ādhāraśakti up to the lotus level), form an embodiment (*mūrti*), meditate on the Goddess, recite her MŪLA mantra, and invoke her into the embodiment. Manonmanī is then honored with *upacāras* of sandal, flowers, and the like.

She is vermillion in color, dressed in red, three-eyed,
And wears a nectar-like moon sliver as her crown.
Abounding in youth, she bends over
From the weight of her large round pendent breasts.
Endowed with many ornaments, she sits on a lotus,
Her form transferred from the BĪJA mantra.
She holds fetter and goad, makes gestures of security and generosity.
I bow to the Goddess, source of the whole world.

The priest meditates in this way and honors the Goddess. Then in the eight pots, starting from the east, he invokes the Rivers with the following mantras, then worships them with all the services.[167]

I honor Gaṅgā.
I honor Yamunā.
I honor Narmadā.
I honor Sarasvatī.
I honor Sindhu.
I honor Godavarī.
I honor Kaverī.
I honor Tāmraparṇī.

Carrying the pots on their heads, the celebrants circumambulate the city, along with the Trident, accompanied by all the instruments. They then take them to a holy bathing place such as a river for the purpose of bathing.

This is the procedure for collecting holy water.

17. *The Festival of Powder*

One should begin the powder festival after the offering of tribute on the day after the collecting of holy water.[168]

[167] The eight Rivers in the eight directions around Manonmanī likewise receive full invocations, with thrones (*āsana*), embodiments (*mūrti*), visualization (*dhyāna*), and invocation using their MŪLA mantras, says *MĀŚ* (p. 300). According to *MĀŚ*, services should include incense and lamp, feeding, betel, illumination, and mantra-recitation.

[168] The central action of the *cūrṇotsava*, the festival of powder, is grinding substances into a powder that is sprinkled over divine and human participants in the *mahotsava*. In fact, Aghoraśiva recommends two different times for the *cūrṇotsava*. Here it forms part of the final bathing sequence, the morning after the *tīrtha-saṅgrahaṇa* and before the final *tīrthasnāna*. This puts it on the morning of the ninth day, after the priest has performed the normal *nityapūjā* and *balidāna*. In the schedule of processions, Aghoraśiva also recommends that *cūrṇotsava* be performed on the sixth day of the festival, after the morning procession. *MĀŚ* sets out procedures for both the "sixth day powder festival" (pp. 193–199) and the "powder festival on the morning of the final bathing day" (pp. 301–9). The two powder festivals are almost exactly the same.

In front of the temple, the priest should draw lotus designs on two platforms.[169] He has the auspicious day proclaimed. He covers the platforms with *darbha* grass. On one platform he sets up the Trident.[170] He should have a mortar made from wood of the *plakṣa*, ficus, holy fig, banyan, or some other suitable tree, and a pestle from wood of the acacia tree, with all proper features. They are placed there by other people, and the priest sprinkles them while reciting ASTRA and consecrates them with the fourfold consecration. He covers the mortar and pestle with a cloth. Reciting the BRAHMADAIVATYA mantra, he should honor the Rudra-pot and the eight surrounding pots of the World-guardians in between the mortar and the Trident.[171]

Or else he may worship Śiva.

He then places on the eight petals of the lotus design surrounding the mortar, starting in the east, the following substances: *dūrvā* grass, the *sahadevī* herbs, saffron, sesame, betel, sandal, fruit, and ash.[172] He consecrates them with the fourfold consecration. He honors the mortar as the Earth, and the pestle as Mount Meru. Then he puts the substances into the mortar.[173]

[169] Aghoraśiva, along with *MĀŚ*, leaves the initial location for the *cūrṇotsava* simply as someplace in front of the sanctum. Other Āgamas like *Ajitāgama* (27.284) and *Rauravāgama* (18.125) recommend it be performed in the *āsthāna-maṇḍapa*, the audience pavilion.

In this ritual area, Aghoraśiva specifies that two platforms be set up, one for the Trident and the other for the mortar and pestle, with an arrangement of nine pots in between the two. More elaborately, *MĀŚ* recommends four *sthaṇḍilas* (for the sixth day *cūrṇotsava*) or five *sthaṇḍilas* (for the ninth day): (1) Trident, (2) nine-pot arrangement, (3) mortar and pestle, (4) *bherī* drum and drumstick, and (5) oil-pot (pp. 193, 302). The first three are arranged along a west-east axis, with Trident to the west and mortar to the east. The *bherī* drum is north of the mortar, and the oil-pot to the west of the drum.

[170] According to the *MĀŚ*, the priest needs first to prepare himself. He does so by imposing mantras on himself (*sakalīkaraṇa*), then going through the sequence of self-purification rites from *nityapūjā*, through the worship of the soul. These acts empower him to set up the Trident. *MĀŚ* specifies that the priest should construct a sixfold throne at the base of the Trident, then form an embodiment, visualize the deity, and invoke him with the MŪLA mantra. The text goes on to recommend that the priest next worship the enlivened Trident with *upacāras* including incense, lamps, food-offerings, betel, illumination, and ending with mantra-recitations.

[171] It is unusual to invoke Rudra, not Śiva, into the center of a pot, to surround him with Lokapālas, and to do so with a Vedic mantra, *Brahmadaivatya*. The more common practice for a nine-pot arrangement, which Aghoraśiva suggests as an alternative, is to have a central Śiva-pot surrounded by the eight Vidyeśvaras.

MĀŚ likewise recommends a central Rudra-pot with an entourage of eight Lokapālas. The priest, it elaborates, should go through the usual invocation sequence of throne-construction, embodiment, invocation with Rudra's MŪLA mantra, and so on. Once Rudra and the Lokapālas are installed, they should be honored with *upacāras* such as incense, lamp, food-offerings, and mantra-recitations (pp. 303–4).

[172] These are the substances that will be mixed and ground together in the mortar to make the *cūrṇa*. *Ajitāgama* gives the simplest recipe here, recommending just one ingredient, *rajanī* (saffron). As with Aghoraśiva, *MĀŚ* proposes an arrangement of eight substances placed around the mortar, similar to that of *MV* but not exactly the same: *dūrvā, sahadevī, koṣṭha* (?), *rajanī*, betel, ghee, fruit, and sandal. It adds several more substances as well: ashes beside the mortar, sandal-oil to its south, and vermillion flowers to the north (pp. 195–96).

[173] *MĀŚ* adds another element to the powder festival, prior to the grinding. The *bherī* drum and the drumstick, installed on the fourth *sthaṇḍila*, must also receive their proper ritual attentions. These follow the procedures of the *bherītāḍana*, described in section 9 above. Drum and stick are consecrated with the fourfold

The Rudragaṇikās grind them into a powder with strokes of the pestle, while the PADA mantra is recited or devotional hymns are sung.[174] That powder is mixed into saffron, with oil, ghee, and sandal water. The officiating priest takes the powder along with gold and puts them into bowls. They are consecrated.[175] He has that powder given to the principal Śiva-liṅga along with ashes, and puts a vermillion turban on it, rubs it with the ointment, feeds it, and presents incense and lamp. He puts the powder on all the processional icons, rubs them with the ointment, and displays the lotus gesture.[176] Then he puts it on himself, and on all the others, and gives them turban, saffron, fruit, betel, and the like.[177] They circumambulate the city or town with the Trident, and return to the temple.

---

consecration, and dressed with a multicolored cloth and a flower belt. Deities are invoked, most notably Rudra into the center of the drum. After a brief honoring of the drum, the priest strikes it three times with *dūrvā* grass, as Vedic hymns are recited. Then he summons the chief drummer, blesses him, and puts a flower garland on his hand. At the priest's command the drummer throws a flower onto the middle of the drum, and plays the *Nanditāla* rhythm.

Likewise, in the case of the ninth-day *cūrṇotsava*, the oil-pot in the fifth *sthaṇḍila* must be purified, consecrated, protected, and finally have a divine presence invoked into it (p. 306).

174 The question of who gets to pound the substances appears to have been a point of contention. While Aghoraśiva allows the Rudragaṇikās as a group to grind the powder, *MĀŚ* insists on a single Rudragaṇikā, with all good qualities, to serve as churnswoman (pp. 197–98). Other Āgama texts propose other grinders:

Ajitāgama: chief priest and others, including *yajamāna*
Rauravāgama: the devotees (*bhaktajana*)
Suprabhedāgama: chief priest with devotees
Dīptāgama: chief priest with Rudragaṇikās and devotees

Meanwhile, others recite either the PADA (word) mantra, most often called the VYOMAVYĀPIN mantra, which consists of eighty-one *padas* (see above, note 89), or *bhaktastotras*, devotional hymns, which in Aghoraśiva's context would most likely have been the Tamil songs of the Śaiva *nāyaṉmārs*.

175 The consecration is the usual *catussamskāra*. At this point *MĀŚ* suggests that the vessel containing the newly ground powder be placed on the head of a *paricāraka* and processed around the temple, accompanied by a suitable musical fanfare. The powder party then enters the sanctum, for the distribution of powder (p. 198).

176 According to *Ajitāgama*, the officiant divides the *cūrṇa* into three parts, one for the Śiva-liṅga, another for the festival images and Trident, and the third for the human participants (27.288–89). This sets out the common hierarchy of recipients that Aghoraśiva accepts as well. The *mūlaliṅga* is first recipient, then the processional icons. *MĀŚ* emphasizes that Somāskanda is first among these festival images.

To display the *padma-mudrā* (lotus gesture), the priest places his two hands together at their bases, spreads the eight fingers out to form the eight petals, and folds the two thumbs inward to form the pericarp (see Janaki 1986 and *SP* I Pl. I, "Mudrā").

177 As with the churning itself, the distribution of the ground *cūrṇa* to human participants is a matter of some dispute among the Āgamas. Aghoraśiva gives first place to the officiating priest, then leaves the "all the others" indeterminate. Some Āgamas like *Ajitāgama* do not even grant the priest first pick, but simply have it distributed to all the people. *Dīptāgama* singles out the *yajamāna* as first recipient. *MĀŚ* provides a more stratified order of distribution, emphasizing the officiants: first the chief priest, then *ṛtvigs*, all brahmins, and finally the mass of devotees (p. 309).

Alternatively, the priest may set up the main pot as the principal weapon and the surrounding pots as the Weapons, starting with the thunderbolt, and worship them.[178]

These are the procedures for the festival of powder.

Immediately afterward, one should perform the sprout ceremony as previously, and go on to the final bath at the holy place.

18. Final Bath at the Holy Bathing Place

For all participants this bath removes the pollution caused by contact with those not to be touched, it brings about the grace of holy bathing places, it brings delight to all the gods, it engenders the four aims of humans starting with righteousness, and it leads to high states of attainment such as sharing in Śiva's world.[179]

One should take the Trident together with Śakti, the processional icons starting with Somāskanda, the sprouts, parasol, yak-tail fans, and the like together with the pots of holy bathing water, accompanied by the sounds of various instruments and hymns to the bank of the holy bathing place.[180] There one should set up the deities in a temporary pavilion or other structure that is already

[178] This alternative procedure seems to involve only the identification of the pots in between the Trident and the mortar. Rather than invoking Rudra and the eight Lokapālas, Aghoraśiva suggests, one may also invoke *astra*, the Trident as Śiva's principal weapon, in the central pot, and the eight Weapons of the Lokapālas, starting with Indra's thunderbolt in the eastern pot.

[179] The *tīrthasnāna* involves a trip to a *tīrtha*, a holy bathing place, seen as a *yātra*, a pilgrimage. The deities, various festival paraphernalia, and the devotees make the pilgrimage together. The *tīrthasnāna* together with the following *dhvajāvarohana* (lowering of the flag) serve as the final, concluding rites of the *mahotsava*. The *tīrthasnāna* may also be referred to as *avabhṛta* (bath of "removal"), and it occupies much the same position in the Śaiva festival that the *avabhṛta* of the sacrificer does in a Vedic public sacrifice. Here it offers final purification for both the icons and the worshipers.

Aghoraśiva's *phalaśruti* here indicates several of the aims: its purificatory role, its homology to other forms of pilgrimage, and the pleasure it brings to the deities. Aghoraśiva adds that those devotees who share in the final bath also come to share in Śiva's world. This may refer to the state of *sālokya*, one of the lower forms of liberation within the Śaiva Siddhānta system, as outlined in the *Śaivaparibhāṣā* of Śivāgrayogin.

[180] *MĀŚ* calls this the "pilgrimage of the icons" (*bera-yātra*) (p. 311). The journey should be performed at midday of the ninth festival day, after completing morning worship and the festival of powder. According to *MĀŚ*, the icons first leave their customary places and assemble in the sanctum, then proceed to the holy bathing place.

In the simplest Āgama formulations, the Trident alone acts as primary pilgrim (*Ajitāgama* 27.293). In *Rauravāgama*, the Trident and the principal festival icon make the pilgrimage. Here Aghoraśiva prescribes that the Trident as King of Weapons (*astrarāja*), along with its Śakti, lead the promenade of Somāskanda and other festival icons. Among other items taken along on this pilgrimage should be the third set of sprouts (*aṅkura*) planted during *aṅkurārpaṇa* of the preparatory ceremonies for the festival, and now carried on a platter (*pālika*), and the nine pots of Manonmanī and the eight Rivers established the previous night during *tīrthasaṅgraha*. *MĀŚ* suggests that this group first make a circumambulation of the town, then set out on the pilgrimage to the holy bathing place, along with all the devotees.

prepared.[181] On a platform in front of it, the priest should have the Manonmanī pot brought and put down in the center, and the eight pots of Gaṅgā and the other Rivers all around, along with the sprout platter. He worships them in the special manner. The priest invokes Durgā in the northwest, and invokes the thirty-three Vedic divinities, the eighteen members of Śiva's troop, and the World-guardians in the presence of the Trident.[182] He removes the protective cord from all the deities, starting with the Trident. He puts the pots along with the platters into the middle of the bathing place, and with the pots performs an *abhiṣeka* bath for each of the icons, starting with Śiva and ending with the Trident. Then the presiding priest should bathe himself, along with all the people.[183]

Then the priest should dismiss the gods of the bathing place and return to the temple. He should perform an *abhiṣeka* for every deity, each with its own pot. He feeds them and presents incense and lamp. He enters the temple. Everyone in the assembly hall gives grains of unhusked rice for blessing into the hand of the presiding priest, accompanied by the sounds of the Vedas, and the priest sprinkles them with the grains of rice, accompanied with blessings.[184] All return to their own places.

[181] The *tīrtha* may be located on the ocean, a river, or other water-source. The icons should be placed in a pavilion so that they face the water (*MĀŚ* p. 311). Aghoraśiva recommends that a *prapā*, a light pavilion without base, be set up at the site. See above, note 13, on the *prapā*. As Dagens points out, the *prapā* is often used for water-based rites such as *jalādhivāsa* and *snāna* (1984: 97).

[182] It is not clear why Durgā should be invoked in the northwest corner of the *sthaṇḍila* containing nine pots. Nor is it certain where the Trident should be placed in relation to this *sthaṇḍila*. Aghoraśiva specifies that a large group of lesser divinities be invoked near, or in the presence of, the Trident before it receives its *abhiṣeka* bath. The thirty-three deities consist of the twelve Ādityas, the eight Vasus, the eleven Rudras, and the two Aśvins. The eighteen Gaṇas, members of Śiva's troupe, constitute an unnamed group.

[183] There are two key ritual actions here. First, the priest has the bathing pots that were prepared during *tīrthasaṅgrahaṇa* employed in giving an *abhiṣeka* bath to all the icons, starting with the Śiva (i.e., Somāskanda) icon and ending with the Trident. Second, the priest enters the water at the bathing place. Aghoraśiva does not state it, but other Āgamas specify that the priest holds the Trident as he bathes (*AĀ* 27.301). The other festival icons, by contrast, do not enter the water. The devotees are then encouraged to bathe. *Ajitāgama* stresses the great benefits of sharing in this final bath: "All those people full of devotion who bathe there together with the priest and the Trident are freed from their accumulated sins, even heinous ones like murdering a brahmin" (27.301–2).

[184] Grains of unhusked rice (*akṣata*) here absorb the benedictions or blessings (*āśis*) pronounced by the priest, and then confer those blessings back onto the recipients. The priest holds a plate in his hand, and the devotees place blessing-rice (*āśyakṣata*) on it. Then, as other priests recite blessings, the principal priest sprinkles the grains of rice over the heads of the devotees.

MĀŚ (pp. 415–19) provides examples of blessings (*āśīrvāda*) that brahmins may pronounce, not only for the participants in the festival but also for the temple and all the special pavilions, for the musical instruments, for the festival paraphernalia, and so on.

> O Lord, through your compassion may the meaning of the mantra of well-being (*svasti*) become true and fruitful; be gracious, O Great Lord.

Prayers request also that the festival itself may be correct and proper.

> During the rites of this nine-day *mahotsava* dedicated to the Lord of Lords, the Great God who carries out the five fundamental activities of emission, maintenance, reabsorption, veiling, and grace for the

These are the procedures for the final bath at the holy bathing place.

19. The Bath with Pots

One should bathe the deity with pots in order to remove the leftover powder of Śiva's festival, to bring about well-being among the people, to attain the favor of the god, and to gain proximity to Indra and the other gods.[185]

The priests should perform special fire rites in each of the fire-pits, and then offer special complete oblations in the fire-pits.[186] The presiding priest joins together the lords of each fire-pit into the principal one and honors Śiva. Again he offers a complete oblation.

He worships the pots starting with the Śiva-pot in the special manner, then joins them together and offers incense and lamp.[187] Honoraria should be given to the officiating priest and others, as described previously, and to the temple attendants and others are given cloth, gold, and the like.[188] They raise the pots onto their heads as previously, circumambulate the temple, and return to the central sanctum.[189] They set the pots down there.

---

good of all the worlds and all beings, the Supreme Lord who joins with the Goddess Tripurasundarī, even if there should be an error in the mantras, a flaw in the ritual actions, or a mistake in the observances, please allow everything to be made good, as directed in the procedures of the holy treatises, by your grace.

[185] The *ghaṭasnāna* (bath with pots) is, along with the final bath and the flag-lowering, one of the rites bringing the festival to its completion. In the *ghaṭasnāna*, the central act involves giving an *abhiṣeka* bath to the principal Śiva-liṅga with the Śiva-pot that has been maintained during the festival in the *yāgaśālā*. The fire-rites of the *yāgaśālā* are also brought to a close.

In his *phalaśruti* Aghoraśiva focuses on the benefits this rite brings to its human participants: well-being (*sthiti*, literally "preservation") to all the people, Śiva's grace (*prasāda*) for some, and proximity (*sāmīpya*) to the worlds of the gods. Yet it is also meant to bring pleasure to Śiva, who may be tired from the exertion of the festival.

[186] The starting location for *ghaṭasnāna* is the *yāgaśālā*. At the beginning of the festival, during the Trident Ceremony (section 11), a set of ten pots were installed there, and likewise a set of either nine or five fires were kindled and consecrated. The separate fires have been maintained and honored through the festival with twice-daily *homa* rites. Now they are once again honored with a final set of oblations. As before, the presiding *ācārya* offers oblations in the principal firepit, while the *mūrtipas* serve the lateral ones. *Rauravāgama* suggests that the *brahmamantras* and *aṅgamantras* accompany the initial oblations, and that the complete oblation be accompanied by the Vedic mantra beginning *sviṣṭam agne* (*Tai Br* 2.4.1.4).

[187] The pots here are the Śiva-pot, the Śakti-pot (*vardhanī*), and the eight Vidyeśvara pots installed on the alter of the *yāgaśālā* during the Trident Ceremony. They are reunited or joined together (*samyojana*) here by mixing together some of the water.

[188] *Dakṣiṇā* (honoraria) are given at this point to the *ācārya* and other ritual officiants, such as the *ṛtvigs* and *mūrtipas*. Aghoraśiva refers to a previous specification of what this *dakṣiṇā* might consist. Gifts are also given to *paricārakas* and other temple functionaries.

[189] During the Trident Ceremony the pots were first set up and enlivened in the temple sanctum, in front of the Śiva-liṅga, and then carried by the *paricārakas* around the temple and to the *yāgaśālā*. The converse movement takes place now, with the *paricārakas* carrying the pots back into the sanctum, where they will be employed in bathing the Śiva-liṅga.

The officiating priest imposes the six paths, and then performs an *abhiṣeka* bath for the principal liṅga.[190] He gives an *abhiṣeka* bath to the pedestal with the Śakti-pot, and around the liṅga in each direction with the Vidyeśvara pots. He performs an imposition of Śrīkaṇṭha on the Goddess image and does an *abhiṣeka* of her with a pot.[191] He offers a large serving of oblation food, presents incense and lamp, and then goes to the fire-hall.

The priest offers 108 oblations in the Śiva-fire, reciting MŪLA, AGHORA, and ASTRA mantras together with ŚIRAS. He gives a complete oblation. He joins the fire with the Lord of Sacrifice, and then, in the manner taught by his preceptor, the priest joins the Śiva-pot, Śakti-pot, and the deities of the five entourages into their own places. He dismisses him also.[192]

Then one may entertain the deity with water-sports and the like. One should give it a large helping of oblation food and then have a bath given to the icon.[193]

These are the procedures for the bath with pots.

20. *The Flag-Lowering Ceremony*

The rite of lowering the flag, preceded by the sounding of the *brahmatāla* rhythm, should be performed on the day of the final bath, either in the forenoon or at night.[194] This rite removes all faults and protects what is

[190] The *ācārya* imposes the mantras of the six paths (*ṣaḍadhvanyāsa*) onto the *mūlaliṅga* (see note 89 above). The *abhiṣeka* here consists of a bath using the contents of the Śiva-pot. *Ajitāgama* (27.311) recommends the recitation of the ŚIVA-GĀYATRĪ mantra during this *abhiṣeka*, and ŚAKTI-GĀYATRĪ while bathing the pedestal with the Śakti-pot. For ŚIVA-GĀYATRĪ, see *SP*, p. 58 n. 4.

[191] The image of Devī stands beside the *mūlaliṅga* in the sanctum. The *śrīkaṇṭha- nyāsa* consists in the imposition of the letters of the alphabet, along with corresponding divine powers, onto different parts of the body (see note 122 above).

[192] The priest returns to the *yāgaśālā* and carries out a final reunification and dismissal of the deities who have been invoked and present there during the festival. After the final oblations in the central fire, he unites (*samyojana*) it with Yāgeśvara, Śiva as Lord of Sacrifice. As Brunner-Lachaux observes, Yāgeśvara designates Śiva presiding in the Śiva-pot, whose principal duty is to protect the sacrifice (*SP* 2 p. 78 n. 1). The final dismissal, following the paradigm of *nityapūjā*, involves reabsorbing the five entourages who have surrounded the Śiva-pot since the Trident Ceremony back into the central form of Śiva, and then dismissing that form of Śiva as well (Davis 1991: 157–58).

[193] Such pleasant diversions as *jalakrīḍā* take place after the official conclusion of the festival. In *jalakrīḍā*, the movable icon (*bimba*) of Śiva (accompanied by his consort, and perhaps by others of his household) is placed on a boat and floated around in a tank or other body of water. If supplementary sports are done, the deity must be given a good-sized meal (*prabhūtahavis*) and a bath afterward.

[194] If the ceremony of raising the flag marks the official beginning of the festival, its lowering (*dhvajāvarohaṇa*) symmetrically forms part of the closing ceremonies. *Dhvajāvarohaṇa* should be performed on the same day as the *tīrthasnāna*. As *Dīptāgama* says, one should perform the *tīrtha* bath during the day, and that night one should complete the *dhvajāvarohaṇa* and the Caṇḍeśa festival (Bhatt, ed., *AĀ* 27.317). The central action involves lowering the flag, of course, but it also includes a final worship of festival icons and a silent offering of tribute.

left over. Following the very best method, the priest should unite the deity located in the banner with the Bull, and then unite that Bull with the Bull image located in front of Śiva.[195] He joins the deities of the Bull's entourage into that entourage, and worships all of them according to the usual procedures.[196]

On that day one should offer tribute silently.[197]

Because a portion of the oblation food is intended for all the deities, at the conclusion of the fire rites, the priest should offer a final tribute in silence.

The officiating priest should go up to the Somāskanda icon, and honor it with a throne extending from Śakti up to Śakti. He imposes the thirty-one *kalās* on it, following the stick-method and the bald-head method, and also performs an imposition of Śrīkaṇṭha.[198] Then he meditates on Somāskanda:

Aghoraśiva fails to outline procedures for lowering the flag, but *MĀŚ* fills the gap with detailed directions (pp. 311–19). To a considerable extent, these rites replicate the earlier ones of *dhvajārohaṇa* (section 8) and *bherītāḍaṇa* (section 9). After various initial rites, the priest constructs three *maṇḍalas* near the base of the flagpole, on which are placed the Trident, the icon of Caṇḍeśa, and the *bherī* drum with drumstick. (In raising the flag, the flag is in the center *maṇḍala*, now occupied by Caṇḍeśa.) The presiding priest sprinkles the ground with water, and performs a sequence of purification rites drawn from *nityapūjā*. Repeating the actions of *bherītāḍaṇa*, he imposes the mantras of the six paths on the Trident (see note 89), and honors the same set of deities inhabiting the Trident. In the second *maṇḍala* Caṇḍeśa is likewise invoked and worshiped. Finally the *bherī* drum and drumstick are purified, dressed, and worshiped as the site of multiple divinities.

The priest then turns his attention to the flagpole. As in the flag-raising ceremony, he constructs a throne "from Śakti up to Śakti" at the base (note 77), reconstitutes the pole as a *vidyādeha* (note 79), invokes Sadāśiva, and honors the various deities in the pole with all sixteen *upacāras* (note 81). Again as in *bherītāḍaṇa*, the priest strikes the drum three times with a bundle of grass, while the same mantras are recited (note 96). The priest summons the chief drummer and directs him to begin. The drummer now plays the *gaṇeśvara-tāla*, not *nanditāla* as in the earlier rite. As the drum strikes and other instruments pitch in, and as singers recite prose and verse praise compositions (*gadya-padya*), the chief priest and mūrtipas quickly unfasten the rope from the pole and lower the flag.

[195] If one characteristic feature of the *mahotsava* is the multiple manifestations of divinity, at the close of the festival there is an inverse need to reabsorb or reunite those manifestations back into their sources. Here Aghoraśiva deals with three supports of Vṛṣabha the Bull: the temporary support of the festival Bull-banner, the permanent large Bull icon in the temple courtyard, and the smaller Bull more proximate to the Śiva-liṅga in the sanctum. The priest must reunite what is temporary and peripheral into that which is more permanent and central. Aghoraśiva refers to the ritual action here as *yojana* or *saṃyojana* (joining, uniting), as does *MĀŚ*, but neither provides instructions on how this unification is to be carried out.

[196] The *āvaraṇa* (entourage) here is the group of eight Nandins (Ukṣana, etc.) surrounding the Bull, who were also imposed onto the festival flag (note 60). As with the Bull of the banner, the deities of the entourage must be joined into their more permanent counterparts surrounding the fixed Bull icon.

[197] Silence is a rare commodity during the *mahotsava*, with all its recitations, proclamations, singers singing, drums beating, and instruments playing. Now, at the close of the festival is a moment of silence, termed *maunabali* (silent tribute) or *maunotsava* (silent procession). The central action here is the priest offering *bali* at all the tribute-pedestals, mirroring the earlier *bali* offerings during *bherītāḍaṇa* (section 9), though this time with no drums and no musical instruments.

[198] Before the *maunabali*, the festival icons should receive a final worship. According to *MĀŚ*, this should take place in the sanctum, in the presence of the primary Śiva-liṅga. For Aghoraśiva, this final *pūjā* involves just the image of Somāskanda, as the principal festival form of Śiva, and the separate Goddess icon that accompanies Somāskanda. More ambitiously, *MĀŚ* calls for the worship of the three deities that form the Somāskanda icon

> With his right leg hanging free and his other bent under,
> Together with the goddess Umā, and Skanda in between,
> He holds a lotus in his pair of hands.
> I honor the Lord with Umā and Skanda.

He worships Somāskanda abundantly, along with his limbs, and also honors the five entourages.[199] He meditates on the Goddess in a manner that will be described later, and worships her.[200] The priest should request good fortune for the whole world.

After that he requests leave, and taking a vow of silence, he stands with his hands folded together in prayer. The deities starting with the Trident should be placed on palanquins, and the rice-liṅga put on a plate. Before, when the flag is taken down, it is accompanied by the sounds of all the instruments. Now, with everyone maintaining a vow of silence and reciting AGHORA in their hearts, with no instruments playing, the priest, accompanied by sword, shield, Trident, and other weapons, presents tribute either half the size of a peacock egg or the size of a chicken egg, along with sandal, flowers, and other offerings, at all the tribute pedestals starting with the central pedestal, to each deity in its place.[201] He dismisses the gods of the junctures, in proper order as previously. After circumambulating, the priest enters the temple. He takes down the deities from their conveyances and puts them back in their own places. Then he dispatches all the leftovers and the rice-liṅga into the water.

These are the procedures for taking down the flag.

(that is, Śiva, Umā, and Skanda) individually, and then for the honoring of the other festival icons, starting with icons of the Goddess and Skanda, and concluding with those of Trident and Caṇḍeśa.

Aghoraśiva provides brief technical details for the worship of Somāskanda. The throne should reach from "Śakti up to Śakti," that is, from Ādhāraśakti to Parāśakti. The priest should impose the *brahmamantras* following the *daṇḍabhaṅgi* and the *muṇḍabhaṅgi* (note 120). He should impose thirty-one *kalās*, rather than the more common thirty-eight imposed on Sadāśiva (see *UKĀ* 3.23–25). And he should also perform a *śrīkaṇṭha-nyāsa* (note 122).

199 Aghoraśiva indicates here that Somāskanda should first be worshiped with his limbs (*aṅga*) in their integral positions (*layāṅga*), as constituent parts of his body (that is, crown, face, and so on), and then in their enjoyment positions (*bhogāṅga*) as separate members of his entourage. See *KKD*, "Worship of the Integral Body," p. 153 n. 149 for this sequence in *nityapūjā*.

200 The Devī icon receives its own worship. Aghoraśiva's allusion to a future visualization of the Goddess probably refers to that of Parameśvarī, the Goddess in her supreme form, given in the Festival of Dancing Śiva (section 24).

201 *MĀŚ* describes this as a silent procession of the deities (*maunotsava*). Aghoraśiva emphasizes the silent offering of tribute (*maunabali*). As in the tribute offerings described earlier in the festival (sections 9 and 13), the offering begins at the *brahmasthāna*, the central tribute-pedestal near the Nandin image (note 100). It then proceeds in a *pradakṣiṇa* order within the temple court from east to northeast. The presiding deities of the junctures (*sandhi*) are the eight Lokapālas.

According to MĀŚ the silent circumambulation concludes at the flagpole, where a final illumination ceremony (*nīrājana*) is held, before returning the deities to their own places.

21. *The Festival of Caṇḍeśa*

After this one should bring the icon of Caṇḍeśa to the sacrificial pavilion, and perform an *abhiṣeka* on him with his own pot.[202] The priest worships Caṇḍeśa according to the procedure, and decorates Caṇḍeśa with the leftover garlands and other remnants of the festival.[203] As expiation, the priest should offer 100, 1000, or 500 ghee oblations into the fire, and then dismisses him as well. With all the devotees, he should circumambulate the temple, accompanied by the triple symphony.[204] Then he returns to his own place. This is the procedure for the festival of Caṇḍeśa.

22. *Worship of the Priest*

The patron worships the priest, then gives him an honorarium—
He should give him cows, land, gold, jewels, cloth, and other valuables.
When the heart of the priest is gratified, Paramaśiva is also pleased.

[202] *Ajitāgama* (27.318–19) explains that Caṇḍeśa is the leader (*nāyaka*) of all the fierce (*caṇḍa*) gaṇas, so he receives an allotment of *pūjā* offerings. In *Kāmikāgama* (*PKĀ* 4.525) he is portrayed as an "angry emanation of Paramaśiva." Caṇḍeśa has his own shrine to the northeast of the main temple sanctum, and during *nityapūjā*, as one of the final acts of worship, he receives Śiva's leftovers (*nirmālya*) as his offering (*KKD* "Worship of Caṇḍeśvara," pp. 196–99; cf. Davis 1991: 154–57). Nirmalamaṇi comments that the offering to Caṇḍeśa also removes any errors of deficiency or excess that the worshiper may have committed during *pūjā*. Within the larger *mahotsava*, the festival of Caṇḍeśa likewise occurs at the end of the ceremonies, and performs an expiatory function.

The location of the Caṇḍeśa festival varies among the texts. *Ajitāgama* recommends an *abhiṣeka* be performed for Caṇḍeśa in his own shrine, or on a *sthaṇḍila* immediately in front of it (27.320–22). Aghoraśiva here recommends taking the Caṇḍeśa icon from his shrine to the *yāgamaṇḍapa* for the *abhiṣeka* and following expiatory fire-oblations. *MĀŚ* does not discuss these offerings, but rather focuses on the subsequent procession of Caṇḍeśa and an illumination ceremony that takes place near the flagpole (pp. 330–31).

[203] Aghoraśiva here refers back, most likely, to the treatment of Caṇḍeśa *pūjā* outlined in the *nityapūjā* section of the *KKD*. This procedure involves a visualization of Caṇḍeśa:

> Fearsome Caṇḍa, who originated from the fire of Rudra, is black in color. Carrying a trident and axe, he is fierce, with four faces and four arms. Great flames pour from his mouth. He has twelve red eyes and is adorned with a crescent moon in his crown of matted locks. He has snakes as bracelets, and a snake is his sacrificial thread. Holding a string of *akṣa* beads and a water pot, he is seated on a white lotus. He destroys the pain of those who bow in devotion.

The worshiper then imposes a mantra on the image, invokes Caṇḍeśa into the image, imposes the *aṅgamantras*, and then presents the leftover offerings for Caṇḍeśa's consumption. He recites mantras and makes a request that Caṇḍeśa "perfect" for him the ritual actions just completed.

[204] *MĀŚ* elaborates on the circumambulation of Caṇḍeśa (pp. 330–31). One should lift the Caṇḍeśa icon onto a palanquin or shield-like platform, and decorate him with clothing, ornaments, and garlands, as well as with umbrella, yak-tail fan, and lamp. Along with all the devotees, he sets out from his shrine, and goes in circumambulatory order to the flagpole. There a ceremony of illumniation and other rites are performed. Finally he returns to his shrine and receives *pūjā* offerings there. Aghoraśiva's mention of a *tauryatrika* ("triple symphony") refers most likely to the threefold performance of vocal music, instrumental music, and dance.

The patron honors the priest, along with the assisting priests, just like Śiva.[205] The priest is put onto a chariot, palanquin, or other vehicle, and circumambulates the city, accompanied by many musical instruments, dance and song, the sounds of Vedas and other hymns. He is also accompanied by the host of devotees and by all the people, starting with king and patron, carrying parasol, yak-tail fans, and other signs of lordship, and many kinds of lamps. He should be taken to his own home by the vehicle.[206]

This is the procedure for the festival of the priest.

23. *Raising the Deity onto the Chariot*

One performs the raising of the deity onto the chariot on the seventh day.[207] On the night before that, the priest should prepare a protective cord.[208] At dawn the priest performs all the daily rites up through daily worship, including a special bath and consecration, according to the usual procedures.[209] He should offer the fire-rites, including the offering of

[205] At the close of the *mahotsava*, the *yajamāna* must honor the chief priest (*ācārya*) and present an honorarium (*dakṣiṇā*) to him. Ths honoring is a common feature of Śaiva public ceremonies, such as liṅga consecration rites (see *SP* 4 p. 100), as well as being a long-standing feature in Indic public ritual from the Vedas onward. For discussions of the role and significance of *dakṣiṇā* in the Vedic system of ritual, see Heesterman 1959 and Malamoud 1976: 156–57.

As well as pleasing Śiva, this concluding act confers many benefits, as *MĀŚ* (p. 334) observes in a *phalaśruti*: victory, prosperity, virtue, good fortune, auspiciousness, pleasantness, fame, long life, sons, and good luck. *Kāmikāgama* ranks the presentations according to quantity. For a chief priest, the lowest *dakṣiṇā* consists in five gold coins (*niṣka*), middle is twice that amount, and the highest is fifteen coins (*UKĀ* 6.395–96). *MĀŚ* also specifies that others beside the chief priest shold receive *dakṣiṇā*: the assisting priests (*ṛtvigs*), adepts (*sādhakas*), scholars (*bodhakas*) and all those who carry out temple duties, starting with the temple attendants (*paricārakas*).

[206] Carrying the chief priest in a vehicle just as the deities have been carried, accompanied by all the same royal insignia, makes visible the lordship that the *ācārya* has exercised throughout the *mahotsava*. Aghoraśiva's account here corresponds closely with that of *MĀŚ* (pp. 332–34), which adds only a few details. In the *ācārya's* procession, says *MĀŚ*, Rudragaṇikās should accompany him on both sides. Once the *ācārya* is delivered to his own home, one should honor the brahmins, and please all the devotees of Śiva by distributing betel.

[207] Aghoraśiva departs from his chronological approach to deal with the preparations for the largest of festival processions, the grand *rathayātra* that takes place on the morning of the seventh day. These preparations include both the consecration of the chariot itself, which involves the imposition of many divinities onto its parts, and the adornment of the icons and all participants in the procession with a special moist paste (*ārdra-paṅka*) and vermillion turbans.

[208] Procedures for the preparation of the protective cord (*rakṣā*) here follow those in section 12 above.

[209] The bathing (*snāpana*) and consecration (*abhiṣeka*) are given to the main liṅga and the processional icons, *MĀŚ* specifies. *MĀŚ* sets out a much more elaborate preparatory sequence, which centers around the consecration of a "chariot pot" (*ratha-kumbha*). After the priest has performed the normal rites of *nityapūjā*, prescribes *MĀŚ*, he should proceed to the *yāgamaṇḍapa*, construct a rice-platform, inscribe an eight-petalled lotus, and place a pot in the center. The priest then goes to the center (*brahmasthāna*), sits on a prepared seat, and performs a series of self-purification rites that lead up to granting him the "hand of Śiva" (*śivahasta*). (The procedure of imposing the *śivahasta* is described most fully in the context of Śaiva initiations, such as *SP* 3 pp. 96–102, and *KKD*, "The Making and Placing of the Hand of Śiva," in Surdam 1984: 19–21.) With the special

oblation food up through the expiation rite, according to the usual method of fire-rites. Then, according to his abilities, he should offer make offerings into the fire: ghee while reciting MŪLA, firewood while reciting ĪŚĀNA, oblation food reciting AGHORA, puffed rice reciting HṚDAYA, sesame reciting VĀMA, jaggery reciting KAVACA, and bilva with NETRA. In the northeast he should offer substances and grain, reciting HṚDAYA and the *vyāhṛtis*. He gives a complete oblation. He restrains the Lord of the Sacrifice, puts on a protective cord, and then shows to the deity a full pot, a plate of sesame, and a cow with its calf. He gives them to brahmins.

He honors Gaṇeśa and feeds him sweetmeats. He feeds payasam to all the deities. Then in a large silver bowl he mixes vermillion, aloe, camphor, sandal, turmeric, and other powders with water. He adds flowers of *pāṭali*, water lily, jasmine, white lotus, *campaka*, and the like to the paste in the bowl. He covers the bowl with a vermillion cloth, and places it on a platform in front of Śiva. He honors the bowl by reciting KLĪM, the seed-syllable of KĀMA, and the moist paste itself by reciting MŪLA. He consecrates it and presents incense and lamp.[210] Then he gives that paste to all the icons, starting with the principal liṅga. The officiating priest puts the moist paste on himself and the assisting priests, and they put on vermillion turbans. Then he gives the moist paste and turbans to all the people, starting with the king, the patron, and the devotees.

Next he should have the chariot sprinkled with the five cow-products and water from the auspicious-day pot.[211] He consecrates the chariot with the

---

powers of the Śiva-hand, the priest now consecrates the chariot-pot with the fourfold consecration, imposes mantras on it, visualizes it as made of the supreme light (*paramajyotis*), invokes Śiva into it, and honors it with the usual services. Once the pot is sufficiently divinized, the priest imposes a series of deities onto it, from the bottom to the top, which corresponds to the set of deities that will subsequently be imposed onto the chariot. Each deity is invoked with its own mantra and honored with *upacāras*. After the priest has honored all the deities in the *ratha-kumbha*, he goes on to perform the fire-rites, also in the *yāgamaṇḍapa*.

[210] *MĀŚ* (pp. 208–9) provides directions that correspond closely to those of Aghoraśiva, and add a few significant details. After honoring the bowl with the seed-syllable KLĪM, the priest should perform *upacāras* for the bowl. Then he meditates that Śiva is in the moist paste while reciting MŪLA to invoke Śiva's presence into it. After the normal offerings are made to this new support of Śiva, the priest gives a protective cord (*rakṣāsūtra*) to the paste (wrapped, no doubt, around the bowl), and has it carried in procession around the temple. The procession returns to the *garbhagṛha*, so that the paste can then be applied to icons and human participants.

[211] The chariot will serve as a mobile *prāsāda* for the mobile deity during the procession. Texts such as *Mayamata* (ch. 31), *Mānasāra* (ch. 43), and *Kāmikāgama* (*UKĀ* ch. 71) provide technical specifications for the construction of festival chariots. This would form part of the specialized knowledge of the *śilpin*. However, since it is destined to serve as a divine support, construction and preparation of the chariot for use in the festival involve ritual procedures, calling upon the priest's expertise as well. So a later compilation, the *Viśvakarmīya Rathalakṣaṇa* (apparently drawing on the *Vijayatantra*, one of the primary Śaiva Āgamas), prescribes the rites of "collecting chariot materials" (*ratha-saṅgrahaṇa*) and "setting up the chariot" (*ratha-sthāpana*), where *ācārya* and *śilpin* make various sacrificial offerings and purify the parts of the chariot prior to the festival (chs. 3–4).

As far as I know, there have been no full historical studies of these extraordinary festival structures. K. V. Raman describes the festival *ratha* of the Varadarajaswamy temple in Kanchipuram, evidently dedicated by the Vijayanagara ruler Krishnadevaraya in 1517 (Raman 1975: 178–79). This may be the earliest extant festival chariot.

fourfold consecration, and has the deity hoisted onto it and placed there. Then he honors all the deities on the chariot.[212] On the wheels:

I honor the Sun.
I honor the Moon.

On the four sides, he worships:

I honor Hara.
I honor Vajrin.
I honor Ekāṅghri.
I honor Dvidaṇḍaka.

On the chariot banners he honors the hundred Rudras. On the pillars he honors the Four Powers, Dharma and the rest. On the platform:

I honor Sadāśiva.

On the joints, he worships:

I honor Dakṣiṇāmūrti.
I honor Viṣṇu.
I honor Brahman.
I honor Skanda.

On the corners of the chariot, he honors the World-guardians. On the ropes:

I honor the Snakes.

Then he honors the deities of the chariot in order.[213]

He should have the chariot decorated with colored banners, hanging cloths, and other ornaments, and at the doorways in the cardinal and

See Michell 1991 for a valuable description of modern temple chariots in south India. For interesting comments by modern *śilpins*, distinguishing chariots from shrines, see Parker 1987: 295.

The "water from the auspicious-day pot" (*puṇyāha-jala*) involves a simple sprinkling of water that has received the *puṇyāha* blessing (see note 17 above).

[212] Aghoraśiva depicts the divinization of the chariot as a matter of imposition (*nyāsa*) of mantra-powers. The priest touches the various parts of the chariot structure while reciting the mantras that invoke each deity. *MĀŚ* calls for an *abhiṣeka* of the chariot with the waters from the *ratha-kumbha*, into which the deities have already been invoked (p. 211).

[213] The identities of these deities are for the most part straightforward. Hara, the "seizer," is a common name for Śiva or Rudra. Vajrin, who possesses the thunderbolt, denotes Indra. Ekāṅghri, the "one-footed one," elsewhere appears in the āgamas as a Kṣetrapāla. Dvidaṇḍaka, the "one who holds two staffs," remains obscure. The hundred Rudras appear elsewhere in Śaiva ritual as lords of the 108 worlds (*bhuvaneśvara*) in the *nivṛttikalā* (see *dīkṣāvidhi* in *SP* 3 pp. 232–38). The Four Powers, Dharma, Jñāna, Vairāgya, and Aiśvarya, are familiar from other aspects of Śaiva ritual, such as the construction of divine thrones (see note 44 above, and Davis 1991: 122–25). The Snakes (*uragas*) are the eight Nāgas: Ananta, Mahāpadma, Takṣaka, Kulika, Śaṅkha, Vāsuki, Padma, and Kārkoṭa (*SP* 4 p. 396).

intermediate directions there should be stalks of *saimha*, plantain, and areca, nicely adorned with coconuts, colored banners, and the like.

Visualizing the charioteer to be Brahman, the priest should invoke Śiva's Pāśupata weapon into the umbrella, and worship the Bull in the banner. The priest should visualize Sadāśiva.[214]

> Luminous with five colors,
> He makes the gestures of security and generosity,
> And with four hands he also holds trident and noose.
> He has six feet, but one stomach, and one face with three eyes.
> On a sixfold throne he is full of good auspices.
> He is the support of all the elements.
> With a footstool, he sits on a great seat, one leg resting on the
> other thigh.
> His stomach is called the seat of the gods, and he has a heart,
> And two high shoulders strong as pillars.
> He is known as the source of all good fortune.

After visualizing Sadāśiva in this form, the priest honors him.

In this way he should have the Goddess, Skanda, Gaṇeśa, and Caṇḍeśa each raised onto their own chariots. He smears them with the moist paste, reciting HṚDAYA, and gives them vermillion turbans, reciting KAVACA. He feeds them fruit, cake, and other edibles, and he honors them with red flowers. Gifts are distributed. All the devotees, starting with the officiating priest, should be pleased with gifts such as cloth, gold, fruit, and betel. Then, at a good moment and an auspicious part of the *rāśi*, during a phase (*lagna*) suitable for movement, preceded by hymns of well-being, they circumambulate the city, accompanied by all the instruments.[215]

[214] Sadāśiva is more often visualized (*bhāvanā*) than fabricated in physical form. For another *dhyānaśloka*, see *PKĀ* 4.329–34, translated in Davis 1991: 116. Here, evidently, the Somāskanda image serves (as the Śiva-liṅga would in daily worship) as the base onto which the priest visually imposes Sadāśiva, as a more comprehensive form of Śiva.

[215] The calculation of the starting time for the chariot procession calls upon specialized knowledge on the part of *ācārya* or *daivajña*. The twelve *rāśis* (signs of the zodiac) can be divided into three phases (*lagna*): steady (*sthīra*), movable (*cala*), and mixed (*ubhaya*). These phases are suitable for different types of ritual actions. A steady phase is the appropriate time for performing the establishment of a fixed liṅga (*liṅga-pratiṣṭhā*), while a mixed phase is best for establishing *utsavamūrtis*, since they will be worshiped both in place and in motion. The proper phase for setting out on a procession, accordingly, is a movable phase.

In its circumambulation of the city, the chariot follows the "chariot street" (*ratha-mārga*), also called the "auspicious route of Śiva" (*PKĀ* 25.2), a broad avenue on the periphery of the settlement just inside the town wall. In *Mayamata's* town-plan, the merchant's quarter should be on the inner side of the *ratha-mārga* (MM 10.78–79).

As is its wont, *MĀŚ* provides a detailed list of the sounds and instruments that should accompany the circumambulation. Brahmins should march along shouting "Well-being!" (*svasti*). There should be drums (*bherī*,

Afterward he has the deities taken down from the chariots and returned to the temple. He bathes the icons. Clothes and other gifts are presented to the people who assist with the chariot, from the head artisan to the brakemen who stop it. Oblation food is distributed, and gifts are given to everyone.[216]

This is the procedure for raising the deity onto the chariot.

24. *The Festival of Dancing Śiva*

24A. THE BLACK BALM.

> Accomplishing all ends that one desires, obtaining good sons,
> Removing all sins, even that of killing a brahmin,
> And destroying all of one's enemies—
> Whoever sees Śiva's dancing form will obtain these fruits.[217]

Then the priest has Dancing Śiva taken to the assembly pavilion. On the night after the eighth day of the festival, he performs the protective cord rite, as described previously.[218] He should put fruit, betel, and the like in the deity's hand. He decorates both Dancing Śiva and his consort with colorful cloth and the like, and gives them food and so on. He circumambulates the temple with them, and places them in the assembly hall. There they spend the remainder of the night watching the entertainments.[219]

---

devadundubhi), cymbals (*jhallarī, tālatraya*), conches (*saṅkha*), and horns (*kāhalī*) playing, as well as several other unidentified instruments. The Rudragaṇikās dance alongside the chariot.

[216] *MĀŚ* (pp. 214–16) proposes a lengthy choreography for the conclusion to the chariot procession. At the end of the chariot's circumambulation of the town, worshipers offer various *upacāras* to the deity, including the fitting service of fanning the god with palm leaves (*tālavṛntānila*). Still outside the temple proper, the deity is taken down from the chariot and placed in a pavilion, where he is surrounded in state with regalia, with the chanting of Vedas, with music and dance. To remove the fatigue of the journey, says *MĀŚ*, one should give Śiva energizing food, including sugar-cane juice, cakes made of mung beans and molasses, bananas and other fruits. Brahmins are fed also, and gifts of cloth and other items are presented to all those who have assisted with the chariot, starting with the *śilpin*. The deity is lifted up, leaves the street, and to the accompaniment of the triple symphony (*tauryatrika*) he reenters the temple. First Śiva may be taken to the *brahmasthāna*, where he presides over a *pariveṣaṇa* assembly (see note 151 above). Then, finally, the priest returns the deity to his own proper place, and has it given a special bath (*mahāsnapana*), consecration (*abhiṣeka*), and other offerings of worship.

[217] The festival of Dancing Śiva centers around the well-known Chola period icon of Śiva most commonly known as Naṭarāja. In iconographic texts, this particular form of Śiva dancing is called *bhujaṅgatrāsita*, Śiva "frightened by a snake." Even though Śiva's dance here is frantic (*tāṇḍava*), he does this dance to protect the world, and so this form of Śiva should be viewed as unthreatening (*aghora*), not as terrifying (*ghora*) (*MĀŚ*, pp. 234–35, quoting *Kāraṇāgama*). R. Nagaswamy (2003: 84–91) describes this ritual based on the *Mahotsavavidhi* and other texts quoted in *MĀŚ*.

[218] The rite of tying the protective cord (*rakṣā, kautuka*) prepares the icon for its participation in the festival. See section 12 above.

[219] Aghoraśiva refers to "both" here to indicate both the Dancing Śiva icon and that of his beloved, Gaurī or Śivakāmī, who accompanies Dancing Śiva always on his left. She will be visualized subsequently as the Supreme

The next day the priest performs the rites concluding the festival. That evening he prepares two platforms in front of the deity, draws lotus designs on them, and strews them with *darbha* grass and flowers. In the middle of one, he places black aloe wood.[220] Beginning with the worship of Gaṇeśa and a proclamation of an auspicious day, he prepares a pot of pacification water, according to proper procedures, and honors it.[221] He performs a fire-sacrifice, starting with the consecration of the fire-pit and ending with a complete oblation, according to the method explained in the fire-rite chapter. In the fire-pit he honors Maheśvara. He offers to him 108 oblations each of fire-sticks, puffed rice, mustard seed, wheat, sesame, and other offerings, while reciting MŪLA. He offers bilva leaves, lotus, as well as the three sweet things, plantain, jackfruit, and mango. When he completes offering the substances, he recites the *vyāhṛtis*, and gives a complete oblation.[222]

He should bathe and ornament the deity. Then he puts the black balm on a plate filled with rice, and covers it with a cloth. He sprinkles it with water from the pacification pot. He cleans it with water mixed with fragrant things such as camphor, reciting ASTRA, and protects it by reciting KAVACA. He endows it with mantra powers by reciting the *brahmamantras* and the *aṅgamantras*, and worships it reciting MŪLA. He displays the cow gesture before it. Then he presents it with services of worship: foot-water, sipping water, *arghya*, incense, lamp, and so on. He makes oblations with various liquids, and prepares a powder. He abandons the fire.

The priest circumambulates the temple with the black balm, accompanied by conches and *dundubhi* drums, along with the sounds of other instruments.

Goddess, Parameśvarī. The entertainments (*vinoda*) refer to performances of dance, music, and anything considered pleasing to the deities.

[220] The preparation and application of a black fragrant balm (*kṛṣṇagandha*) is one of the central rites of the festival of Dancing Śiva. Smearing this balm, says *Kiraṇāgama*, is done in order to make Dancing Śiva black (*MĀŚ*, p. 239). According to Aghoraśiva, the base of this lotion is black aloe or agallochum (*agaru*), a fragrant resinous heartwood. However, other texts cited by *MĀŚ* call the decoction *yakṣakardama*, mud of the Yakṣas. According to the older Vedic Śrautasūtra of Kātyāyana, *yakṣakardama* is a combination of five fragrant substances: agallochum, sandal, camphor, musk, and *kākola* berries (*Amarakośa* 2.6.3.34). *Kāraṇāgama* calls for a mixture of agallochum and a little sandal, formed into a thick paste with molasses (*gula*) and honey.

In *Kāraṇāgama*, as cited in *MĀŚ* (p. 234), the black balm is connected with the three fetters (*mala, karman, māyeya*) that according to Śaiva Siddhānta bind the human soul. One should place gross impurities at the feet of the guru, and subtle impurities should be given over to Dancing Śiva, says *Kāraṇāgama*. So the application and subsequent removal of the black balm enacts Śiva's role in the removal of the impurities that veil (*tirobhāva*) the full powers of the soul. After this destruction of impurity, Dancing Śiva is decorated and adorned all in white.

[221] On the *śānti-kumbha*, the pot of pacifying water, see note 65 above.

[222] The method here is drawn from the procedures for *agnikārya* given in the rules for daily worship (*KKD*, "The Daily Fire Ritual," pp. 178–85), but with additional oblation offerings. Among these offerings, the "three sweets" (*madhutraya*) may denote sugar, honey, and ghee, as the Sanskrit lexicographers suggest. Alternatively, it may correspond to the Tamil *mukkani*, three sweet fruits—plantain, jackfruit, and mango—mixed with honey and ghee.

He enters the sanctum, and presents it before the principal liṅga. Next he places it in front of Maheśvara. Atop the throne, which reaches from Śakti up to Śakti, he performs onto the icon an imposition of thirty-one *kalās*, following the stick method and the bald-head method, and an imposition of Śrīkaṇṭha.[223]

The priest envisions the form of Dancing Śiva:

> On his golden head the moon rests in his splayed matted hair.
> The Goddess stands near, as high as his head.
> He wears the white flower, *mudrarāja* flower, and peacock feather,
> And his garment is the skin of a tiger.
> In his right hands the gesture of security and a *ḍamaru* drum,
> And in his left is fire, while the other extends out straight.
> He stands on the back of Apasmāra who lies outstetched.
> His right leg is bent like a thunderbolt, and his left foot lifted.
> His sandals glow with hundreds of jewels,
> With a flag and small bells in the middle.
> On his right earlobe hangs a crocodile earring,
> On his left a leaf earring.
> He is smeared with ash, has three eyes, and is joined by Umā.
> I worship Śiva, the Lord of Dance.[224]

Then he visualizes the Supreme Goddess, Parameśvarī.

> Dark in hue, with two eyes, two arms, in a triple-bend posture.
> Her right foot is curled, and she holds a lotus in her right hand.

[223] Here the physical form of the Dancing Śiva and his consort are endowed with mantra powers, following procedures employed in other parts of the festival when Śiva is invoked in a comprehensive form. On the throne "from Śakti up to Śakti," see note 77 above, where the masonry base serves as the throne for the flagpole. On the stick and bald-head methods of imposing mantras, see note 120. In this case, however, it is not the more typical five *brahmamantras* or the thirty-eight *kalās* imposed, but rather an alternative group of thirty-one *kalās*. According to *Kāmikāgama* (*UKĀ* 3.23–25), the thirty-one *kalās* are employed in certain special circumstances. On the imposition of Śrīkaṇṭha, see note 122.

[224] The priest's visualization here corresponds closely to the physical form of Dancing Śiva typical of Chola period bronze sculpture. Compare *Mayamata* 36.67–80, which provides directions for two types of Dancing Śiva forms, the *bhujaṅgalalita* (playing with a snake) as well as the better-known *bhujaṅgatrāsita*.

MĀŚ (p. 279) cites *Kāmikāgama* on the significance of Dancing Śiva's iconography:

> The *ḍamaru* drum represents Śiva's activity of emanation. The straight arm signifies maintenance. Reabsorption takes the form of fire. Śiva's bent leg represents veiling, and the gesture of security is Śiva's grace. So Dancing Śiva is the form (*svarūpa*) of Śiva's five fundamental activities (*pañcakṛtya*).

This corresponds to the interpretation of the iconography of Dancing Śiva made famous for Western audiences by Coomaraswamy 1968.

Her other hand hangs down. She wears a wealth of bracelets.
So should the Supreme Goddess be envisioned.[225]

In these forms the priest worships both, and presents incense, lamp, and other tokens of respect. He feeds them payasam made with wheat flour, along with fruit, cake, and other foods, and gives them betel. Then he performs the smearing of the black balm.

The priest has the balm smeared on the foreheads of Dancing Śiva and the Goddess while reciting AGHORA, on their hands while reciting ŚIKHĀ, and all over while reciting SADYOJĀTA.

Then he has it smeared on all the icons beginning with the principal liṅga.

For the female icons it may be put on their foreheads and necks, reciting their own MŪLA mantras or HṚDAYA.

Next the presiding priest puts it on himself, along with the image-protectors, and has it given to all the devotees, starting with the mantra adepts.[226]

The priest has the deity raised up onto a jeweled lion-throne.[227] Gaurī is on his left, and the priest is on his right. The king is on the left side or in front. Male and female dancers and drummers perform song and dance on both sides, and the dancing is done, accompanied by the instruments, up to the shrine of the Seven Planets.[228] They enter the temple and then perform the illumination ceremony and other rites, as previously.

Next the deity is placed in the assembly pavilion, and given *arghya* made with eight substances.[229] The god is fed and given flowers, and is honored with illuminating lights and other services.

Then the priest has the deity bathed with the five cow-products and other substances, presents pure camphor, and consecrates him as previously. The

[225] Here too the visualization parallels the physical image of Śivakāmī, the form of Gaurī or Pārvatī that regularly accompanies Dancing Śiva images.

[226] The mantra-adepts (*sādhakas*) constitute a special category of Śaiva ascetics who have undergone the full sequence of Śaiva initiations and also a special adept-consecration (*sādhakābhiṣeka*). They are not eligible to perform ritual on behalf of others and serve no necessary ritual function in the festival, but as religious virtuosi their presence adds an element of auspiciousness to the *mahotsava*. On *sādhakas*, see especially Brunner 1975.

[227] The lion-throne (*simhāsana*) is a type of pedestal intended for kings and deities, with images of lions serving as legs. For a standing image like Dancing Śiva, its height should be one-fifth the height of the image. See *Mayamata* 32.13–19 for royal lion-thrones, and 34.51–56 for lion-thrones meant for deities.

[228] This appears to involve a procession within the temple complex to a shrine devoted to the Planets. In Śaiva Siddhānta texts the usual group of Planets numbers nine: the Sun in the center, surrounded by the Moon, Mars, Mercury, Saturn, Jupiter, Rāhu, Venus, and Ketu (in circumambulatory order, starting from the east). So in the daily "Worship of the Sun," according to Aghoraśiva, the eight planets are honored as the entourage of the central Sun (*KKD* pp. 82–83). Here the Seven Planets would seem to denote a group that omits the Sun and Moon from the list.

[229] The *arghya* of eight substances is *viśeṣārghya*, prepared with water, milk, tips of *kuśa* grass, husked rice, flowers, sesame, barley, and white mustard (as specified by Nirmalamaṇi, quoting *PKĀ*, in his commentary on the *KKD*).

priest rubs white paste over the entire body of the deity, and decorates him with all-white jasmine flowers and with white cloth. He feeds him rice cooked in milk, and presents incense and lamp. At the time of procession, they proceed very slowly in a processional row.

Accompanied by Vedic recitation, dance, song, and other festive sounds, the processional row should proceed as before to a location in front of the entry tower or in front of the flagpole. All the ceremonies beginning with illumination are performed as before, and they enter the temple. The priest worships the deity with all the services. The remainder of the night is spent in viewing entertainments.[230]

At the break of day, the priest honors the Lord of Dance, and has him ornamented. At a riverbank or the like, he gives him a holy bath, as before.[231] He removes the protective cord, and they circumambulate the city or village. In a pure place, the priest should announce the punishment of bad people, the protection of the good, and the settlement of all disputes. The lovers' quarrel of Śiva with the Goddess is brought to an end, and they enter the temple without any circling around.[232] All are put in their own places, and they are given bath and *abhiṣeka*. Finally the pure dance is performed.

This is the procedure for the black balm ceremony.

25. *The Wedding Ceremony*

Afterward, on the tenth, seventh, or fifth day, the priest should celebrate the marriage and have the festival of wedding vows performed according to the marriage procedures, with all the necessary services.[233]

[230] "As before" here refers back to the procedures of other processions, especially the chariot procession, where the deity may be honored at the end of the procession in a pavilion outside the temple *gopuram* (note 216). Entertainments (*vinoda*) are not specified by Aghoraśiva. This is a context within which concerts of music and dance might be given for the divine audience. In a later period dramatic performances were incorporated into such temple entertainment ceremonies. See Peterson 1998 on the Tamil *kuravañci* dance-drama in temple *mahotsavas* of eighteenth-century south India.

[231] The procedures here would follow those of the *tīrthasnāna*, in section 18 above. The icon is not submerged. Rather, pots of *tīrtha* water are prepared (as in section 16), and poured out over the icon at the bathing spot.

[232] The "lovers' quarrel" (*praṇaya-kalaha*) is only mentioned, with no details. Likewise, *MĀŚ* refers to the "removal of the anger between the Goddess and her lover" as a rite of the tenth day, in its account of a thirteen-day festival (p. 179). As with Aghoraśiva's account, this is followed by a special bath and an *abhiṣeka* and the performance of *śuddhanṛtta*.

[233] The "wedding" (*vaivāha* or *kalyāṇa*) of Śiva and the Goddess is such an important feature of many contemporary south Indian *mahotsavas*, such as the Cittrai festival in Madurai (Harman 1989), that Aghoraśiva's terse prescription here is surprising. Many other Āgamas fail to mention *vaivāha* at all.

MĀŚ provides some details in its account of the thirteen-day festival (pp. 179–80). (See Table 6B for a summary of the schedule of the thirteen-day festival, according to *MĀŚ*.) The *vaivāha* takes place at midday on the tenth day of the festival. At a pavilion near a holy bathing place, the Goddess is gratified with food and other

26. *The Festival of the Goddess*

One should conduct the festival of the Goddess for nine days, seven days, three days, or one day.[234]

On the night of the eleventh day, the priest should have everything decorated and sprinkled, beginning with the Indra chariot.[235] He should give a special bath and an *abhiṣeka* to the deity, as before, and ornament him. The priest has all the deities raised onto their own vehicles. While the deities are circumambulating the city, they should stop at a temporary pavilion in the

---

offerings. Respectable married women (*suvāsinīs*) honor the Goddess, and she is raised onto a jeweled pedestal, accompanied by singing and auspicious sounds. She is taken to the temple, surrounded by a retinue of seven sword-bearing women, and proceeds to the wedding pavilion (*kalyāna-maṇḍapa*), where she is placed next to Śiva. The priest performs the wedding. Then Śiva and the Goddess are raised onto the Bull, and taken in procession, accompanied by all the usual festive instruments, regalia and festoons, dance and song, and so on. *MĀŚ* uses the term *bhrāmayati* (to wander, roam) rather than *pradakṣiṇayati* (to circumambulate), suggesting a more relaxed route for this particular procession. At the completion of their honeymoon ramble, the deities return to the temple.

[234] The first line in Aghoraśiva's account envisions the Festival of the Goddess as an independent *mahotsava*, while the remainder of the section treats the *utsava* as an adjunct to the *mahotsava* of Śiva.

MĀŚ provides extracts from *Lalitāgama* and *Vātulāgama* which describe the Devī-festival as a celebration lasting several days (pp. 361–75). *Lalitāgama* begins its account by distinguishing three forms of Śakti or the Goddess:

1. Yogaśakti or Parameśvarī, who resides in the pedestal of the *mūla-liṅga;*
2. Bhogaśakti or Viśvayoni, a separate goddess image, maintained in the *garbhagṛha* as a consort of Śiva; and
3. Vīraśakti, an independent image of the goddess, who might reside in her own sanctum.

This festival has to do with Vīraśakti. (On the threeforld division of Śakti, see also *SP* 4 p. xxv and p. 264 n. 1.) In its procedures, the Goddess festival parallels many rites of the Śiva *mahotsava*, with one key difference. As *Vātulāgama* puts it, during the Śiva festival the Goddess processes in her own vehicle, but in the Goddess festival Śiva does not appear in the procession (*MĀŚ* p. 369).

In the Goddess festival, the priest performs many of the same preliminary rites, including the worship of Gaṇeśa, the *vāstuhoma*, gathering of earth, sprouting seeds, and beating the drum. At crucial moments, though, the Goddess is substituted for Śiva. So for instance, on the flagpole the priest imposes goddesses (Parāśakti, Bhuvaneśvarī, Mahālakṣmī, Manonmanī) instead of the constituents of Sadāśiva. When raising the flag one recites the MŪLA mantra of the Goddess rather than that of Śiva. For the tying of the protective *kautuka*, according to *Vātulāgama*, the priest should go to the pavilion of Gaurī and honor the principal Śakti image there, and tie the first *kautuka* on that icon. This presupposes a separate sanctum of the Goddess with its own fixed image (*mūlaśakti*) as well as processional icon.

During the twice-daily processions, the parade is led by Gaṇeśa and Skanda, then the Goddess, and Caṇḍeśa brings up the rear. The texts go on to specify the schedule of processions. Like Śiva, the Goddess in her festival appears on different vehicles for each procession. See table 6C for the order of processions according to *Vātulāgama*.

Celebrating the independent festival of the Goddess brings many benefits: long life, good health, mastery, increase in property and wealth, sons, friends, and wives, sovereignty, and happiness (*MĀŚ* p. 375).

[235] Aghoraśiva here describes a brief festival of the Goddess as part of the Śiva *mahotsava*. The eleventh day, then, places it on the second day after the official close of the festival. Aghoraśiva's account corresponds to the procession on the eleventh night prescribed in *MĀŚ* for the thirteen-day festival (p. 180).

The Indra-*vimāna* is a smallish chariot that appears like a small shrine. According to *Manasāra* it is one of the seven types of *ratha* (43.112–123).

northeast direction.[236] It is decorated with flowers, banners, and the like. They take Śiva from his vehicle and place him in the middle of the pavilion. All the other deities, starting with the Goddess and ending with Caṇḍeśa, along with the king, the patron, and musicians, should circumambulate Śiva three times. When they return to the temple, Śiva and the Goddess should bring to an end their quarrel and watch entertainments in front of the entry tower or in front of the temple.[237] Then they enter the temple, according to proper procedures.

This is the procedure for the festival of the Goddess.

27. The Festival of the Devotees

The priest now places the icons of the Devotees and others in front of Śiva or in a pavilion.[238] He gives a special bath and an *abhiṣeka* to the icons, both fixed and mobile, and decorates them. He prepares the festival powder as previously.[239] Holding the Devotee icons, the priest has the powder presented to the initiated Śaiva devotees, starting with preceptors and adepts, and to all the devotees.[240] He gives them *kuṅkuma* turbans, *pavitra* rings, garlands, and the like. He has the

[236] The northeast direction, with Īśāna as its Lokapāla, is considered the most appropriate zone of Śiva.

[237] Here as above (note 232), the "lovers' quarrel" is mentioned with no further detail. According to *MĀŚ*, Śiva and the Goddess are mounted together on the Indra-*vimāna* with great joy, but during the circumambulation of the city they become angry at one another by the time they reach the northeast corner. By the time they return to the temple their quarrel has been resolved (p. 180). The entertainments (*vinoda*), as during the festival of Dancing Śiva, would feature pleasing dances and music (note 230).

[238] The festival of the devotees (*bhaktotsava*) honors those humans who exemplify special devotion to Śiva. Aghoraśiva does not specify the identity of these devotees, but in south Indian practice of his time they would most likely have been the sixty-three *nāyaṉmārs* or Tamil devotional saints (see note 148 above). Within a temple there would have been both mobile and fixed icons (*calācalabera*) of the Devotees, and Āgamas such as *Kāmikāgama* provide rules for ritual establishment of *bhakta-beras* (*UKĀ* ch. 66). Nor does Aghoraśiva specify the proper time for this ceremony, though his textual placement of it following the festival of the goddess indicates it would occur after the official conclusion of the nine-day festival. In its account of the thirteen-day festival, *MĀŚ* locates the festival of devotees on the evening of the thirteenth day, in between the festival of Caṇḍeśa and the honoring of the priest (p. 181).

[239] The preparations of *cūrṇotsava* (see section 17) are repeated, no doubt in an abbreviated form, as part of the *bhaktotsava*.

[240] The categories of initiated Śaivas are a result of the level of initiation and consecration. The *samayin* (common Śaiva) has received the basic or common form of Śaiva initiation (*samayadīkṣā*). The *putraka* (son of Śiva) has received a secondary or special initiation (*viśeṣadīkṣā*). The final stage of Śaiva initiation, liberating initiation (*nirvāṇadīkṣā*) makes one a full Śaiva initiate (*haradīkṣita*). After liberating initiation, one may undergo an additional consecration to become a *sādhaka* (mantra-adept), or (if he is from an *ādiśaiva* lineage) a priestly consecration (*ācāryābhiṣeka*) to become an *ācārya*. Aghoraśiva spells out the categories of initiates and procedures of the various initiations earlier in the *KKD* (see Surdam 1984: lxxiv). Of these, the priests and mantra-adepts rank highest, on account of their greater ritual status and greater resulting powers. "All the devotees" refers to all others devoted to Śiva who have not undergone any initiatory rites.

TABLE 6B Processional Vehicles and Events (Thirteen-day Festival) According to *Mahotsavavidhikrama Āgamaśekhara*

Day and Time	*Vehicles*	*Other Events*
1st Morning	*Raṅga* (Cart)	
1st Evening	*Simha* (Lion)	
2nd Morning	*Sūrya* (Sun)	
2nd Evening	*Candra* (Moon)	
3rd Morning	*Bhūta*	
3rd Evening	*Kheṭaka* (Platform)	
4th Morning	*Nāga* (Snake)	
4th Evening	*Vṛṣabha (Bull)*	*Pariveṣaṇa* (Perambulation)
5th Morning	*Nandin* (Bull)	
5th Evening	*Rāvana*	
6th Morning	*Śibikā* (Palanquin)	*Cūrnotsava* (Powder Festival)
6th Evening	*Gaja* (Elephant)	
7th Morning	*Ratha* (Chariot)	
7th Evening		*Prāyaścitta* (Expiation)
8th Morning	*Puruṣāmṛga*	*Mṛgayātrā* (Hunting) with *Bhikṣātana*
8th Evening	*Aśva*	*Rudragaṇikās*
9th Morning	*Mānavāndālī* (Swing held by man)	
9th Evening	*Vyāghra* (Tiger)	*Kṛṣṇagandha* (Black Balm Ceremony)
10th Morning	*Puṣpamañca* (Flower-dais)	*Kalyāna* (Wedding Ceremony)
10th Evening	*Vṛṣabha*	
11th Morning	*Bhadrapīṭhā* (Throne) or *Ratnasimhāsana* (Lion-throne)	
11th Evening	*Indra-vimāna* (Shrine)	*Devī-yātrā* (Goddess Procession) *Vinoda* (Entertainments)
12th Morning	*Hamsa* (Swan)	
12th Evening	*Kalpavṛkṣa* (Tree of Plenty)	
13th Morning	*Vṛṣa* (Bull)	*Cūrṇotsava* (Powder Festival) *Tīrthayātrā* (Bath at Holy Place)
13th Evening	*Simhapīṭhā* (Lion-pedestal)	*Caṇḍeśotsava* (Festival of Caṇḍeśa) *Bhaktotsava* (Festival of Devotees) *Ācāryapūjā* (Honoring Priest)

Source: Mahotsavavidhikrama Āgamaśekhara, pp. 175–82.

Devotees praised with devotional hymns. He gives betel and other presentations to the devotees of Śiva. They circumambulate the city and return to the temple.[241]

[241] The account of *bhaktotsava* in *MĀŚ* (pp. 331–32) adds only a few details to Aghoraśiva's description. The icons of the Devotees are placed on palanquins or on portable thrones (*bhadrapīṭhas*), and during the circumambulation they are accompanied by all the devotees of Śiva. The devotional hymns (*bhaktastotra*) and other songs are sung. During the time of Aghoraśiva, devotional hymns would most likely refer especially to the Tamil hymns of the *nāyaṉmārs* collected in the *Tirumuṟai*.

TABLE 6C Processional Vehicles and Events (Nine-day Goddess Festival) According to Āgama Sources Quoted in *Mahotsavavidhikrama Āgamaśekhara*

Day and Time	*Vātulāgama*	*Deviyānakramavidhi*
1st Morning		*Mañca (Dais)*
1st Evening	*Hamsa* (Swan)	*Śuka* (Parrot)
2nd Morning	*Mṛga* (Deer)	*Aja* (Ram)
2nd Evening	*Simha* (Lion)	*Bhūtika* (Imp)
3rd Morning	*Sūrya* (Sun)	*Mṛga* (Deer)
3rd Evening	*Puṣpa-vimāna* (Flower-shrine)	*Sūrya* (Sun)
4th Morning	*Candra* (Moon)	*Hamsa* (Swan)
4th Evening	*Vṛṣabha* (Bull)	*Candra* (Moon)
5th Morning	*Śuka* (Parrot)	*Makara* (Crocodile)
5th Evening	*Makara* (Crocodile)	*Vṛṣa* (Bull)
6th Morning	*Mañca* (Dais)	*Kheṭaka* (Platform)
6th Evening	*Gaja* (Elephant)	*Gaja* (Elephant)
7th Morning	*Ratha* (Chariot)	*Ratha* (Chariot)
7th Evening	*Śeṣa* (Snake)	*Prāyaścitta* (Expiation)
8th Morning	*Śibikā* (Palanquin)	*Śibikā* (Palanquin)
8th Evening	*Aśva* (Horse)	*Aśva* (Horse)
9th Morning	*Aja* (Ram)	*Nāga* (Snake)
9th Evening	*Indra-vimāna* (Indra-shrine) *Kṛṣṇagandha* (Black-balm ceremony)	*Indra-vimāna* (Indra-shrine)
10th Morning		*Raṅga* (Cart)
10th Evening		*Simha* (Lion)

Sources: Vātulāgama, quoted in *MĀŚ*, pp. 373–75; *Devīyānakramavidhi*, quoted in *MĀŚ*, pp. 375–76.

He has all the icons put in their own places and offers them food, incense, and lamps. He has cloth and other gifts presented to those who know the Śaiva songs.

This is the procedure of the festival of the Devotees.

28. *Pacification Rites for the Festival*

On the following day the priest first offers a large bathing ceremony. He performs, in order, a fire-rite for pacification, a fire-rite for the manifestations, and a fire-rite for the directions.[242] He offers an *abhiṣeka*. Then he

[242] The issue of pacifying (*śānti*) any undesirable effects of ritual errors committed during the festival is usually treated under the rubric of *prāyaścitta*, or rites of expiation. Here Aghoraśiva provides only an outline, but an appendix to *Śivapratiṣṭhāvidhi*, attributed to Aghoraśiva, gives an exposition of *prāyaścitta* in the context of *pratiṣṭhā*, the establishment of a liṅga (*ŚPV* pp. 302–18). *MĀŚ* also provides a lengthy prescription for expiations at the close of a festival (pp. 334–50). Simpler directions may be found in texts such as *Rauravāgama* (44.34–45).

Common to all are three separate fire-rites: *śāntihoma* (oblations for pacification), *mūrtihoma* (oblations for the manifestations), and *diśahoma* (oblations for the directions). To each is attributed the power to quell or remove the faults (*doṣa*) that may have arisen in the course of the festival. At their simplest, these *homas* involve setting up fire-pits around the temple, often in the four cardinal directions, and making a series of oblation

allows the icons to rest, in order to remove their fatigue from the festival activities.

29. Śiva's Five Activities and the Festival

They say the festival is fivefold.
It has rites of maintenance, emission, reabsorption,
Veiling and grace. These are Śiva's five fundamental activities.[243]
The sprout ceremony, the marriage, the raising of the flag,
And the tying of the protective cord are known as rites of emission.
The processions of vehicles, the fire rites, and the distribution
  of tribute—
These are called rites of maintenance. Now the rites of reabsorption
Are said to be the nighttime powder festival,
Raising the icons onto the chariot,
And the festival of black balm—so it is explained in the Āgamas.
The silent procession is veiling. Grace is the procession of Śakti,
The beginning and end of the bathing day,
And the festival of lovers' quarrel.
So one encounters Śiva's five activities, starting with emission,
In the festival.[244]

---

offerings, reciting a different mantras for each. So for *diśahoma*, according to *Rauravāgama*, one makes one hundred oblations each of fifteen separate items, reciting a different mantra with each item, in each of four fire-pits around the temple. More complex formulations add arrangements of pots, into which divine powers are invoked. So in *mūrtihoma*, one should invoke Śiva and Manonmanī into two central pots, and Śiva's eight manifestations (*mūrti*) into the eight pots surrounding them (*ŚPV* p. 217). The eight manifestations, an ancient list of Śiva's names or forms, are Bhīma, Īśvara, Paśupata, Bhava, Rudra, Mahādeva, and Ugra.

The *ŚPV* also recommends the use of four distinct ASTRA mantras. In the *diśahoma*, according to *ŚPV* (pp. 306–14), the priest constructs four *sthaṇḍilas* with fire-pits in the cardinal directions, and invokes a different ASTRA into the pots and fires of each:

east	ŚIVĀSTRA
south	AGHORĀSTRA
west	PĀŚUPATĀSTRA
north	PRATYAṄGIRĀSTRA

Each has its own mantra formula (given in *SP* 4 App. III), and its own form to be visualized.

243 Śiva's *pañcakṛtya*, the five fundamental activities by which he shapes and activates the cosmos, is a core theological concept in Śaiva Siddhānta. See Davis 1991: 42–43 for a brief précis. The idea that these activities are embedded in the particular rites of the *mahotsava* appears to have been a common one, for the *MĀŚ* provides an elaborate account containing five different formulations (pp. 356–61). See Barazer-Billoret 2000 for an interesting discussion of these themes as a "theologizing" of the festival.

244 *MĀŚ* (pp. 356–61) repeats the formulation used by Aghoraśiva, and goes on to include four other formulations of the relationship between individual festival rites and Śiva's activities.

This concludes the procedures for the great festival, starting with the festival of Gaṇeśa and ending with the festival of the Devotees, in the "Light on Ritual Procedures," composed by the illustrious preceptor Aghoraśiva, also known as Parameśvara.

B. Procedures for Monthly and Other Festivals

30. *Principles for Determining Auspicious Times*

The exact time of the *saṅkrānti* is difficult to determine,
even for those of acute insight.[245]
And so for that reason, a period of thirty *nāḍīs*

One follows the chronological sequence of festival actions. The opening rites such as *mṛtsaṅgraha, aṅkurārpaṇa*, and raising the flag are acts of *sṛṣṭi* (emission); the repetitive daily fire-rites and processions of the first six days are *sthiti* (maintenance); the chariot procession, hunting procession, and the black balm ceremony associated with Naṭarāja are acts of *samhāra* (reabsorption); concluding acts of dismissal such as taking down the flag, the silent procession, and removal of the protective cords are *tirobhāva* (veiling); and the postfestival procession of the Goddess is *anugrāha* (grace).

Another striking formulation relates the sequence of the festival to the gradual process of liberation of the bound soul (*paśu*). In this account, the raising of the festival flag on the first day signifies the conception of the embodied person. Acts of the second through fourth days involve the person's acquisition of fetters, and the gradual consumption of *karman*. By the fifth day, the power of the five senses is removed, and on the sixth day the *paśu* overcomes the forces of attraction and repulsion. On the eighth day the *paśu* is able to gain a consistent connection with god and transcends the body, and on the ninth and final day the *paśu* is freed from subsequent rebirth.

Although the five formulations *MĀŚ* cites are not consistent with one another, there are several repeated associations. The rites of sprouting seeds, marriage, and raising the flag are regularly figured as acts of *sṛṣṭi*. The fire-rites and offerings of tribute appear repeatedly as acts of *sthiti*. The black balm ceremony is seen as *samhāra*. The silent procession is an act of *tirobhāva*, and the procession of the Goddess is regularly associated with Śiva's *anugrāha*.

[245] Throughout this section of the *Mahotsavavidhi*, Aghoraśiva mixes passages of verse concerning the calculations of timing and the fruits of various ritual acts with brief prose expositions of the ritual actions to be undertaken at those times. First he takes up the calculation of timing for the monthly festival (*māsotsava*).

Festival timing is determined according to both solar and lunar calendrical movements. Monthly festivals follow solar movements. Briefly, the sun's movement over the course of the year has two major phases: a northern progress (*uttarāyana*) roughly from mid-January to mid-July, when the sun is waxing, and a southern progress (*dakṣiṇāyana*) from mid-July to mid-January, when it is waning. During its two progresses the sun moves through a series of twelve *rāśis*, literally "groups," understood as solar or zodiacal habitations. Each *rāśi* corresponds to thirty degrees or one-twelfth of the ecliptic. The names of the *rāśis* are largely equivalent to the Greek zodiac names, from which the system was adapted. See diagram 6.

Saṅkrānti, "passage" or "entry," here refers to the sun's transition from one course to another. Moments of transition from northern to southern progresses and southern to northern (parallel to the solstices) are particularly important moments. Similarly the half-way points (*viṣuvat*) during the sun's two progresses (parallel to the equinoxes) are considered significant. Moments of transition are occasions for special ritual action (see Merrey 1982).

before and after is considered auspicious.[246]
When the sun's southern progress is starting,
the first thirty *nāḍīs* will be auspicious,
and at the end of the sun's northern progress also,
so say the Śaiva Brāhmaṇas.
Both the *saṅkrānti* and the equinox of both progresses,
southern and northern, are special.
During the sun's southern progress,
when it enters the *rāśis* of the Bull, Scorpion, Pot, and Lion,
this is known as the "Footprint of Visnu,"
and this is more fruitful than the equinox.[247]
When the sun moves into the *rāśis* of the Virgin,
the Twins, the Fish, and the Bow,
brahmins call this the "Eighty-six Faces,"
and consider it even more auspicious.
The sixteen *nāḍīs* before and after the sun's passage
into one of these *rāśis* is also auspicious.
When the *rāśis* Scales and the Ram are present,
ten *nāḍis* before and after are auspicious.
At the start of a new progress of the sun,
when Viṣṇu is active, at an equinox,
at one of the Eighty-six Faces,
at the end of the sun's northern passage,
at a *saṅkrānti* when an eclipse is seen,
at times of marriage, death, and birth,
and also during voluntary vows at night,
rites such as bathing and gift-giving should be performed.
At those times also one should perform worship of Śiva
and festivals of the god.
Those *nāḍis* closest to the *saṅkrānti* are considered the very best.

So at the time of the *saṅkrāntis* also, the priest should perform an *abhiṣeka* for the Lord, accompanied by a special bath and other rites, as described

[246] A *nāḍī* here refers to a measure of time equal to one-half a *muhūrta*, which is one-thirtieth of a full day or forty-eight minutes. Thus, thirty *nāḍīs* equals a half-day, twelve hours. This period provides some leeway in the performance of a *māsotsava*.

[247] The sun's entry into each *rāśi* also constitutes a *saṅkrānti*. (For various qualities of the different *rāśis*, see Kane 1968–74: 5.561–69.) The further designation of these monthly *saṅkrāntis* as "Visnu's footprint" (*viṣṇupada*) or "Eighty-six Faces" (*ṣaḍaśītimukha*) covers the *saṅkrāntis* that are not solstice or equinox. This classification is drawn from Sūryasiddhānta treatises, but its significance to Śaiva ritual is not clear.

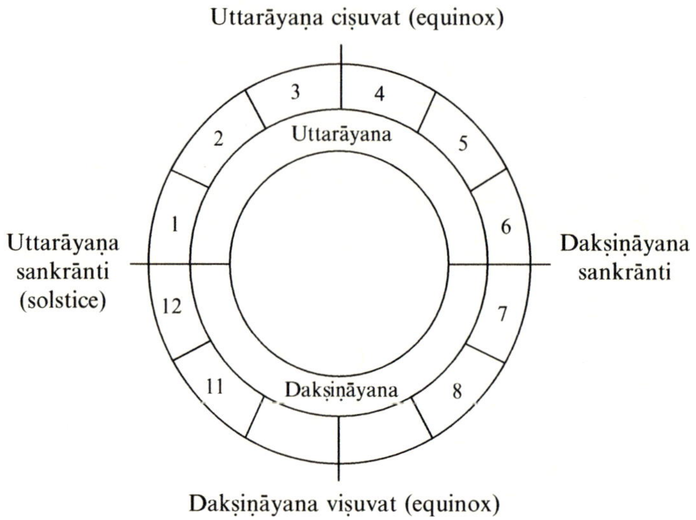

DIAGRAM 6. Solar Calendar and Māsotsava. Sources: Pandurang Vaman Kane, *History of Dharmaśāstra (Ancient and Mediaeval Religious and Civil Law)*, 2d ed. (Poona: Bhandarkar Oriental Research Institute, 1974), vol. 5, pp. 561-69; Karen L. Merrey, "The Hindu Festival Calendar," in *Religious Festivals in South India and Sri Lanka*, eds. Guy R. Welbon and Glenn E. Yocum (Delhi, Manohar, 1982).

Half-year	Month (rāśi)	Zodiac	Gregorian	*Saṇkrānti*
Uttarāyana				
	1. Makara (Crocodile)	Capricorn	Jan-Feb	solstice
	2. Kumbha (Pot)	Aquarius	Feb-Mar	viṣṇupada
	3. Mīna (Fish)	Pisces	Mar-Apr	ṣaḍaśītimukha
	4. Meṣa (Ram)	Aries	Apr-May	equinox
	5. Vṛṣa (Bull)	Taurus	May-June	viṣṇupada
	6. Mithuna (Twins)	Gemini	June-July	ṣaḍaśītimukha
Dakṣināyana				
	7. Karka (Crab)	Cancer	July-Aug	solstice
	8. Simha (Lion)	Leo	Aug-Sept	viṣṇupada
	9. Kanyā (Virgin)	Virgo	Sept-Oct	ṣaḍaśītimukha
	10. Tulā (Scale)	Libra	Oct-Nov	equinox
	11. Vṛścika (Scorpion)	Scorpio	Nov-Dec	viṣṇupada
	12. Dhanus (Bow)	Sagittarius	Dec-Jan	ṣaḍaśītimukha

previously.[248] He has the primary liṅga and other icons adorned with all their ornaments. Then, accompanied by all the instruments, he leads the group of processional images including Gaṇeśa, Somāskanda, and the other deities, and the Devotees in a circumambulation of the town, city, or the temple. Returning, he places them at the *brahmasthāna* or in front of the Bull, and performs the Illumination Ceremony and other concluding rites.[249] He returns the images to their own locations.

> One who carries this out does not contract any fault
> for that month, within the entire realm.
> Therefore one should perform the monthly festival
> completely and with full effort.

These are the procedures for the monthly festival.

31. *Festival of the New Moon*

Next are the procedures for the festivals of the two lunar fortnights.[250]

> On the eighth day and the fourteenth when the moon is waning,
> or one-eighth of the new moon, it becomes very minute.

[248] The special bath (*snapana*) and consecrating bath (*abhiṣeka*) have not been fully described previously in the *Mahotsavavidhi*, and it is not clear what description Aghoraśiva alludes to here. The procedures for the special bath are outlined in Āgamas like *Rauravāgama* (chs. 20–24), which provides instructions for baths involving 9, 25, 49, 108, and 1,009 pots. In each case the officiant marks out a geometrical design with the proper number of squares. Properly decorated water pots are set up in each square, and specific substances are added to the water in each one. Mantras are used to invoke deities into each pot. The pots are then used to give a holy bath to the central Śiva-liṅga (as here), or some other designated recipient. According to *Rauravāgama* (23.1–2), the bath with 108 pots is particularly efficacious for occasions such as the solstices, equinoxes, and other *saṅkrāntis*—that is, the times of *māsotsava*.

[249] The *brahmasthāna*, or central location of the site, here designates the temple's central *balipīṭha* (see note 100). The *nīrājana* ceremony here refers to the relatively simple actions employed at the conclusion of each daily procession during the *mahotsava* (as specified in section 14), not the more elaborate Illumination Ceremony performed near the end of the *mahotsava* (described in section 15).

[250] Fortnightly festivals (*pakṣotsava*) follow lunar movements, namely, the phases of the moon. A lunar month, like a solar year, consists of waxing and waning halves: the movement from the new moon (*amāvāsyā*) to the full moon (*pūrṇimāvāsyā*) is the waxing or bright fortnight (*śuklapakṣa*), and the movement from full moon to new is the waning or dark fortnight (*kṛṣṇapakṣa*). Each lunar month is divided into thirty *tithis* or lunar days, so each *pakṣa* consists of fifteen *tithis*. Within each fortnight the *tithis* are given numerical namesthe "first *tithi* of the bright fortnight" and so on.

Since the new moon and full moon represent transitions from one movement to another, they are moments for enhanced ritual activity. Here Aghoraśiva specifies two fortnightly festivals as the "new moon festival" (*amāvāsyotsava*) and the "full moon festival" (*paurṇamāsyotsava*). The initial section in verse here provides a technical discussion of exceptions and modifications.

When the moon is first seen it is called Sinīvālī.
When it is completely lost, it is Kuhūrmatā.[251]
If the new moon should begin at midday,
one should perform the rites on the following day.
It cannot be on the fifteenth day,
because that is touched by an evil spirit.[252]
If not, then the new moon day, diminished by one *ghaṭika*,
is on the first day of the fortnight.[253]
In that case, even though touched by an evil spirit,
the rites devoted to gods and ancestors should be performed.
Even when the new moon falls during the first days of the fortnight,
if it extends over the first half of the day,
even though touched by an evil spirit,
the rites of the gods should be performed always.
During the *rāśis* Scales, Crocodile, Fish, Virgin, and the Twins,
worship offered at the new moon, even touched by an evil spirit,
will be especially efficacious.
When the fourteenth day is complete,
one obtains unending merit, along with joy and the rest.
One should perform the festival of the gods on the fourteenth,
and the holy bath on the new moon day.
When the new moon day is associated with Monday,
the seventh with Sunday, or the fourth with Tuesday,
the fruit is equal to that at an equinox.
But when the new moon is on Monday,
that will be equal to Śivarātri.
One should stay awake at night,
and then perform the divine festival.
When the new moon is associated with the star Ārdra,
if it falls on a Monday, one will obtain
the fruit of a crore of sacrifices, austerities, and gifts,
by performing the festival then.

[251] The two godesses Sinīvālī and Kuhūrmatā go back to Vedic observations. Sinīvālī is the presiding deity of the first day of the new moon when it rises just barely visible. Kuhūrmatā, daughter of Aṅgiras, is identified with the new moon when it rises invisible.

[252] The fourteenth *tithi* of the dark fortnight is identified as *bhūta* (here, evil spirit), and so the following day would be "touched" by that *bhūta*.

[253] A *ghaṭika* is a period of time equal to twenty-four minutes, or the same as a *nāḍī*.

So on the new moon day, the priest should have a large *abhiṣeka* performed, along with a bath of the five cow products, for the principal liṅga and for all the icons that have been installed for processions.[254] The priest has them adorned with all their ornaments, and then fed a large meal. He leads the god, joined with parasol, yak-tail fan, and other regalia and with many colorful lamps, and accompanied by many musical instruments, on a circumambulation around the village, hamlet, or on another route, but without any offering of tribute.[255] Then he brings them to the *brahmasthāna* and performs the Illumination Ceremony and other concluding rites, as described previously. Finally he returns the god to its own place.

> The mortal who does this obtains an auspicious state.
> If he desires sons he obtains sons,
> and if he desires daughters he will gain a beautiful daughter.
> One desiring money gains abundant wealth,
> and one who wants liberation will attain it.
> Rain will not come at the wrong time,
> and he will be free of disease and accidents.
> One attains everything one desires
> just by offering a festival on the new moon.

These are the procedures for the festival of the new moon.

32. *Festival of the Full Moon*

Now come the procedures for the festival of the full moon.

> The full moon is considered twofold: Rākā and Anumatī.
> The day before the full moon is Anumatī,
> and it goes with the later one.[256]
> The day at the end of the fortnight is called the fifteenth,
> and that is considered the full moon day.
> If the full moon comes on the sixteenth day that is best,

[254] The procedure for the *amāvāsyotsava* is similar to that for the *māsotsava*. Initial observances take place in the temple sanctum and involve both the Śiva-liṅga and the processional icons. The *mahābhiṣeka* or large consecrating bath refers to a bathing (*snapana*) of the liṅga with many pots (see note 248).

[255] The *Mahotsavavidhi* here speaks of the "god" in singular, without identifying the particular processional form of Śiva who is at the center of fortnightly festivals. Modern temple practice suggests it would be Candraśekhara, Śiva who wears the moon in his crown, appropriate for these festivals tied to the moon's movements (see L'Hernault and Reiniche 1999: 60). Candraśekhara would be accompanied by the goddess Umā, and Gaṇeśa would presumably lead the procession.

[256] Rākā is the goddess who presides over the full moon day, sometimes considered the consort of the full moon. Anumatī presides over the previous day, when the moon rises one digit less than full.

on the fifteenth day is medium, and
if on the fourteenth that is considered lowest.
If it comes on the seventeenth day, that is sinful.
Starting with the first day of the fortnight,
all days start with sunrise, until the next sunrise.
The full moon is called "complete"
since the rites of the gods done then are pure.
The second and third, fourth and fifth days,
the sixth and seventh, the eighth and ninth,
and the eleventh yoked to the twelfth,
and the fourteenth and full moon days are joined together.
Even though the new moon is touched by the day of evil spirits,
when two *tithis* are united, that is very fruitful.

Here also the priest should perform all the preparatory rites, starting with the worship of Gaṇeśa up to the feeding, as described previously. One should take the gods, starting with Gaṇeśa, adorned with all their ornaments, on a circumambulation of the city or the like.[257] Then one places them back in their own places, as described before.

By these rites he destroys blemishes and faults,
by the command of Śiva.

These are the procedures for the full moon festival.

33. *Procedures for Festivals Related to the Stars*

One should calculate from the setting of the sun
and the rising of the moon,
and on that very star one should fast, except if the star is Śravaṇa.[258]
After the sun sets and the moon rises, for three *muhūrtas*
one should fast, bathe, and offer worship on that day.
On a day in which the star appears before midnight,

[257] The procedures given here refer back to earlier models. The preparatory rites from the preliminary worship of Gaṇeśa up through the meal (*naivedya*) would include the bathing rite (*snapana*) and adornment of the processional images, as in the new moon festival. Here the processional party is given as "Gaṇeśa and the others." Again judging from modern practice, Candraśekhara would be the central icon.

[258] *Ṛkṣa*, star, is here used as the equivalent of *nakṣatra*, a constellation or lunar mansion, of which there are twenty-eight. The moon's relation to these fixed constellationsits habitation of the lunar mansionschanges over a cycle of twenty-seven and one-third days. Here the *ṛkṣotsava* is a nighttime ceremony involving fasting, worship observances, and a procession. The lengthy verse portion links the festivals of specific *nakṣatras* with the fruits resulting from each.

one should perform the vow of that star,
and break the fast only at sunrise.
Those who worship Śiva on Kṛttikā obtain happiness.
One who desires children should worship on Rohiṇī.
One who worships on Mṛṛgaśiras becomes illustrious;
on Ārdrā one obtains all riches,
and on Punarvasu one gains land.
Worshiping Śiva on Puṣya leads to prosperity,
on Āśleṣa to many sons,
on Makhā to preeminence among one's own people,
and on Pūrvaphalgunī to great happiness.
Performing the rite on Uttaraphalgunī one gains generosity.
The one who worships Śiva on Hasta becomes best among the good,
and on Cittā one obtains a beautiful wife.
On Svātī one gains merchandise,
and on Viśākha one gets many desirable things.
When performed on Anurādhā it grants imperial sway,
on Jyeṣṭhā abundant riches,
and on Mūla good health.
Worshiping on Ādyāṣāḍhā one attains fame,
and on Uttarāṣāḍhā even more fame.
On Śravaṇa one gets pleasures and enjoyments,
and on Dhaniṣṭhā much money.
Worshiping on Abhijīt one becomes a knower of the Vedas,
and on Bhiṣaj, where Vāruṇa presides, one becomes skilled in medicine.
On Proṣṭhapada one acquires goats and sheep,
and on Uttarabhadrapada cows.
On Revatī Viṣṇu sleeps,
and on Aśvinī he wakes up.
Whoever worships on Bharaṇī gains long life.
Therefore one should make every effort to offer a festival on these stars.
Whether a common Śaiva, son of Śiva, mantra adept, or full Śaiva initiate,
the one who fasts on Ārdrā, Śiva's star,
gains the fruit of a hundred thousand horse-sacrifices,
a hundred crore of sacrifices, a crore of daughter-gifts,
multiplied by a crore of crores.[259]
And the sinful one who does not perform this on Śiva's star

[259] The verse here refers to the four categories of initiated Śaivas, based on their level of initiation and consecration.

will go to hell.
Men of the brahmin, *kṣatriya, vaiśya, śūdra,* and intermediate classes,
unmarried women or widows, those of good minds, ascetics,
initiated or not initiated, and best of brahmins—
at night they should offer worship, food, bath, and gift-giving,
toward the star,
they should look at the God of Gods, bow and praise him,
and according to their abilities
present gold, cloth, and food to brahmins.

So after the evening worship, and omitting the ghee-bath, the priest should properly honor all the deities, to the extent of his resources, and feed them a large oblation-meal. He should then make a circumambulation of the city or temple with Somāskanda, accompanied by parasol, yak-tail fan, and other regalia, and many colorful lamps. He performs an illumination rite, as described previously, and returns the image to its resting place.

The mortal who performs this rite joins with Rudra, no doubt about it.
For him, calamities and cruel afflictions from the planets are prevented.
He is exempt from all disease, and gains long life and happiness.
Within one year the brahmin certainly gains a good son.

34. The Weekly Festival

If Śiva's star comes on Sunday that is very salutary.[260]
If it comes on Monday it gives happiness.
On Tuesday it grants victory in battle.
On Wednesday it grants all that one desires,
and on Thursday it gives knowledge along with the sacred treatises.
On Friday one gains great wealth,
and on Saturday one is protected against sudden death.
Knowing this, one should diligently worship Śiva then.

This concludes the procedures for festivals, starting with the *brahmatāla* and ending with the festivals related to the stars, in the "Light on Ritual Procedures," composed by the illustrious preceptor Aghoraśiva, also known as Parameśvara.

[260] Here a weekly festival (*vārotsava*) is linked to the day of the week on which Śiva's star, Ārdrā, may fall. The particular days on which this festival may occur are assigned their special results. Aghoraśiva does not provide any procedural recommendations for the weekly festival.

Note on the Sanskrit Text

This devanagari text of the *Mahotsavavidhi* is based on the two published editions of the text, edited by M. Alagappa Mudaliyar in 1910 and by C. Swaminatha Gurukkal in 1974 (largely a reprint of the 1910 edition). I have not been able to locate any manuscripts that Alagappa Mudaliyar might have used for his 1910 edition. Both these published texts are in grantha script, and neither is a critical edition in the modern scholarly sense. There are numerous nonregular features in these editions, including irregular sandhi and the introduction of spaces to separate words. I have made no effort to produce a critical edition of the text myself. I have simply tried to choose the best readings between the two editions available to me. In a few cases I have made corrections recommended by N. R. Bhatt. The aim has been to produce a devanagari text that approximates as closely as possible the *Mahotsvavidhi* as it was available to generations of south Indian Śaiva temple priests.

महोत्सवविधि क्रमः

प्रथमं वृषयागञ्च ध्वजारोहं द्वितीयकम्।
बृहत्तालं तृतीयञ्च चतुर्थञ्चांकुरार्पणम्॥
यागशाला लक्षणञ्चास्त्रयागमतः परम्।
सप्तमं बलिदानञ्च यानक्रममथाष्टकम्॥
नवमं परिवेषञ्च दशं नीराञ्जनक्रमम्।
एकादशं कौतुकञ्च द्वादशं तीर्थसंग्रहम्॥
चूर्णोत्सवं त्रयोदश्यां चतुर्दश्यां तु तीर्थकम्।
अवरोहं पञ्चदशं षोडशं स्नपनं भवेत्॥
वैवाहिकं सप्तदशं भक्तोत्सव मतः परम्।

इत्यादिभेदेनोत्सवं ज्ञात्वा शैवादिदैविकान्तभेदेनोत्तमोत्तमनवाहोत्सवविधिर् विधीयते॥

तद्यथा - तत्पूर्वरात्रावधिवासनमारभेत्। तत्राचार्यादयः आरोहणाद्यवरोहणपर्यन्तमेकभुक्तोऽधश्शयनतैलाभ्यञ्जनस्त्रीसंपर्कपरान्न- भोजनादिराहित्यः त्रिषवणस्नायिनः वपनपूर्वकं हतं वासः परिधाय संकल्पपूर्वमिष्टदेवतां नमस्कृत्य एवमाचरेत्।

तत्र पूर्व ध्वजारोहणं पूर्वेद्युः वपनं कार्यम्।

प्रथम द्वितीय तृतीय चतुर्थ पञ्चम षष्टि सप्ताष्ट नवाहेषु द्विवारं बलिः कार्यः। तीर्थदिने प्रातर्बलिं दत्वा चूर्णोत्सवं तीर्थमारभेत्।

नवाहोत्सवं ध्वजारोहणपूर्वमेव कार्यम्॥

१ नक्षत्रादिनिर्णयः

मार्गशीर्षमासे आर्द्रान्तं पुष्ये पुष्यान्तं माघे माघान्तं फल्गुने उत्तरफल्गुन्यन्तं चैत्रे चित्रान्तं वैशाखे विशाखान्तं ज्येष्ठे ज्येष्ठान्तं मूलान्तं वा आषाढे उत्तराषाढान्तं पूर्वाषाढान्तं वा श्रावणे श्रवणान्तं भाद्रपदे पुर्वभाद्रपान्तं आश्विने अश्विन्यन्तं कार्तिके कृत्तिकान्तमेवं सद्दक्षाणि।

समुद्रतीरे पर्वणि नद्यादौ पर्वयुक्ते वियुक्ते वा माघे सितषष्ठ्यन्तं ज्येष्ठे कृष्णाष्टम्यन्तं वा अथवा आचार्यभूपयजमानदेवग्रामादि नक्षत्रेषु वा कर्तुर् अभीष्टनक्षत्रे वा तीर्थं कारयेत्।

समुद्रे पूर्वाह्ने पुष्करादिष्वपराह्ने नद्यां मध्यदिने तीर्थं ग्राह्यं नक्षत्रादित्ये सायाह्ने तीर्थं ग्राहयेत्।

ऋक्षद्वये तिथिद्वये वा एकस्मिन् मासे संप्राप्तेऽपरे विष्वयनसंक्रान्त्यादि योगयुक्तश्चेत् पूर्वमेव ग्राह्यं।

आरोहणादितीर्थान्तमेकस्मिन् मासे श्रेष्ठं विष्वन्तमयनान्तं ग्रहणान्तं वेति तीर्थमारभेत्।

शैवादित्यशिवोत्सवे प्रातःकाले अवभृतं निशि प्रातः ध्वज इति निशिसायं दिवाप्रातः ध्वजारोहणं कारयेत्।

ध्वजे ध्वजं न कर्तव्यं कर्तव्यं वृषभध्वजं।

अन्येषां ध्वज आरब्धे महादोषः प्रजायते॥

एकवास्तुनि वा ग्रामादौ वा देवोत्सवमध्ये नुः कल्याणं न कारयेत् कृतश्चेद् राज्ञो राष्ट्रस्य दोषो भवति।

२ विनायकोत्सवम्

उत्सवारम्भपूर्वे वाहनादिरथान्तं नवीकृत्य देवधामादिवीथ्यन्तान् कदलीस्तम्भपूगस्तम्भनालिकेरलिकुचादितत्कालोचितफलपल्लवपुष्पमालादर्पणद्वारतोरणवितानध्वजमालादिभिर् अलंकृत्य प्रपादिविश्राममण्टपान्तं चालंकृत्य सम्मार्जनजलसेचनादि कारयित्वा भूशुद्धिं कारयेत्।

भद्रकाल्युत्सवान्ते विघ्नेश्वरस्य नवाह सप्ताह त्र्यहं एकाहं वा उत्सवं कारयेत्।

तद्यथा - विनायकस्कन्दवीरशास्ता पञ्चविंशतिबेरस्कन्दचण्डेशशिवास्त्रभक्त विग्रहादिसहितान् विशेषतः पञ्चगव्य पुरस्सरं संपूज्य अलंकृत्य आचार्य ऋत्विक्भूपयजमानाः ब्राह्मणैस् तौर्यत्रिकैस् सह शुभे लग्ने उत्सवार्थं विघ्नेश्वरपूजा पुरस्सरं महादेवशब्दं विशिष्टं पुण्याहं वाचयित्वा स्नपनपूर्वं विघ्नेशं संपूज्य मोदकभक्ष्यभोज्यादिनैवेद्यन्तं दत्वा ब्राह्मणान् भोजयित्वा अविघ्नमस्त्विति प्रार्थ्य देवालयकर्मरतान् सर्वान् दीनान्धान् कृपणाधान् भोजनाच्छादनैः सन्तोष्यास्त्रराजं चण्डेश्वरञ्च विनायकपूर्वं रथे वा शिबिकादौ वा आरोप्य दर्पणछत्रचामरादिनानाध्वजसहितं गन्धपुष्पधूपदीपनानावाद्यवेदघोषसहितं ग्रामं प्रदक्षिणीकृत्यास्थानमण्डपे निवेशयेत्।

३ दारुसंग्रहणम्

ततः शिलाग्रहणवत् दारुसंग्रहणं कुर्यात्।

बिल्वखादिरदेवदारुचम्पकार्जुनाशोकशिरीषवेणु इत्यादिवृक्षाणां एकं अग्रमूलं परीक्ष्य शिवंसंपूज्य बलिं विधाय निरुध्य परशुना छिन्द्यात्।

पूर्वे चोत्तरे चैशान्यां पतितं चेच्चोभनमन्यधातु संत्यजेत्।

तच्चतुरश्रीकृत्य आदाय शिल्पिना सह रथे च आरोप्य आनीय गव्येन स्नाप्य कौतुकं अग्रे बध्वा पुनः पुण्याहं वाचयित्वा स्नानमण्डपे निधाय गन्धतैलादिना विमृज्य सर्वेषां ताम्बूलं दक्षिणाञ्च दापयेत्।

४ ध्वजदण्डम्

तत्र स्थण्डिलं विधाय मध्ये दण्डं विन्यस्य वस्त्राद्यैरलङ्कृत्य मालादिभिः विभूष्य धूपदीपौ दत्वा वेदाश्रवस्वश्रवृत्तभागेषु शिवभागादितः तत्वत्रयं सेश्वरं संपूज्य प्रणनोत्थाप्य तत्स्थाने विवेश्य सामान्यप्रतिष्ठोक्तवत्

प्रतिष्ठापयेदिति स्थूप्यन्त चूलिकान्तं वा शुकनासान्तं वा यष्टित्रय फलकात्रयं उपदण्डद्वय घण्टासहितं अष्टाधिकशतदर्भकूर्चयुक्तं दर्भरज्जुवेष्टितं वलयसहितं कारयेदिति दारुसंग्रहदण्डप्रतिष्ठाविधिः।

५ मृत्संग्रहणम्

नदीतीरादिस्थले पूर्वोक्तवत् मृत्संग्रहणं कृत्वा विघ्नेश्वरादिबेरसहितं नानावाद्यवेदघोषसहितं गत्वा पूर्वोक्तवत् मृत्संग्रहणं कृत्वा तन्मृदं परिचारकैः माहेश्वरैः रुद्रगणिकाभिः गजाद्यैर् वाहयित्वा पुरं प्रदक्षिणीकृत्य प्रासादं प्रविश्य अङ्कुरार्पण वेदिकायां निक्षिप्य विघ्नेशं मोदकाद्यैर् अपूपैर् इक्षुदण्डनालिकेरकपित्थमातुलङ्गककदल्यादि तत्कालोचित फलैश् चणकमुद्गताम्बूलादि निवेद्य सर्वोपचारैः पूजयेदिति मृत्संग्रहणविधिः।

६ अङ्कुरम्

ध्वजाङ्कुरन्तु प्रथमं द्वितीयं चोत्सवाङ्कुरम्।
तीर्थाङ्कुरं तृतीयमिति पूर्वोक्तवत् कुर्यात्॥

इत्यङ्कुरार्पणविधिः।

७ वृषयागः

ध्वजारोहणपूर्वेद्युः रात्रावधिवासन क्रियां कारयेत्।

ततः शिवं संपूज्य विज्ञाप्य वितानाद्यैर् वृषस्थानमलङ्कृत्य गुरुर् उत्तराभिमुखो भूत्वा स्थिरासनं पूर्वोक्तवत् अङ्गन्यासादिकं कृत्वा अर्घ्यं संसाध्य वृषेशं संपूज्य मुद्रान्नं निवेद्य तस्याग्रे स्थण्डिलं विधाय अङ्गुल्यादिभिः मध्ये पद्मं विलिख्य कुशैः पुष्पैः परिस्तीर्य नवकलशान् संस्थाप्य मध्यकुम्भे वृषभं षडुत्थासनपूर्वं संपूज्य पूर्वादीशान्त दिक्षु

उक्षाय नमः
गोपतये नमः
शृङ्गिणे नमः
नन्दिने नमः
वृषपतये नमः
वृषाणिने नमः
शङ्कुकर्णाय नमः
महोदराय नमः

इत्यासनादि मूलमन्त्रैर् अभ्यर्च्य
यद्वा लोकपालान् संपूज्य

ध्वजपटमुक्तवन्नवहस्तादिकं पञ्चभागैकविस्तारं विस्तारसमं पुच्छं पुच्छार्धं शिरः सितं सूक्ष्मं श्लक्ष्णं कार्पासादि सम्भवं तत्त्रिभागं कृत्वा मध्यभागे वृषभं त्रिभागैकभागे वा समालिख्य तेन रत्नेन शृङ्गकर्णाङ्कुराणि पीतेन पुच्छमक्षीणि श्वेतकृष्णेन कृत्वा तत्पुरस्तात् पूर्णकुम्भं तत्पश्चात् दीपं घण्टां श्रीवत्सं स्वस्तिकं शेषमङ्गलरूपाणि च विलिख्य ध्वजयागमारभेत्।

अथवा दण्डदीर्घं दण्डनासविस्तारं पूर्ववत् पटं विन्यस्य पुण्याहं वाचयित्वा पञ्चगव्यादिभिः प्रोक्ष्य वृषे चलासनं संपूज्य तस्याग्रे स्थण्डिलं कृत्वा अग्निकार्योक्तमार्गेण होमञ्च विधाय बेरशुद्ध्यनन्तरमन्यत्र स्थण्डिलद्वयं संपाद्य वृषपटमध्ये न्यस्त्वा हेमतूलिकया सूर्यसोममन्त्राभ्यां अक्षिमोचनं वृषगायत्र्या वा विधाय-

तीक्ष्णशृङ्गाय विद्महे वेदपादाय धीमहि।

तन्नो वृषः प्रचोदयात्॥

अक्षिमोचनानन्तरं गोदर्शनादिसर्वं विधाय मृद्भिः पञ्चगव्येन सिताम्भसा च प्रोक्ष्य दर्पणे गव्यादिभिः स्नाप्य जले अधिवासयेत्।

जलादुत्तिर्य यागशालायां ध्वजपटमानीय वृषगायत्र्या पुनः गव्यादिना संप्रोक्ष्य स्थण्डिले संस्थाप्य वृषे षडुत्थासनं संपूज्य मूर्तिं ध्यानपुरस्सरं सङ्कल्पयेत्।

पश्चात् वाससा आच्छाद्य ब्रह्माणि विन्यस्य धूपदीपौ दत्वा निद्राकुम्भं संस्थाप्य उक्षादीन् परितः विन्यस्य पूजयेत्।

वृषमूले स्थित्वा मूर्धादिपादपर्यन्तं चतुस्त्रिंशत् तत्वानि साधिपानि विन्यसेत्।

तद्यथा -

सदाशिवतत्वाय नमः

सदाशिवतत्वाधिपाय ब्रह्मणे नमः

इत्यारभ्य

पृथिवीतत्वाय नमः

पृथिवीतत्वाधिपाय श्रीकण्ठाय नमः

इत्यन्तं संपूज्य त्रिखण्डं परिकल्प्य पुष्पमालाप्रतिसरं दत्वा पूर्ववत् भागत्रयं सङ्कल्प्य प्रतिभागं पूर्वादिक्रमेण -

क्ष्मावह्नियजमानार्कजलवातेन्दुखानि च। इति मूर्तय।

उक्षा गोपति शृङ्गी नन्दि वृषपतिर् विषाणि शङ्कुकर्ण महोदरान् मूर्त्यधिपान् विन्यस्य जीवन्यासं तन्मूलेन कृत्वा स्थापनाद्युपचारैः संपूज्य भस्मदर्भतिलैः प्राकारत्रयं बहिर् विदध्यात्।

लोकपालान् अध्येष्य कुण्डे

आधारशक्तये नमः

इत्यग्नौ संपूज्य आहुतित्रयं दत्वा

आत्मतत्त्वे विद्यातत्त्वे शिवतत्त्वे ब्रह्मविष्णुशिवेभ्यो नमः

इति संपूज्य प्रत्येकं आहुतित्रयं दत्वा क्ष्मामूर्तीः

तदधिपेभ्यो नमः

इति संपूज्य प्रत्येकं आहुतित्रयं दत्वा मूलब्रह्माङ्गानि च प्रत्येकं शतमर्धं वा हुत्वा पूर्णां दत्वा गुरुः शान्तिकुम्भहस्तः वृषसमीपं गत्वा शान्तिकुम्भजलेन प्रोक्ष्य तन्मूलेन कुशमूलमध्याग्रैर् भागत्रयं सङ्कल्प्य संस्पृश्य जप्त्वा हुत्वा वर्मणावकुण्ठ्य निरुध्य तत्त्वाधिपानाज्ञां श्रावयित्वा ज्ञानशक्तिं विन्यस्य निरुध्य होमैर् वेदादिघोषैः वा नृत्तगीतमहोत्सवैर् भक्तितो एकरात्रं वा कुर्यात्।

वृषाधिवासनं दिक्बलिञ्च निवेद्य गुरुः पूर्ववत् स्वपेदिति वृषाधिवासविधिः।

८ ध्वजारोहणम्-

अपरेद्युः प्रातस्नानादिकं कृत्वा सङ्कल्प्य सकलीकृत्य सामान्यार्घ्यं संसाध्य नित्यवद् आत्मपूजाविधिं सर्वं विधाय पटं कुम्भादीन् यथाक्रमेणाभ्यर्च्य वह्नावपि समिदाज्य चरुभिर् अष्टोत्तरशतं हुत्वा पूर्णां दत्वा निरुध्य मण्टपादिषु मण्डलत्रयं कृत्वा परिचारकमाहूय अस्त्रेण संप्रोक्ष्य सोष्णीषं उत्तरीयं च धारयित्वा पटकुभादि सहितं उद्धृत्य अस्त्रादिचण्डेशान्तं सर्वतोद्यसमायुक्तं शङ्खदुन्दुभिनिर्घोषैर् वेदादिघोषैस्सह ग्रामप्रदक्षिणं कृत्वा आलयं प्रविश्य पटमेकस्मिन् अस्त्रराजमेकस्मिन् कुम्भमेकस्मिन् स्थण्डिलत्रये निधाय पुण्याहं वाचयित्वा पञ्चगव्यार्घ्योदकेन सह प्रोक्ष्य वृषं कुम्भजलेन प्रोक्ष्य उक्षादिघटैरभिषिच्य गन्धाद्यैरलङ्कृत्य हविश्चणकादि निवेद्य अस्त्रराजमपि तत्कुम्भजलेन अभिषिच्य अलङ्कृत्य निवेद्य जपान्तं संपूज्य अस्त्रराजस्य रजनीचूर्णं दत्वा स्वयञ्च धृत्वा राज्ञां भक्तानां परिचारकानां सर्वेषाञ्च रजनीचूर्णं दापयेत्।

ततो ध्वजदण्डमलङ्कृत्य गायत्र्या घण्टायां अभ्यर्चयेत्।

देवं रथादौ समारोप्य शूलं अग्रे अग्रतः आचार्यः पृष्ठतः यजमानः भक्तजनैस्सर्वैस्सार्धं सर्वतोद्यसमायुक्तं मङ्गलाङ्कुरसहितं पूर्णकुम्भसहितं नानाविधचत्रचामरदीपसंयुक्तं यात्रादानसहितं दिग्विदिक्षु गीतनृत्तबलिदानसहितं पुरं प्रदक्षिणीकृत्य आलयं प्रविश्य ध्वजस्थाने समानीय पुण्याहं वाचयित्वा सवेदिकमभ्युक्ष्य शक्त्यादिशक्त्यन्तं वेदिकायां अभ्यर्च्य-

ध्वजदण्ड ध्यानम्,

एकं च पादं द्विभुजं त्रिणेत्रं रोमावलीराजित दर्भरज्जुम्।
श्वेताङ्गरूपं शुकनासिकान्तं आरूढ पद्मासन दण्डरूपम्॥

इति ध्यात्वा-

दण्डे सदाशिवमावाह्य यष्टिफलकासु शक्तित्रयं उपदण्डे सूर्यसोमौ रज्जौ तक्षाधिदैवत्यं पटे वायुं ध्वजे वृषं क्रमेणाभ्यर्च्य मुद्गान्नं पायसं वा वृषाय निवेद्य धूपदीपौ दत्वा ब्राह्मणानां स्वर्णादि दत्वा ध्वजपटं समुद्धृत्य रज्जुना

बन्धयित्वा करिष्यमाणं उत्सवं क्रियत इति शिवं विज्ञाप्य ब्रह्मताल पठनं कृत्वा विघ्ननिरसनार्थं असंख्य नालिकेरबलिं दत्वा सुमुहूर्ते नानावाद्यसहितं देशिको दण्डमूले स्थित्वा अर्घ्येणारोपितपरिचारकं च प्रोक्ष्य स्वयमादौ स्पृष्ट्वा मूर्तिपैस्सह शीघ्रमारोपयेत्। सव्यक्रमेण रज्जुना सह वेष्टनं कृत्वा दण्डमूले बन्धयेत्।

अथ प्रभृति तीर्थान्तं वृषं त्रिकालं द्विकालं वा पूजयेत्।

पश्चात् कुम्भान्तिकं गत्वा प्रायश्चित्तं हुत्वा वृषयागाग्निं विसृजेत्।

दिग्विदिक्षु शुद्धनृत्तं कार्यमिति ध्वजारोहणविधिः।

बलिपिण्डप्रमाणम्।

नारिकेलप्रमाणं तु पञ्चविंशति पिण्डकं।
दण्डपीठेन शुद्धं स्यात्
तत्पिण्डं प्राशयेन्नारी अपुत्री पुत्रमाप्नुयात्।
व्याधिघ्नं सर्वदोषघ्नं वृषोश्चिष्टं शिखिध्वज॥

ध्वजारोहणफलं

यत्रैतत् क्रियते राष्ट्रे ध्वजयष्टिनिवेशनम्।
नाकालमृत्युस्तत्रास्ति नालक्ष्मीः पापकृत्स्वपि॥
नोपसर्पभयं तत्र नोपरागो न विभ्रमः।
विपरीताश्च मतयोः योगिनामपि भूयसा॥
स्वकालवर्षी पर्जन्यः सुभिक्षं विजयी नृपः।
शान्तानि सर्वभूतानि पयस्विन्यः पयोभृतः॥
कृतघ्नो ब्रह्महा गोघ्नो दृष्टाध्वजनिवेशनम्।
प्राप्नोति पापनिर्मोक्षं किमु कर्तुः कुलत्रयम्॥
कृते महाध्वजारोहे तत्कोटिगुणितम् फलम्।

९ भेरीब्रह्मतालविधिः।

उक्तं उत्सवपद्धत्यां सर्वदेवप्रियार्थकम्।
सायरक्षावसाने च भेरीं सन्ताड्यते यथा॥
देवाग्रे ध्वजाग्रे वा देवताह्वानक्रियां समारभेत्।
तत्र स्थण्डिलत्रयं कृत्वा एकस्मिन् शूलं तत्पुरतो पटं तदग्रे भेरीं न्यस्य दक्षिणे घोणदण्डं विन्यसेत्।

ततस्त्रिशूले तत्त्वभुवनवर्णपदमन्त्रकलादीन् विन्यसेत्।

तद्यथा - मध्यपत्रे

शिवतत्त्वाय नमः

शिवतत्त्वाधिपाय रुद्राय नमः

वामपत्रे

विद्यातत्त्वाय नमः

विद्यातय्त्वाधिपतये विष्णवे नमः

दक्षिणपत्रे

आत्मतत्त्वाय नमः

आत्मतत्वाधिपाय ब्रह्मणे नमः

फलकायां

पार्वत्यै नमः

कुम्भदेशे सेनान्यै नमः

तदास्ये

विघ्नराजाय नमः

दण्डाग्रे

मदनाय नमः

भास्कराय नमः

दण्डमूले

चण्डेश्वराय नमः

आग्नेयादिसप्तदलेषु

ब्राह्म्यै नमः

माहेश्वर्यै नमः

कौमार्यै नमः

वैष्णव्यै नमः

वाराह्यै नमः

माहेन्द्र्यै नमः

चामुण्ड्यै नमः

पश्चिमदलमध्ये

ज्येष्ठायै नमः

कुबेरदलमध्ये

कात्यायन्यै नमः

शूलमूले - एकादशरुद्रा द्वादशादित्याष्टवसवश्च अश्विनिदेवता अष्टादशगणाश्चावाह्य अभ्यर्च्य तानाहूयाशिषश्चोक्त्वा भेरीं सन्ताडयेत्।

ततो भेरीं विचित्रवस्त्रेणावेष्ट्य मध्ये रुद्रं सप्तकीलेषु मातृन् कीले नवग्रहांश्च रज्जुषु वासुकीं प्रहरे षण्मुखं क्रमेणाभ्यर्च्य गन्धादिभिरलङ्कृत्य भेरीताडनं कुर्यात्।

आचार्यं शस्त्रं बिन्दुरूपं ध्यात्वा दर्भेण त्रिवारं ताडयेत्।

तन्नादं प्राणिनां श्रवणपथं चेत् अपेतकिल्बिषा भवन्ति।

पश्चात् वाद्यकमाहूय यज्ञसूत्रमुत्तरीयञ्च गन्धमाल्यादि धारयित्वा तद्धस्ते पुष्पं दत्वा सोपि आचार्यानुज्ञया भेर्यां पुष्पं निक्षिप्य वाद्यं स्कन्धे समारोप्य नन्दितालेन ताडयेत्।

ततः शिवादिसर्वदेवांश्च अष्टादशगणांश्च इन्द्रादिदिक्पतींश्च समुद्रान् पर्वतान् द्वीपान् पातालान् सकलांश्च आहूय श्रावयेत्।

ततः मध्यादिदेवताह्वानार्थं अस्त्रराजसोमास्कन्ददेविविनायकस्कन्दनन्दिचण्डभक्तविग्रहादिसहितं सर्वमङ्गलैस्सह वृषस्थानमाश्रित्य पूजाबलिं दत्वा नृत्तगीतवाद्यादिभिः सन्तोषं ब्रह्मस्थानमाश्रित्य तन्मण्डले पुण्याहप्रोक्षणादि सर्वं विधाय ध्यात्वा संपूज्य नैवेद्यार्थं बलिं दत्वा अनन्तरं तालं ब्रह्मतालं रागं वङ्कुलं नृत्तं समपादं पण् पञ्चमं वाद्यं गुच्छपुटं इत्यादिभिस्सन्तोष्य अनन्तरं इन्द्रदिशमाश्रित्य तन्मण्डले पूर्ववत् आसनादिबल्यन्तं कृत्वा तालं समतालं नृत्तं भुजङ्गं पण् कौमेशीं वाद्यं साचपटमिति कृत्वा आग्नेयां दिशि अग्नेः पूजादिबल्यन्तं कृत्वा रागं वराटि तालं मत्ता वरणं नृत्तं मण्डलं पण् कोल्लि वाद्यं उद्धरितमित्यादिभिः सन्तोष्य याम्यदिशि यमं पूजादिबल्यन्तं विधाय रागं रामगिरि तालं भृङ्गिणीतालं नृत्तं दण्डपादं पण् कौशिकं वाद्यं मिलितमट्टयं इत्यादिभिः सन्तोष्य नै-ऋते नि-ऋते नि-ऋतिं पूजाबलिं दत्वा रागं भैरवी तालं मल्लतालं नृत्तं भुजंगत्रासं पण् नट्टभाषा वाद्यं लम्बकमित्यादि कृत्वा वारुणे वरुणं पूर्ववत् बलिदानं कृत्वा रागं कुञ्जरी तालं नागतालं नृत्तं आकुञ्चिकं पण् श्रीकामरं वाद्यं सिंहनादमिति कृत्वा वायव्यां वायुं पूर्ववत् बलिं दत्वा रागं देशागिरि तालं बलितालं नृत्तं भुजङ्गलमितं पण् तक्काशि वाद्यं जम्पटमिति कृत्वा उत्तरे कुबेरं पूर्ववत् ध्यात्वा बलिं दत्वा रागं गौढिकं तालं गौलितालं नृत्तं आकुञ्चितं पण् कौशिकं वाद्यं पञ्चममिति सन्तोष्य ईशाने ईशानं पूर्ववत् ध्यात्वा संपूज्य बलिं दत्वा रागं तुण्डीरं तालं ढक्करी नृत्तं ऊर्ध्वपादं पण् शालापाणि वाद्यं कुम्भवाद्यं इत्यादिभिः सन्तोष्य इन्द्रादिभिः क्रमेण प्रदक्षिणीकृत्य आलयं प्रविश्य ध्वजमूले बलिपीठे वा विशेषं क्षिपेदिति ब्रह्मतालविधिः।

१० यागशालार्चनाविधिः

ततः पूर्वोक्तप्रकारेण मङ्गलाङ्कुरं निर्वृत्यानन्तरं यागशालार्चनं।

देवाग्रे वा ईशानाग्नेये सौम्यवारुणे वा पञ्चहस्तादिमण्टपे पश्चिमद्वारं विधाय तन्मध्ये यथोक्तवेदिका दर्पणोदरवद् उपवेदिका सहिता कार्या।

तद्बहिः पूर्वादीशान्तकुण्डानि क्रमेणाश्रयान्यर्धचन्द्र त्रिकोणवृत्त षड्कोण पद्माष्टकोण कुण्डानि – चन्द्रेशानयोर्मध्ये वृत्तं वा चतुरश्रं वा-

यद्वा - पञ्चपक्षे वृत्तं प्रधानं ईशाने चतुर्दिक्षु चतुरश्राणि कुण्डानि।

अथवा - एकं वृत्तं चतुरश्रं वा कृत्वा गोमयेनोपलिप्य वितानध्वजचात्रदर्भमालादिद्वारतोरणमङ्गलाष्टकयुक्तं -

दर्पणं पूर्णकुम्भं च वृषभं युग्मचामरं।
श्रीवत्सं स्वस्तिकं शङ्खं दीपो देवाष्टमङ्गलमिति॥
वज्रं शक्तिं च दण्डं च खड्गं पाशं तथाङ्कुशं।
ध्वजं गदा च शूलं च पद्मचक्रमिति॥

दशायुधसहितं स्रुक् स्रुवादिकारकसमूहयुक्तं विधाय सायाह्ने उत्सवारम्भं कुर्यादिति यागशालालक्षणविधिः

अस्त्रयागविधिः।

आचार्यो ऋत्विग्भिस्सह सायं संध्यां विशेष संध्यां च निर्वृत्य आलयं प्रविश्य देवाग्रे स्थण्डिलं विधाय अस्त्रेण संप्रोक्ष्य कुम्भान् सुस्निग्धान् सुदृढान् नवान् हेमादिमृण्मयान्तान् निष्कलङ्कान् सकूर्चान् सपिधानान् वस्त्रफलपल्लवसूत्रसहितान् सहिरण्यरत्नादिसंयुक्तान् यथोक्तलक्षणान् अस्त्रेण वारिणा प्रक्षाल्य धूपयित्वा हृदा गन्धतोयेनापूर्य स्थण्डिलोपरि मध्ये शिवकुम्भं उत्तरे वर्धनीं परितोष्टघटान् संस्थाप्य मूर्तिमन्त्रेण कुम्भं शक्त्या वर्धनीं च अनन्तादिशिखण्ड्यन्तान् कलशेषु संपूज्य तत्परितः नन्द्याद्यायुधां च परिचारकमाहूय शिवकुम्भवर्धन्यौ च क्रमेण धारयित्वा वज्रादिचक्रान्तं शङ्खदुन्दुभिनिर्घोषैर् वेदादिघोषैश्च विमानं प्रदक्षिणीकृत्य यागशालां प्रवेश्य वेदिकामध्ये अष्टद्रोणशालिभिः सदर्भतण्डुलैः तदर्ध तिललाजैः सप्तधान्यैश्च परिस्तीर्य तन्मध्ये शिवकुम्भवर्धन्यौ विद्येश्वरघटाश्च संस्थाप्य धर्मादिसूर्यान्तस्थाने संस्थाप्य ऋत्विग्भिर् यजमानैः सह गुरुर् विनायकपूजापुरस्सरं पुण्याहं वाचयित्वा सौरपूजां नित्यवत् कृत्वा विसृज्यैव समाचम्य सकलीकृत्य सामान्यार्घ्यं संसाध्य पूर्वादिद्वाराणि संपूज्य प्रतिद्वारं द्वौ द्वौ नन्द्यादिचण्डान्तं पूर्ववत् संपूज्य पश्चिमे नित्यवत् द्वारपालान् आराध्य नै-ऋते वास्तुनाथं संपूज्य ब्रह्मस्थानाद् दक्षिणतोदङ्मुखे समुपवेश्य भूतशुद्ध्यादि विशेषार्घ्यं च कृत्वात्मानं गन्धाद्युष्णीषान्तैः मूर्तिपैस्सह अलङ्कृत्य पञ्चगव्यं विधिवत् विधाय पञ्चगव्यार्घ्यजलैः मण्टपशुद्धिं विधाय शिवकुम्भवर्धिन्यौ पूर्ववज्जपान्तं संपूज्य लोकपालान् वाहनायुधसंयुक्तान् ध्यात्वा संपूज्य महालक्ष्मीं गणपतिं गुरुपङ्क्तिं चाभ्यर्च्य सर्वान् शिवाज्ञां श्रावयेत्।

ततः स्थण्डिलाद्दक्षिणतः उपविश्य शिवकुम्भे शक्त्यादिशक्तिपर्यन्तासनं संपूज्य दण्डभङ्गी मुण्डभङ्गी कलाभङ्गी च न्यस्त्वा सर्वाध्वोपेतं शिवं पूर्वोक्तवद् ध्यात्वाताह्य वर्धन्यां श्रीकण्ठन्यासं विधाय-

देवीध्यानम्।

द्विभुजां चारुवदनां सुस्तनां च सुयौवनाम्।
दुकूलवसनां शान्तां किञ्चित् प्रहसिताननाम्॥
सर्वाभरणसंयुक्तां आसने हरवत् स्थिताम्।
करण्डमकुटोपेतां देवीं ध्यायेदनुक्रमादिति॥

ध्यात्वा तन्मूलेनावाह्य तौ पञ्चावरण पञ्चोपचारैः संपूज्य नवेद्य जपञ्च समर्प्य हुत्वा प्रार्थ्य आग्नेयादिकोणेषु धर्मादीन् संपूज्य शिवाज्ञां श्रावयित्वा कुण्डान्तिकं व्रजेयुः।

कुण्डसंस्कारादिपूर्णान्तं विधाय अग्निं नवधा पञ्चधा वा विभज्य पूर्वादि कुण्डेषु निक्षिप्य तत्तच्छिवं साङ्गं संपूज्य चरुहवनप्रायश्चित्ताङ्गं मूर्तिपैः सह जुहुयुः।

तत्तत् कुण्डेषु शिवं विशेषतः संपूज्य -

यज्ञसमिधः।

अश्वत्थोदुम्बरप्लाक्षवटाः पूर्वादिदिक्षु च।
शमीखादिरमायुरश्रीवृक्षाग्न्यादि कोणतः॥
प्रधानेन पलाशं स्यात् स च सर्वत्र सम्मतः।

चरुलाजसर्षपयवतिलमुद्ग माषशिम्बाढक चणक कुलुत्थांश्च हुत्वा द्रव्यान्ते व्याहृतिभिश्च हुत्वा मूलेन अष्टोत्तरशतं सहस्रमर्धं वा पूर्णासहितं जुहुयुः।

ततः शोत्रचन्दनादिकं कृत्वा वह्निं निरुध्य होमरक्षां मूललिङ्गादिबेराणाञ्च दापयित्वा स्वयं च ऋत्विग्भिस्सह धृत्वा तत्रेशाने मारुते वा शूलं समानीय स्थापयित्वा प्रतिदिनं सायं प्रातर् एवमेव कारयेत्।

इत्यस्त्रयागविधिः।

१२ रक्षाबन्धनविधिः।

ततः स्वर्णरजतकार्पासेभ्यो ऽन्यतमं रक्षासूत्रं तिथिरौद्रनवात्मकं षोडशाङ्गुलयामं लिङ्गस्य तन्नाह समं पिण्डिकायां नालसमं स्थलिकायां तण्डुललाजपुष्पैरापूर्य तन्मध्ये पद्ममालिख्य तदुपरि विन्यस्य भस्मरजनी धूर्वागन्धपुष्पफलसुवर्णताम्बूलादि दत्वा तत्सूत्रं त्र्यम्बकेन भस्मना संमृज्य पुण्याहं वाचयित्वा षडुत्थासनपूर्वं अभ्यर्च्य धूपदीपौ दत्वा आलयं प्रदक्षिणीकृत्य अन्तः प्रविश्य शिवं संपूज्य धूपदीपौ दत्वा वासुकिं ध्यात्वा लिङ्गमूले

मूलेन धृत्वा पिण्डिकायां नालभाङ्गे तन्मूलेन बन्धयित्वा त्र्यम्बकेन भस्म समर्प्य तदुपरि रजनीं दत्वा गन्धादिभिरभ्यर्च्य अस्त्रराजस्य मध्यपत्रे बन्धयित्वा अस्त्रादिभक्तान्तबेराणां त्र्यम्बकेन सहृदा दक्षहस्ते बन्धयेत्।

गौर्यादिस्त्रीबेराणां च गौरीमूलमन्त्रेण वामहस्ते कौतुकं बन्धयेत्।

स्वस्य च ऋत्विजां च बलिवाहकस्य भेरीताडनस्य च दशायुधानां च कौतुकं बन्धयित्वा तदुपरि भस्मरजनी समर्प्य ध्वजदण्डमध्ये कौतुकं धृत्वा सपुष्पं ग्रन्थिषु रजन्या सह सुदृढं बन्धयेत्।

सर्वेषां रजनीचूर्णं स्वर्णफलताम्बूलादि दापयेदिति रक्षाबन्धनविधिः।

१३ बलिदानविधिः।

ततो बलिः महोत्सवे सायं प्रातः ब्रह्मस्थानादिध्वजान्तं वा वृषादिबलिपीठान्तं वेति बलिं दद्यात्।

तद्यथा - ब्रह्मस्थानादिस्थानेषु हस्तप्रमाणविस्तारदीर्घं तदर्धं विस्तार द्वादशाङ्गुलं अष्टाङ्गुलं वा घनं मेखलात्रययुतं एकैकपीठं कर्णिकाष्टदलयुतशिलामयं अथवा इष्टिकामयं सारदारुमयं वा सलक्षणं पीठानि निर्मायालेख्य पञ्चचूर्णैस्तत्तद्दिगलं कृत्य द्रोणं वा तदर्धतण्डुलं वा विपच्य बलिपात्रे च आदाय अस्त्रेण संप्रोक्ष्य तदन्यत् स्थालिकायां तदर्धं समानीयान्नलिङ्गं सलक्षणं कुर्वीत।

तद् द्वादशाङ्गुलमुन्नतं नाहं देवाङ्गुलं सपीठं प्रकल्प्य दध्नाचालिप्य विधिवत् प्रतिष्ठाप्यध्यानं-

पाशुपतध्यानं।

त्रिणेत्रं चतुर्भुजं देवं जटामकुटधारिणम्।
वरदाभयहस्तं च वामहस्तेऽक्षमालिकाम्॥
दक्षिणे शूलसंयुक्तं रौद्रदृष्टिसमन्वितम्।
नागाभरणसंयुक्तमूर्ध्वकेशमधोक्षी च॥

एतत् पाशुपतं दिव्यं लिङ्गमध्ये प्रपूजयेत्।

यद्वा - पूर्ववच्छिवं संपूज्य

आचार्यः स-ऋत्विक् दशायुधास्त्रराजयुक्तः भस्माद्युष्णीषान्तैर् अलङ्कृतः परिचारसहितो विचित्रध्वजचत्रचामरादिसहितो नानावाद्यघंटाब्रह्मघोषैश्चैव नृत्तकीनर्तकगायकसहितो बलिं दद्यात्।

नवाहोत्सवे विशेषबलिदेवान् क्रमेण उच्यते।

प्रथमेऽहनि

विघ्नराजाय स्वाहा

द्वितीये

भूतेभ्यः स्वाहा

तृतीये

ऋषिभ्यः स्वाहा

चतुर्थे

इन्द्राय स्वाहा

पञ्चमे

ब्रह्मणे स्वाहा

षष्ठे

विष्णवे स्वाहा

सप्तमे

रुद्राय स्वाहा

अष्टमे

ईश्वराय स्वाहा

नवमे

सदाशिवाय स्वाहा

इत्येतेषु दिवसेषु हविर् लिङ्गपूजान्ते कार्यं।

शुद्धान्नमाज्ययुक्तं दधिप्लुतं कुक्कुटाण्डप्रमाणं क्षिपेत्।

विशेषबलिः।

गोस्थाने रुद्राय कुम्भोदराय कुशेषु लङ्कायै नदीषु गङ्गायै तटाके क्षेत्रमूर्तये सभास्थाने सरस्वत्यै दुर्गायै कोशे महालक्ष्म्यै गोपुरे भीमाय स्वाहा इत्येवं सायं प्रातः बलिं दिशेत्।

ब्रह्मस्थानादि बलिपीठान्तं दण्डान्तं वा आल्यं प्रविश्य बलिपीठे शेषं क्षिपेत्।

अन्नलिङ्गं जले विसृज्य पादौ प्रकाल्याचम्य शुद्ध भस्मनोद्धूल्य प्रवेशयेदिति बलिप्रमाणविधिः।

१४ यानक्रमविधिः

पूर्वोक्तवत् वीथीः समलङ्कृत्य रथे रङ्गे खेटके शिबिकादौ वा नानालङ्कारपुष्पप्रभासमायुक्तं देवं शक्त्या सहितं मूलस्थाने समानीयावाह्य धूपदीपौ दत्वा पुष्पाञ्जलिना अभ्यर्च्य शक्त्यादिभक्तान्तबेरसहितं प्रदक्षिणमुपक्रमेत्।

अग्रतो नानालङ्कारसहितं भेर्यादिवाद्यसहितं शैलार्दितदन्तराले नन्दिं विनायकसुब्रह्मण्यौ मध्ये देव्या सह सोमास्कन्दं अग्रतः पृष्ठतो वा भक्तबेरांश्च तत्पश्चात् चण्डेश्वरं च देशिकः सव्यभागे स्थित्वा मूलमघोरं वासंख्यं जपेत्।

वामभागे नृपः पृष्ठदेशे भृत्याः देवस्य पुरतो नर्तकवंशकगायकमर्दलकाश्च पार्श्वद्वये नृत्तयुक्तानि रुद्रगणिका अग्रे महाशैवाः पृष्ठतो वेदादिघोषसंयुताः तत्पश्चात् चातुर्वर्णोद्भवाः माहेश्वराश्च अनुगच्चन्तः अश्वमेधफलं प्राप्नुवन्ति।

एवं देवं सन्तोष्य प्रथमेऽहनि प्रातः रङ्गं रात्रौ सिंहं द्वितीयेऽहनि सूर्यसोमयन्त्रं तृतीये भूतयन्त्रं रात्रौ हंसं चतुर्थे नागं रात्रौ वृषभं वृषप्रदक्षिणान्तराले परिवेषणं कुर्यात्।

परिवेषणं।

तद्यथा -उद्यानादिष्वं कणेकणे वेदस्तुतिश्रुतिवीणावेणुगायकनृत्तकरुद्रगणिकासहितं फलाद्युपहारैस् ताम्बूलादिभिश्च पदे पदे देवं सन्तोष्य आलयं प्रवेशयेत्।

पञ्चमेऽहनि आन्दोलिका रात्रौ शिखरियुक्ता रावणयन्त्रं षष्ठेऽहनि शिबिकायां खेटका वा समारोप्य चूर्णोत्सवं वक्ष्यमाणवत् कृत्वा कुङ्कुमकुसुम्भहरिद्रादिजलैश्च देवान् संप्रोक्ष्य कुङ्कुमपङ्कैर् देवानालिप्य सर्वान् प्रोक्षयेत्।

रात्रौ गजारूढं सप्तमे रथं रात्रौ कल्पतरौ अष्टमे प्रातः आन्दोलिका रात्रौ अश्वारोपणं कृत्वा यानकाले अश्वारूढा कुन्ताद्यायुधयुक्ताः धनुः खेटकयुक्ताः सर्वालङ्कारसहितरुद्रगणिकाः परितो व्रजेयुः।

अत्रान्तरे दुष्टनिग्रहशिष्टपरिपालनं कृत्वा सकलधर्माधर्मान् श्रावयित्वा आलयं प्रवेशयेत्।

नवाहे पुरुषयन्त्रयुक्तान्दोलिका सखेटके रात्रौ कृष्णगन्धं दशमेऽहनि रत्नसिंहासने शिबिकादौ वा देवं समारोप्य पुरादिकं प्रदक्षिणीकृत्य हर्म्याग्रे ध्वजाग्रे विकृतान्नं परिभ्राम्य तच्चतुष्पथे प्रक्षिपेत्।

अनन्तरं गरुणा सुवासिनीभिः रुद्रगणिकाभिर्वा नीराञ्जनं कारयेत्।

ततो गोपुराग्रे ध्वजाग्रे वा देवाय घटदीपं दत्वा अनन्तरं घटदीपसहिता रात्रिकनीराञ्जनहस्तयुक्ता रुद्रगणिका नृत्तगीतादिभिः सकलवाद्यैस्सह प्रदक्षिणं क्रमात् कृत्वा शैलादिनन्दिविनायकस्कन्ददेवीभक्तचण्डेश्वरैस्सह प्रातः प्रदक्षिणीकृत्य आलयं व्रजेयुः।

ततो मङ्गलगायन्तीभिः सर्ववाद्यैस्सह सोमास्कन्दमालयं प्रवेशयित्वास्थानमण्टपादौ संस्थाप्य प्रच्छन्नपटं कृत्वा महाहविं निवेद्य सर्वोपचारैः सम्पूज्य श्रमहरणार्थं नालिकेरेक्षुसारमुद्गतत्कालोचितफलानि निवेद्य ब्राह्मणान् गन्धपुष्पैरलङ्कृत्य भोजयेत्।

शिवभक्तान् दीनांदींश्च अविचारेण भोजयेत्।

अथवान्यप्रकारेण यानं कुर्यादिति यानक्रमविधिः।

१५ नीराञ्जनविधिः -

नीराञ्जनार्थं स्वर्णरजतताम्रकांस्यादिपात्राणि वितस्तिविस्तार मोष्ठमेकाङ्गुलं पञ्च संगृह्य मण्डलोपरि विन्यस्य गन्धपुष्पादिनाग्निबीजेन ब्रह्मभिरभ्यर्च्य चतुस्संस्कारैः संस्कृत्य शूलमुद्रां धेनुमुद्रां प्रदर्श्य स्वस्तिसूक्तैर् मङ्गलवाचकैः सपिष्टैः पात्रैः दीपमादाय शिरसि निधाय ग्रामप्रदक्षिणं कृत्वा देवस्याग्रे मण्डलके संस्थाप्य देवस्य शिरःप्रभृतिपादान्तं त्रिधा त्रिधा ब्रह्मभिः परिभ्राम्य दर्पणछत्रचामरव्यजनभस्मादि समर्प्य मूलेन शिवाय पुष्पाञ्जलिं दत्वा प्रणम्य गणिकाभिः पूर्ववत् वाहयित्वा पाद्यादिभिस्सह पीठाग्रे वृषाग्रे वा प्रक्षिपेत्।

पादप्रक्षालनादिकं कृत्वा आलयं प्रविशेदिति नीराञ्जनविधिः।

१६ तीर्थसंग्रहणविधिः।

तीर्थस्य पूर्वस्मिन् दिने तीर्थं संग्रहेत्।

रक्षां पूर्ववत् कृत्वा आशिषो वाचयित्वा मण्टपमध्ये मनोन्मनीकरकं तत्परितोष्टकर्करीस्संस्थाप्य मध्ये -

सिन्दूराभां त्रिणेत्राममृतशशिकलां शेखरीं रक्तवस्त्रां

पीनोत्तुङ्गप्रवृत्तस्तनभरनमितां यौवनारम्भणाढ्याम्।

नानालङ्कारयुक्तां सरसिजनिलयां बीजसंक्रान्तमूर्तीं देवीं

पाशाङ्कुशाढ्यां अभयवरकरां विश्वयोनिं नमामि॥

इति ध्यात्वा संपूज्य पूर्वाद्यष्टघटेषु

गङ्गायै नमः

यमुनायै नमः

नर्मदायै नमः

सरस्वत्यै नमः

सिन्धवे नमः

गोदावर्यै नमः

कावेर्यै नमः

ताम्रपर्ण्यै नमः

इत्यावाहनादिसर्वोपचारैः संपूज्य शिरसा वाहयित्वा अस्त्रसमन्वितं सर्वातोद्यसमायुक्तं पुरं प्रदक्षिणीकृत्य नद्यादितीर्थेषु स्नानार्थं संप्रदेशयेदिति तीर्थसंग्रहणविधिः।

१७ चूर्णोत्सवविधिः।

तीर्थसंग्रहदिवसाद् अपरदिनेषु बलिदानात् परं चूर्णमारभेत्।

प्रासादाग्रे स्थण्डिलद्वितये पद्ममालिख्य पुण्याहं वाचयित्वा दर्भैः परिस्तीर्य एकस्मिन् शूलं संस्थाप्य प्लक्षोदुम्बराश्वत्थपटादिवृक्षेण उलूखलं मुसलं खादिरेण सलक्षणं कृत्वा परैः संस्थाप्य अस्त्रेण संप्रोक्ष्य चतुस्संस्कारैः संस्कृत्य उलूखलं मुसलं च वस्त्रेणावेष्ट्य ब्रह्मदैवत्यमिति उलूखलास्त्रयोर् मध्ये रुद्रकुम्भं परितो लोकपालाष्टकलशान् संपूज्य-

यद्वा - शिवं चाभ्यर्च्य

उलूखले परितः पूर्वादिदलेषु दूर्वा सहदेवी कोष्ठं रजनीं तैलफलताम्बूलगन्धपुष्पभस्म संस्थाप्य चतुस्संस्कारैः संस्कृत्य उलूखले पृथ्वीं मुसले मेरुमभ्यर्च्य तदुलूखले प्रक्षिप्य पदमन्त्रेण वा भक्तस्तोत्रेण वा मुसलाघातेन गणिकाभिः चूर्णीकृत्य तच्चूर्णं रजन्यां तैलघृतगन्धाख्योदकेन मिश्रीकृत्य सहिरण्यमाचार्यः तच्चूर्णं

गृहीत्वा पात्रेषु निक्षिप्य संस्कृत्य मूललिङ्गे भस्मना सह दापयित्वा कुङ्कुमोष्णीषं धृत्वा तत्पङ्कैरालिप्य निवेद्य धूपदीपौ दत्वा सर्वेषां बेराणां च चूर्णं धृत्वा तत्पङ्केन आलिप्य पद्ममुद्रां प्रदर्श्य स्वयं च धृत्वा सर्वेषां च उष्णीषरजनीफलताम्बूलादि दत्वा पुरादिकं त्रिशूलेन सह प्रदक्षिणीकृत्य आलयं प्रवेशयेत्।

अथवा - अस्त्रकुम्भं वज्रादिकलशांश्च संस्थाप्य संपूजयेदिति चूर्णोत्सवविधिः।

पश्चात् पूर्ववद् अङ्कुरं कृत्वा तीर्थस्नानमाचरेत्।

१८ तीर्थस्नानं।

सर्वेषां अस्पृष्टैः स्पृष्टदोषनिवृत्यर्थं तीर्थप्रसादसिध्यर्थं सर्वदेवप्रियावहं धर्मादिफलसिध्यर्थं सालोक्यादिपदप्राप्त्यर्थं तीर्थतीरे शक्त्या सह अस्त्रराजसोमास्कन्दाद्यङ्कुरछत्रचामरादि नानावाद्यघोषस्तुतिभिः सार्धं तीर्थकुम्भसहितं विहितप्रपादिके देवान् संस्थाप्य तदग्रे स्थण्डिले मनोन्मनीं मध्ये गङ्गाद्यष्टकुम्भांश्चावतीर्य पालिकयासह संस्थाप्य विशेषतः संपूज्य ईशान्यां दुर्गां आवाह्य त्रिशूलसन्निधौ त्रयस्त्रिंशद्देवताश्च अष्टादशगणांश्च लोकपालांश्च आवाहनं कृत्वा अस्त्रादिदेवतानां कौतुकं विसृज्य तीर्थमध्ये प्रक्षिप्य पालिकैस्सह शिवाद्यस्त्रपर्यन्तं तत्तत् घटैर् अभिषिच्य सर्वजनैः सार्धं स्नानमाचरेत्।

ततः आचार्यः तीर्थदेवानुद्वास्य आलयं प्रविश्य सर्वेषां देवानां स्वं स्वं कुम्भमभिषिच्य नैवेद्य धूपदीपादि दत्वा आलयं प्रविश्य स्थानस्थाः सर्वे आचार्यहस्ते ब्रह्मघोषसहिता आशयक्षतां दत्वा देशिक आशयक्षतैर् आशीर्वादपुरस्सरं स्वं स्वं स्थानं प्रवेशयेदिति तीर्थस्नानविधिः।

१९ घटस्नानविधिः।

हरोत्सवस्य चूर्णार्थं जनानां स्थितिकरणार्थं देवप्रसादसिध्यर्थं इन्द्रादिदेवतासामिप्यसिध्यर्थं घटस्नानं कारयेत्।

कुण्डेषु विशेषहोमं विधाय कुण्डेषु विशेषेण पूर्णाहुतीः जुहुयुः।

तत्तदीशं प्रधाने संयोज्य शिवमभ्यर्च्य पुनः पूर्णां दत्वा शिवकुम्भादीन् विशेषेण अभ्यर्च्य संयोज्य धूपदीपौ दत्वा आचार्यादिभ्यो यथोक्त दक्षिणां दत्वा परिचारकादिभ्यो वस्त्रहेमादि दत्वा पूर्ववत् कुम्भान् उद्धृत्य आलयं प्रदक्षिणीकृत्य गर्भगेहं प्रविश्य संस्थाप्य षडध्वन्यासपूर्वं मूललिङ्गेऽभिषेचयेत्।

वर्धनीं पीठे विघ्नेशकलशान् तत्तत्स्थानेऽभिषिच्य देवीं श्रीकण्ठन्यासपुरस्सरं कलशेन अभिषिच्य महाहविर् निवेद्य धूपदीपौ दत्वा अग्निसदनं यायात्।

शिवाग्नौ सशिरसा मूलाघोरासिना शताधिकं हुत्वा पूर्णां दत्वा अग्निं यागेशे संयोज्य गुरूपदिष्टप्रकारेण कुम्भवर्धन्यादि पञ्चावरणादेव तत्तत्स्थाने संयोज्य तमपि विसर्जयेत्।

अथ देवं जलक्रीडादिभिः सन्तोष्य प्रभूतहविषं दत्वा बिम्बं प्रति स्नपनं कारयेत्।

इति घटस्नानविधिः।

२० अवरोहणम्।

दुष्टनिग्रह शिष्टपरिपालनार्थं तीर्थदिवस पूर्वाह्लादिके रात्रौ वा ब्रह्मतालपठनपूर्वं अवरोहणं कर्तव्यं उत्तमोत्तमप्रकारेणेति ध्वजस्थं वृषभे संयोज्य वृषमपि शिवाग्रे स्थितविग्रहे समारोप्यावरणदेवांश्च तदावरणे संयोज्य यथाविधि पूजयेत्।

तद्दिने मौनबलिः।

होमान्ते हविर्भागं देवतानामिति उक्तत्वात् तन्निमित्तं मौनबलिमारभेत्।

आचार्यः सोमास्कन्दसमीपं गत्वा शक्त्यादिशक्त्यन्तं संपूज्य दण्डभङ्गी मुण्डभङ्गी एकत्रिंशत्कलान्यासं श्रीकण्ठन्यासं च कृत्वा ध्यायेत्।

ध्यानम्।

दक्षालम्बित निद्रितान्यपदयादेवायुतं मध्यतः।
स्कन्देनाब्जकरद्वयेन सहितं सोमं गुहेशं भजे॥

इति साङ्गं पञ्चावरणोपेतं प्रचुरेण संपूज्य वक्ष्यमाणवत् तद्देवीं ध्यात्वाभ्यर्च्य जगतः शुभं प्राथ्य तस्मात् लब्धानुज्ञो मौनव्रतधरो बद्धाञ्जलिपुटो भूत्वा अन्नलिङ्गसमन्वितं अस्त्रादिदेवान् याने समारोप्य गन्धपुष्पादिसंयुक्ता खड्गखेटकास्त्रादिसंयुक्ता बहुरूपं हृदि स्मरन्तो मौनव्रतधरा वाद्यघोषं विना ग्रासार्थं कुक्कुटाण्डमात्रं वा ब्रह्मस्थानादिसन्दिष्टपीठेषु तत्तत्स्थाने वाद्यघोषसहितं ध्वजावरोहणपूर्वं बलिं विधाय पूर्ववत् सन्धिदेवान् यथाक्रमेण विसृज्य प्रदक्षिणीकृत्य आलयं प्रविश्य अवरुह्य पूर्वस्थले विन्यस्य सर्वानपि च अन्नलिङ्गं जले विसर्जयेदित्यवरोहणविधिः

२१ चण्डोत्सवविधिः।

पश्चात् चण्डमूर्तिं यागालये समानीय तत्कुम्भेन अभिषिच्य यथाविधि संपूज्य निर्माल्यादिना विभूष्य प्रायश्चित्तं अग्नौ शतं सहस्रमर्धं वा हुत्वा तमपि विसृज्य आलयं तौर्यत्रिकेण भक्तजनैस्सार्धं प्रदक्षिणीकृत्य तत्स्थाने निवेशयेदिति चण्डोत्सवविधिः।

२२ आचार्यपूजा।

आचार्यं पूजयेत् पश्चात् दक्षिणां च प्रदापयेत्।
गोभूमिहेमरत्नादि वस्त्रान्तानि प्रदापयेत्॥
आचार्यमनसस्तृप्तिस् तस्मात् तृप्तिः परश्शिवः॥इति॥

तमपि ऋत्विग्भिस्सह शिववत् संपूज्य रथे शिबिकादौ वा संस्थाप्य नानावाद्यैर् नृत्तगीतादिभिर् वेदादिघोषैर् भक्तसमितिभिश्च छत्रचामरादिनानाविधदीपैस्सह भूपयजमानसर्वजनैश्च पुरं प्रदक्षिणीकृत्य यानेन सह स्वगृहं प्रवेशयेद् इत्याचार्योत्सवविधिः।

२३ रथारोहणम्

सप्तमेन वा रथारोहणं कार्यं तत्पूर्वरात्रौ रक्षां कृत्वा प्रभाते स्नपनाभिषेकं नित्यपूजावसाने विधाय यथाविधि संपूज्य अग्निकार्योक्तमार्गेण चरुहवनप्रायश्चित्तान्तं पूर्ववत् कृत्वा आज्यं मूलेन समिदीशेन चरुं अघोरेण हृदा लाजं वामेन तिलं कवचेन गुलं नेत्रेण बिल्वं यथाशक्ति हुत्वा ईशाने द्रव्याणि धान्यानि हृदा व्याहृतीभिश्च हुत्वा पूर्णां दत्वा यागेशं निरुध्य रक्षां समर्प्य पूर्णकुम्भं तिलपात्रं सवत्साङ्गां दर्शयित्वा ब्राह्मणेभ्यो दद्यात्।

विघ्नेशं संपूज्य मोदकं निवेद्य देवतानां पायसं निवेद्य पश्चात् रौप्यकटाहे कुङ्कुमागरुकर्पूरचन्दनहरिद्राद्यैर् वारिणा संयोज्य कटाहे पाटल्युत्पलजातिपुन्नागचम्पकाद्यादि पङ्कं निक्षिप्य कुङ्कुमवस्त्रादिना कटाहं परिवेष्य शिवाग्रे स्थण्डिले विन्यस्य कटाहे कामबीजेन अभ्यर्च्य आर्द्रपङ्कं मूलेन अभ्यर्च्य संस्कृत्य धूपदीपौ दत्वा मूललिङ्गादिबेराणां च तद्दत्वा देशिकः स्वयं च ऋत्विग्भिः सह आर्द्रपङ्कं कुङ्कुमोष्णीषं च भूपयजमानभक्तादि सर्वजनानां आर्द्रपङ्कं उष्णीषं ददेत्।

पश्चात् रथं पञ्चगव्यं पुण्याहजलेन संप्रोक्ष्य रथं चतुस्संस्कारैः संस्कृत्य तस्मिन् देवं समारोप्य स्थापयित्वा रथे सर्वान् देवान् प्रपूजयेत्।

चक्रेषु

सूर्याय नमः

चन्द्रमसे नमः

परितः

हरये नमः

वज्रिणे नमः

एकाङ्घ्रये नमः

द्विदण्डकाय नमः

इत्यभ्यर्च्य पताकासु शतरुद्रान् गात्रेषु धर्मादीन्

स्थलिकायां

सदाशिवाय नमः

सन्धिषु

दक्षिणामूर्तये नमः

विष्णवे नमः

ब्रह्मणे नमः

स्कन्दाय नमः

इत्यभ्यर्च्य रथप्रान्तान् लोकपालान् रज्जुषु

उरगेभ्यो नमः

इत्येवं क्रमेण अभ्यर्च्य विचित्रपटवस्त्राद्यैर् अलङ्कृत्य दिग्विदिक्षु द्वारपार्श्वे च सैंहकदलीपूगस्तम्बकं नालिकेर विचित्रपटादिना सुशोभितं कृत्वा ब्रह्माणं सारथ्यं कल्पयित्वा सच्छत्रे पाशुपतास्त्रं आवाह्य सध्वजे वृषमभ्यर्च्य

पञ्चवर्णं महादीप्तं अभयं वरदान्वितम्।
षड्दश्चैककुक्षिं च शूलं पाशं चतुर्भुजम्॥
एकवक्त्रं त्रिणेत्रञ्च षड्बलं मङ्गलान्वितम्।
पादचक्रसमायुक्तं भूताधारं च जाङ्घिकम्॥
प्रौढस्थलं सुजान्वाख्यं उपरिस्थलमूरुकम्।
कुक्षिर्देवासनं प्रोक्तं हृदयं स्तम्भवर्गकम्॥
कूटस्कन्धद्वयं प्रोक्तं सर्वमङ्गलकारणम्।

इति ध्यात्वा संपूजयेत्।

एवं देवीस्कन्दवैनायकचण्डेश्वरांश्च तत्तद्रथे समारोप्य आर्द्रपङ्कं हृदालिप्य कुङ्कुमोष्णीषं कवचेन धृत्वा फलापूपादि निवेद्य रक्तपुष्पैरभ्यर्च्य दानादि दत्वा आचार्यादि भक्तानां वस्त्रहेमफलताम्बूलानि दत्वा सर्वान् सन्तोष्य सुमुहूर्ते शुभांशे चरलग्ने स्वस्तिपूर्वं समस्तवाद्ययुक्तं पुरं प्रदक्षिणीकृत्य रथादवतार्य आलयं प्रविश्य स्नपनपूर्वं स्नापयित्वा शिल्पादिरथनियन्तृणां वस्त्रादि दत्वा महाहविर् निवेद्य सर्वेषां दापयेदिति रथारोहणविधिः।

२४ नृत्तमूर्त्युत्सवः।

कृष्णगन्धविधिः।

इष्टकाम्यार्थसिध्यर्थं सुपुत्रावाप्तिहेतुकं।
ब्रह्महत्यादिहननं सर्वशत्रुनिबर्हणम्॥
यो वा को वा नृत्तमूर्तिदर्शनात् फलमश्नुते।

तदनु नृत्तमूर्तिमास्थानमण्टपे समानीय अष्टम दिन अपररात्रौ रक्षां पूर्ववत् कृत्वा फलताम्बूलादि युक्तं हस्ते कृत्वा चित्रवस्त्रादिना उभावप्यलंकृत्य नैवेद्यादि दत्वा आलयं प्रदक्षिणीकृत्य मण्टपे संस्थाप्य विनोददर्शनेन रात्रिशेषं व्यपोहयेत्।

अपरेद्युर् उत्सवान्तं कारयित्वा सायाह्नसमये देवाग्रे स्थण्डिलद्वितयं विधाय पद्ममालिख्य दर्भैः पुष्पैः परिस्तीर्य तन्मध्ये कालागरुं संस्थाप्य विनायकपूजा पुरस्सरं पुण्याहं वाचयित्वा शान्तिकुम्भं विधिवद् विधाय संपूज्य अग्निकार्योक्तमार्गेण कुण्डसंस्कारादिपूर्णान्तं विधाय तस्मिन् महेशं संपूज्य समिल्लाजसर्षपयवतिलादीन् प्रत्येकं तं मूलेन अष्टोत्तरशतं हुत्वा बिल्वोत्पलकदलीपनसादींश्च मधुत्रयाणि च हुत्वा द्रव्यान्ते व्याहृतिर् हुत्वा पूर्णां दत्वा देवं

संस्नाप्य अलङ्कृत्य स्थलिकायां तण्डुलेनापूरितायां कृष्णगन्धं निधाय वस्त्रेणावेष्ट्य शान्तिकुम्भजलेन प्रोक्ष्य कर्पूराद्यैः सुगन्धिभिर् मिश्रितं अस्त्रेण संशोध्य वर्मणावकुण्ठ्य ब्रह्माङ्गैर् अभिमन्त्र्य मूलेन संपूज्य धेनुमुद्रां प्रदर्श्य पाद्याचमनार्घ्यधूपदीपादि दत्वा सम्पाताभिर्हुतं कृत्वा चूर्णां विधाय अग्निं विसृज्यालयं शङ्खदुन्दुभिः वाद्यघोषसहितं प्रदक्षिणीकृत्य गर्भगेहं प्रविश्य मूललिङ्गे समर्प्य अनन्तरं महेशाग्रे संस्थाप्य शक्त्यादिशक्त्यन्तासने दण्डमुण्डभङ्ग्या च एकत्रिंशत्कलात्मकं श्रीकण्ठन्यासं च विधाय।

सङ्कीर्णज्जटमिन्दुहेमकुररी मुण्डास्थिदेवापगा
श्वेतार्क मुद्रराज पिञ्चकधरं वैयाघ्रकृत्यम्बरम्।
सर्वं सव्यकरेऽभयं डमरुकं वामं प्रसार्यान्यकं
वामेऽग्निं दधतं शयानभरितापस्मारपृष्ठे स्थितम्॥
वक्रीकृत्य स्वदक्षिणं तु चरणं चोद्धृत्य वामं पदं
मध्यस्थध्वजकिङ्किणी मणितुलाकोटिस्फुरत्पादुकम्।
दक्षे नक्रसुकुण्डलं श्रुतिपुटे वामे तु पत्रान्वितं
भस्मा लिप्तमुमायुतं त्रिणयनं वन्दे नटेशं शिवम्॥

इति ध्यात्वा

श्यामा द्विनेत्रा द्विभुजा त्रिभङ्गी सव्यापस्थितकुञ्चिताङ्घ्री।
सव्योत्पलावा कटकान्विताढ्या हस्तावलम्बा परमेश्वरी स्यात्॥

इत्युभावपि संपूज्य धूपदीपादि दत्वा पैष्टेन पायसेन फलापूपादिना च सह निवेद्य ताम्बूलं दत्वा कृष्णगन्धलेपनं कार्यं।

ललाटे अघोरेण शिखया बाह्वौ सर्वत्र सद्येन वा दापयेत्।

पश्चात् सदाशिवादिमूर्तीनां दापयेत्।

स्त्रीबेराणां ललाटे गले तन्मूलेन हृदा वा धारयेत्।

पश्चाद्देशिको मूर्तिपैस्सह धृत्वा सर्वेषां साधकादिभक्तजनानां च दापयेत्।

देवं रत्नसिंहासने तद्वामे गौरीं सव्ये देशिकेन सहारोप्य वामतोऽग्रतो वा नृपः नर्तकनर्तकीमर्दकाश्च उभयोः पार्श्वयोः गेयनर्तनं च कृत्वा वाद्यैस्सह सप्तग्रहपर्यन्तं नटित्वा आलयं प्रविश्य नीराजनादि पूर्ववत् कुर्यात्।

पश्चाद् आस्नानमण्टपे संस्थाप्य साष्टाङ्गं अर्घ्यं दत्वा फलैस्सह निवेद्य नीराजनाद्यैः पूजयेत्।

पश्चात् गव्यस्नपनादीनां संस्नाप्य शुद्धकर्पूरं पूर्ववत् संस्कृत्य फालादिसर्वाङ्गं धृत्वा सुश्वेतैर् जातिपुष्पैः शुक्लवस्त्रैश्च अलङ्कृत्य पायसान्नं निवेद्य धूपदीपौ दत्वा यानकाले पङ्क्तियानं शनैश्शनैः कार्यं।

तत्र वेदनृत्तगीतादिभिः गोपुराग्रे ध्वजाग्रे वा पूर्ववत् पङ्क्तियानं कृत्वा नीराजनादि सर्वं पूर्ववत् कृत्वा आलयं प्रविश्य सर्वोपचारैः संपूज्य रात्रिशेषं विनोददर्शनेन व्यपोहयेत्।

अरुणोदये नृत्तेषं संपूज्य अलङ्कृत्य नद्यादौ पूर्ववत् तीर्थं कृत्वा कौतुकं विसृज्य पुरादिकं प्रदक्षिणीकृत्य शुद्धदेशे कृदुष्टनिग्रहशिष्टपरिपालनं सर्वव्यवहारवाचकं च श्रावयित्वा देव्याः प्रणयकलहं व्यपोह्य परिवेषं विनालयं प्रवेशयेदिति स्वस्थाने संस्थाप्य स्नपनाद्यैर् अभिषिच्य शुद्धनृत्तं कारयेदिति कृष्णगन्धविधिः।

२५ वैवाहिकं।

अनन्तरं दशमे सप्तमे पञ्चमे वाह्नि विवाहं विधिवत् औपचारिकेण कल्याणव्रतोत्सवं कारयेत्।

२६ देव्युत्सवविधिः।

नवाहञ्च सप्ताहं त्र्यहं एकाहं वा उत्सवं कारयेत्।

एकादशदिवसर्रात्राविन्द्रविमानादिसर्वमलङ्कृत्य संप्रोक्ष्य स्नपनपूर्वं देवं अभिषिच्य अलङ्कृत्य देवान् सर्वान् तत्तद्विमानं अधिरोप्य पुरप्रदक्षिणकाले ऐशान्यां दिशि प्रपां पुष्पादिध्वजैर् अलङ्कृत्य तन्मध्ये विमानस्थं शिवमानीय तं देविपूर्वचण्डेशान्तं भूपयजमानवाद्यैस्सह प्रदक्षिणत्रयं कारयित्वालयप्रवेशकाले गोपुराग्रे हर्म्याग्रे वा प्रणयकलह व्यपोहनं विनोददर्शनं च कारयित्वा यथाविधि प्रवेशयेदिति देव्युत्सवविधिः।

२७ भक्तोत्सवविधिः।

अथ भक्तबेरादीन् शिवाग्रे मण्टपे वा संस्थाप्य स्नपनपूर्वं चलाचलबेरानभिषिच्य अलङ्कृत्य चूर्णोत्सवं पूर्ववत् कृत्वा भक्तबेराणां धृत्वा आचार्य साधकादीनां दीक्षितानां भक्तानां चूर्णां दापयित्वा कुङ्कुमोष्णीष पवित्रमालादि दत्वा भक्तस्तुतिभिः स्तुत्वा शिवभक्तानां ताम्बुलादि दत्वा पुरं प्रदक्षिणीकृत्य आलयं प्रविश्य तत्तत्स्थाने सर्वान् संस्थाप्य निवेद्य धूपदीपौ दत्वा शिवगानविदां वस्त्रादि दापयेदिति भक्तोत्सवविधिः।

२८ उत्सवशान्तिः।

अपरेद्युः महास्नपनपूर्वं शान्तिहोममूर्तिहोमदिशाहोमादिकं क्रमेण कृत्वाभिषिच्य श्रमहरणं कारयेत्।

२९ उत्सवपञ्चककृत्यं।

उत्सवं पञ्चधा प्रोक्तं स्थित्युपत्तिलयात्मकम्।
तिरोभावानुग्रहञ्च सृष्ट्याद्यं पञ्चकृत्यकम्॥
अङ्कुरार्पणकल्याणं ध्वजारोहणमेव च।
रक्षाबन्धनमित्युक्तं सृष्टिकर्ममुदाहृतम्॥
वाहनोत्सवसंयुक्तं होमकर्मबलिभ्रमम्।
स्थितिकर्ममिति प्रोक्तं संहारः कथ्यतेऽधुना॥
रात्रिचूर्णसमायुक्तं रथारोहणमेव च।
कालागरूत्सवं चैवं आगमेषु प्रसिद्धितम्॥
मौनोत्सवतिरोभावं शक्तियात्रात्वनुग्रहम्।
तीर्थस्य दिवसाद्यन्ते प्रणयः कलहोत्सवः॥
बीजक्षेत्रे समायुक्तं सृष्ट्याद्यं पञ्चकृत्यकम्।

इति परमेश्वरा परनामधेय श्रीमदघोरशिवाचार्यविरचितायां क्रियाक्रमद्योतिकायां वैनायकोत्सवादिभक्तोत्सवान्तविधिः समाप्तः।

मासोत्सवविधिः।

३० पुण्यकालविधिश्च।

सक्रान्तिसमयस्सूक्ष्मो दुर्ज्ञेयो विशितेक्षणैः।
तद्योगाच्चाप्यधश्चोर्ध्वं त्रिंशन्नाड्यः पवित्रता॥
भविष्यत्ययने पुण्यस् त्रिंशदेव तु दक्षिणे।
अतीत उत्तरे नाड्य इति प्रोक्ता हरद्विजाः॥
सङ्क्रान्ति विषुवं चैव विशेषेणायनद्वयम्।
वृषवृश्चिककुम्भेषु सिंहे चैव तु दक्षिणे॥
एतत् विष्णुपदं नाम विषुवादधिकं फलम्।
कन्यायां मिथुने मीने धनुष्यपि रवेर्गतिः।
षडशीतिमुखाः प्रोक्ताः पुण्याधिकतमा द्विजाः॥
नाड्यः षोडशपूर्वेण सङ्क्रान्तेरपरेण च।
वर्तमाने तुलामेषे नाड्यस्तूभयतो दश॥
भविष्यत्ययने विष्णौ वर्तमाने तथा विषौ।
षडशीतिमुखे चैव ह्यतीते चोत्तरायणे॥
राहुदर्शनसङ्क्रान्ति विवाहात्ययवृद्धिषु।
स्नानदानादिकं कार्यं निशि काम्यव्रतेषु च॥
देवोत्सवं च तत्रैव पूजां कुर्याच्छिवस्य च।
या यास्सन्निहिता नाड्यः तास्ताः पुण्यतमा स्मृताः॥

अथ सङ्क्रान्तिसमयेऽपि पूर्ववत् स्नपनादि पुरस्सरं देवमभिषिच्य मूललिङ्गादीन् सर्वालङ्कारैर् अलङ्कृत्य सर्वातोद्य समन्वितं विनायकसोमास्कन्दादिभक्तबेरसहितं ग्रामं वा पुरं आलयं वा प्रदक्षिणं नीत्वा ब्रह्मस्थाने वृषाग्रे वा पूर्वं नीराजनादि कृत्वा स्वस्थाने निवेशयेदिति।

एवं यः क्रियते राष्ट्रे मासदोषो न विद्यते।
तस्मात् सर्वप्रयत्नेन उत्सवं सम्यगाचरेत्॥

इति मासोत्सव विधिः।

३१ अमावास्योत्सवः।

अथ पक्षोत्सवविधौ
अष्टमेऽम्शे चतुर्दश्यां क्षीणो भवति चन्द्रमाः।
अमावास्यष्टमेंशे वा पुनः किल भवेदणुः॥
द्रष्टचन्द्रा सिनीवाली नष्टचन्द्रा कुहूर्मता।
मध्याह्नाद्या त्वमावास्या परस्था संप्रवर्तते॥
भूतविद्धा तु सा ज्ञेया न सा पञ्चदशी भवेत्।
घटिकैकाप्यमावास्या प्रतिपत्सु न चेत्तदा॥

भूतविद्धापि कर्तव्या दैवपित्र्यपि कर्मणि।
प्रतिपत्स्वप्यमावास्या पूर्वाह्णव्यापिनी यदि॥
भूतविद्धैव सा कार्या दैवकर्मणि सर्वदा।
तुलामकरमीनेषु कन्यायां मिथुने तथा।
भूतविद्धाप्यमावास्या पूज्या भवतु यत्नतः॥
चतुर्दश्यत्र संपूर्णा नन्दाद्याक्षयगामिनी।
देवोत्सवं तु भूतायां अमायां तीर्थमाचरेत्॥
अमा वै सोमवारेण रविवारेण सप्तमी।
चतुर्थी भौमवारेण विषुवत्सदृशं फलं॥
अमा वै सोमवारे तु शिवरात्रि समो भवेत्।
रात्रौ जागरणं कुर्याद् दैवोत्सवमथाचरेत्॥
अमावास्या यदार्द्रायां युक्ता चेत् सोमवासरे।
कोटियज्ञतपोदानफलं प्राप्नोति तद्व्रताम्॥

अथ अमावास्यायां मूललिङ्गाद्यास्थापनोत्थापनबेराणां पञ्चगव्यपुरस्सरं महाभिषेकं कारयित्वा सर्वालङ्कारैर् अलङ्कृत्य महाहविर् निवेद्य ग्रामखेटादिके बलिग्रहणं विना छत्रचामरादिसंयुक्तं अनेकविचित्रदीपिकासहितं नानावाद्यसहितं देवं प्रदक्षिणं नीत्वा ब्रह्मस्थाने समानीय पूर्ववन् नीराजनादि कृत्वा स्वस्थाने निवेशयेत्।

एवं यः कारयेन्मर्त्यः सपुण्यां गतिमाप्नुयात्।
पुत्रार्थी लभते पुत्रान् कन्यार्थी कन्निकां शुभां॥
धनार्थी विपुलानर्थान् मोक्षार्थी मोक्षमाप्नुयात्।
नाकालवर्षी पर्जन्यो न रोगो निरुपद्रवः॥
अमावास्योत्सवेनैव सर्वान् कामानवाप्नुयात्।

इत्यमावास्योत्सव विधिः।

३२ पौर्णमास्योत्सवविधिः।

राका चानुमती चैव पौर्णमासी द्विधामता।
या पूर्वा पौर्णमासी सानुमतिर्योत्तरा सह॥
पक्षान्ता पञ्चदश्याख्या पौर्णमासीति सा स्मृता।
षोडशेऽहन्यभीष्टेति मध्या पञ्चदशेऽहनि॥
चतुर्दशी जघन्येति पापा सप्तदशेऽहनि।
प्रतिपत् प्रभृतयस्सर्वा उदयाद्योदयाद्रवेः।
संपूर्णा इति विख्याता दैवे कर्मणि पावनि॥
युग्माग्नियामभूतानां षण्मन्योर्वसुरन्ध्रयोः।
रुद्रेण द्वादशी युक्ता चतुर्दश्या च पौर्णिमा॥
भूतविद्धाप्यमावास्या तिथ्योर्युग्ममहत्फलं।

तत्रापि पूर्वत् विघ्नेशपूजा पुरस्सरं नैवेद्यान्तं कर्म कृत्वा विघ्नेशादिदेवान् सर्वालङ्कारसंयुक्तान् पुरादि प्रदक्षिणं नीत्वा पूर्ववत् स्वस्थाने समारोपयेदिति।

समस्तविधिवच्छिद्रदोषो नश्येच्छिवाज्ञया
इति पौर्णमास्योत्सवविधिः।

३३ ऋक्षोत्सवविधिः

यत्रोक्तोस्तमयाद्धानुं नयेदुदयमिन्दुना।
तत्रैवोपवसेदृक्षं नक्षत्रं श्रवणं विना॥
यावदस्तमनादूर्ध्वं उद्भवात् त्रिमुहूर्तगा।
तत्रैवोपवसेदृक्षं स्नानं पूजां च तद्दिने॥
यत्रार्धयामादर्वाक्तु नक्षत्रं प्राप्यते दिने।
तन्नक्षत्रव्रतं कुर्याद् उदिते पारणं क्वचित्॥
कृत्तिकासु शिवं पूज्य सौख्यमाप्नोति मानवः।
अपत्यकामो रोहिण्यां सौम्ये ओजस्विवान् भवेत्॥
आर्द्रायां सर्वसम्पत्ति क्षत्रादिति पुनर्वसौ।
पुष्टिं पुष्ये हरं पूज्याश्लेषायां परान् सुतान्॥
मखासु स्वजनश्रेष्ठं सौभाग्यं पूर्वफल्गुनी।
प्रदानशीलो भवति सफल्गुन्युत्तरासु च॥
प्राप्नोति श्रेष्ठतां सत्सु हस्ते तु हरपूजकः।
स्वरूपवन्ती चित्तासु तथा पत्नीमवाप्नुयात्॥
वाणिज्यलाभदा स्वाती विशाखे बहुकामवान्।
कुर्वतां चानुराधायां दद्युश्चक्रप्रवर्तकम्॥
ज्येष्ठास्वर्थसुसम्पत्तिं मूले चारोग्यमुत्तमम्।
आद्याषाढे यशः प्राप्तिर् उत्तरासु यशोन्नता॥
श्रवणे च सुखान् भोगान् धनिष्ठासु धनं महत्।
वेदविच्चाभिजीतीतु भिषत्सिद्धिं तु वारुणे॥
अजाविकं प्रोष्ठपदे विन्देत् गाश्च तदुत्तरे।
रेवत्यां तु हरेस्सुप्यं अश्विन्यां तु तरङ्गमान्॥
पूजकस्तत्तदाप्नोति भरण्यामायुरुत्तमम्।
तस्मात् सर्वप्रयत्नेन ऋक्षेष्वेतेषु चोत्सवम्॥
तत् कोटिकोटिगुणितं आर्द्रायां चोपवासता।
हयमेधसहस्राणि यज्ञकोटिशतानि च॥
कोटिकन्याप्रदानस्य फलं प्राप्नोति शाङ्करे।
समयी पुत्रको वापि साधको हरदीक्षिताः॥

नाचरेद्यस्तु शर्वर्क्षं सपापी नरकं व्रजेत्।
ब्राह्मणा क्षत्रिया वैश्या शूद्राश्चावान्तरा नराः।
कन्या वा विधवा वापि सुमना वा यतिव्रतिः॥
दीक्षितोऽदीक्षितो वापि प्रति-ऋक्षं द्विजोत्तमाः।
रात्रौ पूजां च भुक्तिं च स्नानं दानं च तत्र तु॥
दर्शनं देवदेवस्य कृत्वा स्तुत्वा प्रणम्य च।
ब्राह्मणेभ्यो यथाशक्ति स्वर्णच्छादन भोजनैः॥

अथ सायङ्कालपूजानन्तरं घृतस्नपनं विना यथा विभवविस्तरेण सर्वान् देवान् यथाविधि संपूज्य महाहविर् निवेद्य सोमास्कन्दं छत्रचामरादिबहुविचित्रदीपिकासहितं पुरमालयं वा प्रदक्षिणं कृत्वा नीराजनादि पूर्ववत् कृत्वालयं प्रवेशयेत्।

एवं यः कारयेन्मर्त्यः सरुद्रो नात्र संशयः।
उत्पातास्तस्य नश्यन्ति ग्रहपीडाश्च दारुणाः॥
सर्वव्याधिविनिर्मुक्तश्चिरायुस्सुखमेधते।
एकस्मिन् वत्सरे विप्राः सुपुत्रं लभते ध्रुवं॥

३४ वारोत्सवः।

आदित्यवारे यद्रौद्रं प्राप्ते चारोग्यमुत्तमम्।
सोमे सौख्यप्रदं भौमे संग्रामविजयप्रदम्॥
बुधवारे सर्वकामं गुरौ विद्यास्सशास्त्रकाः।
शुक्रे महद्धनं मन्दे चापमृत्युविनाशनम्॥
एवं ज्ञात्वा प्रयत्नेन शिवं तत्र प्रपूजयेत्।

इति परमेश्वरनामधेय श्रीमदघोरशिवाचार्यविरचितायां क्रियाक्रमद्योतिकायां ब्रह्मतालादि ऋक्षोत्सवान्तविधिः समाप्तः।

References

SANSKRIT SOURCES (EDITIONS AND TRANSLATIONS)

Ajitāgama (AĀ)

Bhatt, N. R., ed. 1964–91. *Ajitāgama*. Publications de l'Institut Français d'Indologie 24. Pondichéry: Institut Français d'Indologie. 3 vols.

Bhatt, N. R., Jean Filliozat, and Pierre-Sylvain Filliozat, trs. 2005. *The Great Tantra of Ajita: Ajitamahātantra*. Kalamulasastra Granthamala, vols. 47–51. New Delhi: Indira Gandhi National Centre for the Arts. 5 vols.

Amarakośa

Colebrooke, H. T. 1990, tr. *Kosha or Dictionary of the Sanskrit Language by Amara Singh*. 3rd revised ed. Delhi: Nag Publishers.

Aṣṭaprakaraṇa

Dvivedi, Vrajavallabha, ed. 1988. *Aṣṭaprakaraṇa*. Yogatantra-Granthamala 12. Varanasi: Sampurnananda Sanskrit University.

Bhogakārikā of Sadyojyoti with Commentary of Aghoraśiva

Borody, W. A., tr. 2005. *Bhoga Kārikā of Sadyojyoti with the Commentary of Aghora Śiva*. Delhi: Motilal Banarsidass.

Kāmikāgama

See *Pūrvakāmikāgama* and *Uttarakāmikāgama*.

Kriyākramadyotikā of Aghoraśiva (*KKD*)

Krishna Sastri, Karunkulam, and Polagam Srirama Sastri, eds. 1927. *Kriyākramadyotikā (or Aghoraśivapaddhati) with the Commentary of Nirmalamaṇi*. Cidambaram: Janansambandham Press.

Davis, Richard H., and Ginette Ishimatsu, trs. 2004. "The Treatise Called the *Kriyākramadyotikā* ('Light on Ritual Procedures') written by Aghoraśivācārya (Daily Ritual)." Unpublished translation, Chennai.

Surdam, Wayne Edward, tr. 1984. "South Indian Śaiva Rites of Initiation: The *Dīkṣāvidhi* of Aghoraśivācārya's *Kriyākramadyotikā*." Ph.D. dissertation, South and Southeast Asian Studies, University of California, Berkeley.

Mahotsavavidhi of Aghoraśiva (*MV*)

Alagappa Mudaliyar, Mayilai, ed. 1910. *Mahotsavavidhi*. Chennai: Sivajnanabodha Press.

Swaminatha Gurukkal, C., ed. 1974. *Mahotsavavidhi*. Chennai: South Indian Archakar Association.

Mahotsavavidhikrama Āgamaśekhara (MĀŚ)

See *Mahotsavavidhi* of Aghoraśiva.

Mānasāra

Acharya, P. K., ed. 1933. *Mānasāra on Architecture and Sculpture*. Manasara Series 3. Oxford: Oxford University Press.

Acharya, P. K., tr. 1933. *Architecture of Mānasāra*. Manasara Series 4. Oxford: Oxford University Press.

Manusmṛti

Olivelle, Patrick. 2005. *Manu's Code of Law: A Critical Edition and Translation of the Mānava-Dharmaśāstra*. South Asia Research, edited by Patrick Olivelle. Oxford: Oxford University Press.

Mayamata (MM)

Dagens, Bruno, tr. 1994. *Mayamatam: Treatise of Housing, Architecture and Iconography*. Kalamulasastra Series 14, 2 vols. New Delhi: Indira Gandhi National Centre for the Arts.

Mṛgendrāgama

Kaul Shastri, Madhusudan, ed. 1930. *Mṛgendrāgama, vidyāpāda and yogapāda*. Kashmir Series of Texts and Studies 50. Bombay: Nirnaya Sagar Press.

Bhatt, N. R., ed. 1962. *Mṛgendrāgama (Kriyāpāda et Caryāpāda) avec le commentaire de Bhaṭṭa-Nārāyaṇakaṇṭha*. Publications de l'Institut Français d'Indologie 23. Pondicherry: Institut Français d'Indologie.

Hulin, Michel, tr. 1980. *Mṛgendrāgama: Sections de la doctrine et du yoga avec la vṛtti de Bhaṭṭanārāyaṇakaṇṭha et la dīpikā d'Aghoraśivācārya*. Publications de l'Institut Français d'Indologie 63. Pondicherry: Institut Français d'Indologie.

Brunner-Lachaux, Hélène, tr. 1985. *Mṛgendrāgama: Section des rites et section du comportement, avec le vṛtti de Bhaṭṭanārāyaṇakaṇṭha*. Publications de l'Institut Français d'Indologie, vol. 69. Pondicherry: Institut Français d'Indologie.

Nādakārikā of Rāmakaṇṭha with the commentary of Aghoraśiva

Filliozat, Pierre-Sylvain. 1984. "Les Nādakārikā de Rāmakaṇṭha." *Bulletin de l'École Française d'Extrême-Orient* 73: 223–55.

Nāṭyaśāstra of Bhāratamuni

Sivadatta, Pandit, ed. 1894. *Nāṭyaśāstra of Bhāratamuni*. Kavyamala 42. Bombay: Nirnaya Sagara Press.

Ghosh, Manmohan, tr. 1967. *The Nāṭyaśāstra (A Treatise on Ancient Indian Dramaturgy and Histrionics)*, 2d ed. Calcutta: Manisha Granthalaya.

Pañcāvaraṇastava of Aghoraśiva

Goodall, Dominic, Nibedita Rout, Sathyanarayanan, S.A.S. Sarma, T. Ganesan, and S. Sambandhasivacarya, eds. 2005. *The Paácāvaraṇastava of Aghoraśivācārya: A Twelfth-century South Indian Prescription for the Visualisation of Sadāśiva and His Retinue*. Collection Indologie 102. Pondicherry: Institut Français de Pondichery.

Prāyaścittavidhi of Aghoraśiva

Shanmukhasundara Mudaliyar, K., ed. 1961. *Prāyaścittavidhi*. Chennai: South Indian Archakar Association.

Pūrvakāmikāgama (*PKĀ*)

Alagappa Mutaliyar, Mayilai, ed. 1909. *Kāmikāgama, Pūrvabhāga and Uttarabhāga*. Chennai: Sivajnanabodha Press.

Swaminatha Gurukkal, C., ed. 1975. *Kāmikāgama, Pūrvabhāga*. Chennai: South Indian Archakar Association.

Rauravāgama (RĀ)

Bhatt, N. R., ed. 1961–88. *Rauravāgama*. Publications de l'Institut Français d'Indologie 18.1–3. Pondicherry: Institut Français d'Indologie. 3 vols.

Dagens, B., and M.-L. Barazer-Billoret, trs. 2000. *Le Rauravāgama: Un traite de rituel et de doctrine śivaites*. Publications du départment d'Indologie 89.1–2. Pondicherry: Institut Français de Pondichéry. 2 vols.

Ṛgveda (RV)

Griffith, Ralph T. H., tr. 1973. *The Hymns of the Rgveda*. Revised ed. Delhi: Motilal Banarsidass.

Van Nooten, Barend A., and Gary B. Holland, eds. 1994. *Rig Veda: A Metrically Restored Text with an Introduction and Notes*. Harvard Oriental Series 50. Cambridge: Department of Sanskrit and Indian Studies, Harvard University.

Śaivāgamaparibhāṣamañjarī of Vedajñāna (*ŚPM*)

Dagens, Bruno, ed. and tr. 1979. *Śaivāgamaparibhāṣamañjarī de Vedajñāna: Le florilege de la doctrine śivaite*. Publications de l'Institut Français d'Indologie. Pondicherry: Institut Français d'Indologie.

Śivaliṅgapratiṣṭhāvidhi

Kumāraswāmi Gurukkal, S., ed. 1994. *Śivaliṅgapratiṣṭhāvidhi*, 2d ed. Kadalur: Sri Archana Printers.

Śivapratiṣṭhāvidhi of Aghoraśiva (*ŚPV*)

Kacchapesvara Sivacarya, K., ed. 1964. *Śivapratiṣṭhāvidhi of Aghoraśiva*. Chennai: South Indian Archakar Association.

Somaśambhupaddhati of Somaśambhu (*SP*)

Subrahmanya Sastri, K. M., ed. 1931. *Kriyākaṇḍakramāvali (Somaśambhupaddhati)*. Devakottai: Sivagamasiddhantaparipalanasangha.

Zadoo, Jagaddhar, ed. 1947. *Somaśambhupaddhati (Karmakaṇḍakramāvali)*. Kashmir Series of Texts and Studies 73. Srinagar: Krishna Printing Press.

Brunner-Lachaux, Hélène, tr. 1963–98. *Somaśambhupaddhati*. Publications de l'Institut Français d'Indologie 25.1–4. Pondicherry: Institut Français d'Indologie. 4 vols.

Subrahmanyapratiṣṭhāvidhi of Aghoraśiva

Alagappa Mutaliyar, Mayilai, ed. 1920. *Subrahmanya Pratiṣṭhāvidhi*. Chennai: Sivajnanabodha Press.

Tattvaprakāśa of Bhojadeva with the commentary of Aghoraśiva

Filliozat, Pierre-Sylvain. 1971. "Le Tattvaprakāśa du roi Bhoja et les commentaires d'Aghoraśivācārya et de Śrīkumāra." *Journal Asiatique* 259: 247–95.

Gengnagel, Jorg. 1996. *Māyā, Puruṣa und Śiva: Die dualistiche Tradition des Śivaismus nach Aghoraśivācārya's Tattvaprakāśavṛtti*. Beiträge zur Kenntnis Südasiatischer Sprachen und Literaturen 3. Wiesbaden: Harrassowitz.

Tattvasamgraha of Sadyojyoti with the commentary of Aghoraśiva

Filliozat, Pierre-Sylvain. 1988. "Le Tattvasamgraha, 'Compendium des essences,' de Sadyojyoti." *Bulletin de l'École Française d'Extrême-Orient* 77: 101–63.

Tattvatrayanirṇaya of Sadyojyoti, with the commentary of Aghoraśiva

Filliozat, Pierre-Sylvain. 1991. "Le Tattvatrayanirṇaya (La determination des trois essences) de Sadyojyoti avec le commentaire d'Aghoraśivācārya." *Bulletin de l' École Française d'Extrême-Orient* 78: 133–58.

Davis, Richard H. 2000. "Sadyojyoti's 'Tattvatraya Nirṇaya.'" *Journal of Oriental Research* 68–70: 191–206.

Uttarakāmikāgama (UKĀ)

Alagappa Mutaliyar, Mayilai, ed. 1909. *Kāmikāgama, Pūrvabhāga and Uttarabhāga*. Chennai: Sivajnanabodha Press.

Swaminatha Gurukkal, C., ed. 1988. *Kāmikāgama (Uttara Bhāgam)*. Chennai: South Indian Archakar Association.

Viśvakarmiya Rathalakṣaṅ ṣa

Kulkarni, R. P. 1994. *Viśvakarmiya Rathalakṣaṇam: A Study of Ancient Indian Chariots*. Delhi: Kanishka Publishers.

SECONDARY SOURCES

Acharya, K. T. 2002. *A Historical Dictionary of Indian Food*. New Delhi: Oxford University Press.

Adicéam, Marguerite E. 1965. Les images de Śiva dans l'Inde du sud, III et IV—Bhikṣātanamūrti et Kaṅkālamūrti. *Arts Asiatiques* 12: 83–112.

———. 1971. Les images de Śiva dans l'Inde du sud: XI—Pāśupatamūrti. *Arts Asiatiques* 24: 23–50.

———. 1973. Les images de Śiva dans l'Inde du sud: XII, XIII, XIV—Sukhāsana, Umāsahitasukhāsana, Umāmaheśvaramūrti. *Arts Asiatiques* 28: 63–101.

Ali, Daud. 1996. "Regimes of Pleasure in Early India: A Genealogy of Practices at the Cola Court. " Ph.D. dissertation, University of Chicago.

———. 2004. *Courtly Culture and Political Life in Early Medieval India*. Cambridge: Cambridge University Press.

Anderson, Leona M. 1993. *Vasantotsava: The Spring Festivals of India*. Reconstructing Indian History and Culture. New Delhi: D. K. Printworld.

Balasubrahmanyam, S. R. 1979. *Later Chola Temples: Kulottunga I to Rajendra III (A.D. 1070-1280)*. Faridabad: Mudgala Trust.

Barazer-Billoret, Marie-Luce. 1999. "La grande fête du temple (mahotsava) d'après les āgama śivaites." Ph.D. dissertation, U. F. R. Orient Monde Arabe, Paris III—Sorbonne-Nouvelle.

———. 2000. "De la fête de Śiva aux 'cinq activités': Un example d'adaptation du rituel à une nouvelle norme." In *La norme et son application dans le monde indien*, edited by Marie-Luce Barazer-Billoret and Jean Fezas. Études Thématiques 11, 107–15. Paris: École Française d'Extrême-Orient.

Bhatt, N. R., ed. 1961–88. See *Rauravāgama*.

———, ed. 1962. See *Mṛgendrāgama (Kriyāpada et Caryāpada)*.

———, ed. 1964–91. See *Ajitāgama*.

———. N.d. *What Is Śaivāgama?* Pamphlet.

Bhatt, N. R., Jean Filliozat, and Pierre-Sylvain Filliozat., trs. 2005. See *Ajitagama*.

Biardeau, Madeleine. 1986. "Semis de grains dans des pots: Réflexions sur une forme." In *Essais sur le rituel 1*. Bibliothèque de l'École ses Hautes Études, Section des Sciences Religieuses, 93–117. Louvain: Peeters.

Branfoot, Crispin. 2001. "Tirumala Nayaka's 'New Hall' and the European Study of the South Indian Temple." *Journal of the Royal Asiatic Society (London)*, Third Series 11: 191–218.

Brunner, Hélène. 1964. "Les categories sociales védiques dans le Śivaisme du sud." *Journal Asiatique* 252: 451–72.

———. 1975. "Le sādhaka: Personnage oublié du Śivaisme du sud." *Journal Asiatique* 263: 411–43.

———. 1977. "Importance de la Littérature Āgamique pour l'Étude des Religions Vivantes de l'Inde." *Indologica Taurinensia* 3–4: 107–24.

———. 1988."L'ācārya śivaite: Du guru au gurukkal." *Bulletin d'Études Indiennes* 6: 145–76.

———. 1999."Le Parārthanityapūjāvidhi: Règle pour le culte quotidien dans un temple." In *Tiruvannamalai: Un lieu saint śivaite du sud de l'Inde: 3. Rites et fêtes*, edited by Françoise L'Hernault and Marie-Louise Reiniche, 263–340. Publications de l'École Française d'Extrême-Orient 156, no. 3. Paris: École Française d'Extrême-Orient.

Brunner-Lachaux, Hélène, tr. 1963–98. See *Somaśambhupaddhati.*

———, tr. 1985. See *Mṛgendrāgama.*

Ceyaraman, N. V. 1966. *Ulā Ilakkiyaṅkaḷ.* Cidambaram: Manivacakar Nulakam.

Colas, Gérard. 1986. *Le Temple selon Marīci.* Publications de l'Institut Français d'Indologie 71. Pondicherry: Institut Français d'Indologie.

———. 1996. *Viṣṇu, ses images et ses feux.* Paris: Presses de l'École Française d'Extrême-Orient.

Coomaraswamy, Ananda K. 1968. "The Dance of Shiva." In *The Dance of Shiva,* 66–78. New Delhi: Sagar Publications.

———. 1977. "Ornament." In *Coomaraswamy, 1: Selected Papers: Traditional Art and Symbolism,* edited by Roger Lipsey, 241–53. Bollingen Series 89. Princeton: Princeton University Press.

Cox, Whitney. 2005. "The Transfiguration of Tiṉṉaṉ the Archer (Studies in Cēkkiḻār's Periyapurāṇam I)." *Indo-Iranian Journal* 48, no. 3–4: 223–52.

Dagens, Bruno, ed. and tr. 1979. See *Śaivāgamaparibhāṣamañjarī.*

———. 1984. *Architecture in the Ajitāgama and the Rauravāgama.* New Delhi: Sitaram Bhartia Institute of Scientific Research.

———. tr. 1994. See *Mayamata.*

Dagens, Bruno, and M.-L. Barazer-Billoret, trs. 2000. See *Rauravaāgama.*

Davis, Richard H. 1991. *Ritual in an Oscillating Universe: Worshiping Śiva in Medieval India.* Princeton: Princeton University Press.

———. 1992. "Aghoraśiva's Background." *Journal of Oriental Research* 56–62: 367–78.

———. 1997. *Lives of Indian Images.* Princeton: Princeton University Press.

———. 2000. "Praises of the Drunken Peacocks." In *Tantra in Practice,* edited by David Gordon White, 131–45. Princeton Readings in Religion. Princeton: Princeton University Press.

———. 2002. "Chola Bronzes in Procession." In *The Sensuous and the Sacred: Chola Bronzes from South India,* edited by Vidya Dehejia, 46–63. New York: American Federation of Arts.

———. 2006. "Who's Who in the Cola Festival." In *Sahṛdaya: Studies in Indian and SouthEast Asian Art in Honour of Dr. R. Nagaswamy,* edited by B. Baumer, C. Prapandavidya, R. N. Misra, and D. Handa, 191–200. Chennai: Tamil Arts Academy.

Davis, Richard H., and Leslie C. Orr. 2007. "People of the Festival." In *Mélanges tantriques à la mémoire d'Hélène Brunner,* edited by Dominic Goodall and André Padoux, 73–97. Collection Indologie 106. Pondicherry: l'Institut Français de Pondichéry.

Day, C. R. 1974 [1891]. *The Music and Musical Instruments of Southern India and the Deccan.* 2d ed. Delhi: B. R. Publishing.

De Neve, Geert. 2000. "Patronage and 'Community': The Role of a Tamil 'Village' Festival in the Integration of a Town." *Journal of the Royal Anthropological Institute* 6, no. 3: 501–19.

Dehejia, Vidya. 2002. *The Sensuous and the Sacred: Chola Bronzes from South India.* New York: American Federation of Arts.

Diehl, Carl Gustav. 1956. *Instrument and Purpose: Studies on Rites and Rituals in South India*. Lund: CWK Gleerup.
———. 1957. "Punyāhavācana." *Orientalia Suecana* 6: 97–106.
Edholm, Eric af. 1984. "Caṇḍa and the Sacrificial Remains: A Contribution to Indian Gastrotheology." *Indologica Taurinensia* 12: 75–91.
Filliozat, Jean, and P. Z. Pattabiramin. 1966. *Parures divines du sud de l'Inde*. Publications de l'Institut Français d'Indologie 29. Pondicherry: Institut Français d'Indologie.
Filliozat, Pierre-Sylvain. 1975. "Le droit d'entrer dans les temples de Śiva au XIe siècle." *Journal Asiatique* 263: 103–17.
———. 1994. "Pandit N. Ramaccandra Bhatt and Śaivāgamas." In *Pandit N. R. Bhatt Felicitation Volume*, edited by P.-S. Filliozat, S. P. Narang, and C. P. Bhatta, 5–14. Delhi: Motilal Banarsidass.
Ganesan, T. 2005. "Śaiva Festival Calendar. " Lecture, Paris-3 University.
Gonda, Jan. 1975. "Skt. utsava—'Festival.'" In *Selected Studies, Vol. II: Sanskrit Word Studies*, 276–86. Leiden: E. J. Brill.
———. 1980. *Vedic Ritual, the Non-solemn Rites*. Handbuch der Orientalistik. Leiden: E. J. Brill.
Good, Anthony. 2004. *Worship and the Ceremonial Economy of a Royal South Indian Temple*. Mellen Studies in Anthropology 14. Lewiston, N.Y.: Edwin Mellen Press.
Goodall, Dominic. 1998. *Bhaṭṭa Rāmakaṇṭha's Commentary on the Kiraṇāgama, Vol. 1, chapters 1–6*. Publications du Département d'Indologie 86.1. Pondicherry: Institut Français de Pondichéry.
———. 2000. "Problems of Name and Lineage: Relations between South Indian Authors of the Śaiva Siddhānta." *Journal of the Royal Asiatic Society (London)*, Series 3, 10, no. 2: 205–16.
Gopinatha Rao, T. A. 1993. *Elements of Hindu Iconography*. Delhi: Motilal Banarsidass.
Harman, William P. 1989. *The Sacred Marriage of a Hindu Goddess*. Religion in Asia and Africa Series. Bloomington: Indiana University Press.
Hart, Kausalya, and Gita Pai. 2003. *Vikrama Cholan Ulaa by Ottakkuthar*. Berkeley: Department of South and South East Asian Studies, University of California.
Heesterman, J. C. 1959. "Reflections on the Significance of the Dakṣiṇā." *Indo-Iranian Journal* 3, no. 4: 241–58.
Hoffman, Lawrence A. 1987. *Beyond the Text: A Holistic Approach to Liturgy*. Jewish Literature and Culture. Bloomington: Indiana University Press.
Hudson, D. Dennis. 1977. "Śiva, Mīnākṣī, Viṣṇu—Reflections on a Popular Myth in Madurai." *Indian Economic and Social History Review* 14: 107–18.
———. 1982. "Two Citrā Festivals in Madurai." In *Religious Festivals in South India and Sri Lanka*, edited by Guy R. Welbon and Glenn E. Yocum, 101–56. Studies on Religion in South India and Sri Lanka 1. New Delhi: Manohar.
Irācārām, Turai. 2000. *Kaviccakaravartti Oṭṭakkūttararuḷiya Mūvarulā*. Chennai: Mullai Nilaiyam.

Ishimatsu, Ginette. 2000. "Aghoraśivācārya: Author of the *Parārthanityapūjāvidhi?*" *Journal of Oriental Research* 67–70: 231–46.

Janaki, S. S. 1986. *Mudrālakshaṇam (Cited in Nirmalamaṇi's Commentary Prabhā on Aghoraśivācārya's Paddhati).* Dharmapuram: International Institute of Saiva Siddhanta Research.

———. 1988. *Dhvaja-stambha (Critical Account of Its Structural and Ritualistic Details).* Madras: Kuppuswami Sastri Research Institute.

Kaali, Sundar. 1999. "Spatializing History: Subaltern Carnivalizations of Space in Tiruppuvanam, Tamil Nadu." *Subaltern Studies* 10: 126–200.

Kane, Pandurang Vaman. 1968–74. *History of Dharmaśāstra (Ancient and Mediaeval Religious and Civil Law)*, 2d ed. Government Orient Series. Poona: Bhandarkar Oriental Research Institute. 5 vols.

Kersenboom, Saskia C. 1987. *Nityasumaṅgalī: Devadasi Tradition in South India.* Delhi: Motilal Banarsidass.

Kramrisch, Stella. 1946. *The Hindu Temple.* Delhi: Motilal Banarsidass. 2 vols.

Krishna Sastri, H. 1920. *South Indian Inscriptions, Vol. 3.* Madras: Superintendent, Government Press.

———. 1923. *South Indian Inscriptions, Vol. 4.* Archaeological Survey of India, New Imperial Series. Madras: Superintendent, Government Press.

Kumāraswāmi Gurukkal, S. 1994. See *Śivaliṅgapratiṣṭhāvidhi.*

L'Hernault, Françoise. 1978. *Iconographie de Subrahmanya au Tamilnad.* Publications de l'Institut Français d'Indologie 59. Pondicherry: Institut Français d'Indologie.

L'Hernault, Françoise, and Mary-Louise Reiniche. 1999. *Tiruvannamalai: Un lieu saint sivaite du sud del l'Inde, 3. Rites et fêtes.* Publications de l'École Française d'Extrême-Orient 156–3. Paris: École Française d'Extrême-Orient.

MacAloon, John J. 1984. *Rite, Drama, Festival, Spectacle: Rehearsals toward a Theory of Cultural Performance.* Philadelphia: Institute for the Study of Human Issues.

Malamoud, Charles. 1976. "Terminer le sacrifice: Remarques sur les honoraires rituels dans le brahmanisme." In *Le sacrifice dans l'inde ancienne*, edited by Madeleine Biardeau and Charles Malamoud, 155–206. Bibliothèque de l'École des Hautes Études, Section des Sciences Religieuses 79. Paris: Presses Universitares de France.

Martin, James L. 1982. "The Cycle of Festivals at Pārthasārathī Temple." In *Religious Festivals in South India and Sri Lanka*, edited by Guy R. Welbon and Glenn E. Yocum, 51–76. Studies on Religion in South India and Sri Lanka 1. New Delhi: Manohar.

Meister, Michael W., and M. A. Dhaky. 1983. *Encyclopaedia of Indian Temple Architecture: South India, Lower Dravidadesa, 200 B.C.-A.D. 1324.* New Delhi: American Institute of Indian Studies.

Merrey, Karen L. 1982. "The Hindu Festival Calendar." In *Religious Festivals in South India and Sri Lanka*, edited by Guy R. Welbon and Glenn E. Yocum, 1–25. Studies on Religion in South India and Sri Lanka 1. Delhi: Manohar.

Michell, George. "Chariot Panels from Tamil Nadu." *Marg* 43, no. 2: 29–52.

Nagarajan, Vijaya. 2000. "Rituals of Embedded Ecologies: Drawing Kōlams, Marrying Trees, and Generating Auspiciousness." In *Hinduism and Ecology: The Intersection of Earth, Sky, and Water,* edited by Christopher Key Chapple and Mary Evelyn Tucker, 453–68. Religions of the World and Ecology. Cambridge: Center for the Study of World Religions, Harvard Divinity School.

———. Forthcoming. *Drawing down Desires: Women, Ritual and Art in Southern India.* Oxford: Oxford University Press.

Nagaswamy, R. 1983. *Masterpieces of Early South Indian Bronzes.* New Delhi: National Museum.

———. 2002. "The Bronzes of Emperor Kulottunga and His Successors." In *The Sensuous and the Sacred: Chola Bronzes from South India,* edited by Vidya Dehejia, 28–45. New York: American Federation of Arts.

———. 2003. "The Festival of Dancing Siva (Nataraja and Kalamukhas)." In *Facets of South Indian Art and Architecture* 1: 84–91. New Delhi: Aryan Books International.

Nilakanta Sastri, K. A. 1932. *Studies in Cola History and Administration.* Madras: University of Madras.

Orr, Leslie C. 2000. *Donors, Devotees, and Daughters of God: Temple Women in Medieval Tamilnadu.* South Asia Research. New York: Oxford University Press.

———. 2004. "Processions in the Medieval South Indian Temple: Sociology, Sovereignty and Soteriology." In *South-Indian Horizons: Felicitation Volume for François Gros,* edited by Jean-Luc Chevillard, 437–70. Pondicherry: Institut Français de Pondichéry.

———. 2006. "Preface." In *Pondicherry Inscriptions,* edited by G. Vijayavenugopal, i–xxvii. Collection Indologie 83, no. 1. Pondicherry: l'École Française d'Extrême-Orient/Institut Français de Pondichéry.

———. 2007. "Singing Saintly Songs: Tamil Hymns in the Medieval South Indian Temple." In *Sacred Songs of the Saints: Medieval and Modern Perspectives on the Tamil Hymns.* Boston: Association for Asian Studies.

Parker, Samuel Kenneth. 1987. "Makers of Meaning: The Production of Temples and Images in South India." Ph.D. dissertation, Anthropology, University of Chicago.

Peterson, Indira Viswanathan, tr. 1989. *Poems to Śiva: The Hymns of the Tamil Saints.* Princeton Library of Asian Translations. Princeton: Princeton University Press.

———. 1998. "The Evolution of the *Kuravañci* Dance Drama in Tamil Nadu: Negotiating the 'Folk' and the 'Classical' in the *Bhārata Nāṭyam* Canon." *South Asia Research* 18, no. 1: 39–72.

Pillay, K. K. 1953. *The Sucindram Temple.* Adyar, Madras: Kalakshetra.

Prentiss, Karen Pechilis. 1999. *The Embodiment of Bhakti.* New York: Oxford University Press.

Raghavan, V. 1958. "Pañca-mahā-śabda."*Indian Linguistics,* Sir Ralph Turner Jubilee Volume 1: 302–10.

———. 1968. *New Catalogus Catalogorum.* Madras University Sanskrit Series 30. Madras: University of Madras.

Ramachandra, T. N., tr. 1990. *St. Sekkizhar's Periya Puranam.* Thanjavur: Tamil University.

Raman, K. V. 1975. *Srī Varadarājaswāmi Temple--Kāñchi: A Study of Its History, Art and Architecture.* New Delhi: Abhinav.

Rangaramanuja Ayyangar, R. 1981. "Music in Temple Rituals." In *Proceedings of the Seminar on Temple Art and Architecture held in March 1980*, edited by K.K.A. Venkatachari, 47–52. Ananthacharya Indological Research Institute Series. Bombay: Ananthacharya Indological Research Institute.

Sabharatna Sivacarya, K. A. 1988. "Urcava Vimarcanam." In *Siva Temples and Temple Rituals*, edited by S. S. Janaki, 92–107. Madras: Kuppuswami Sastri Research Institute.

Sambamoorthy, P. 1931. "Catalogue of the Musical Instruments Exhibited in the Government Museum, Madras." *Bulletin of the Madras Government Museum* n.s. 2, no. 3: 1–25.

Sanderson, Alexis. 2007. "The Śaiva Exegesis of Kashmir." In *Mélanges tantriques à la mémoire d'Hélène Brunner*, edited by Dominic Goodall and André Padoux, 231–442. Collections Indologie 106. Pondicherry: Institut Française de Pondichery.

Smith, H. Daniel. 1981. "Vāhanas in the Cultic Art of South Indian Temples." In *Proceedings of the Seminar on "Temple Art and Architecture" Held in March 1980*, edited by K.K.A. Venkatachari, 12–29. Anantacharya Indological Research Institute Series, vol. 10. Bombay: Ananthacharya Indological Research Institute.

Srinivasan, P. R. 1987. "Darasuram: Epigraphical Study." In *Darasuram: Epigraphical Study, Étude architecturale, Étude iconographique*, edited by Françoise L'Hernault. Publications de l'École Française d'Extrême-Orient, Mémoires Archeologiques 16. Paris:École Française d'Extrême-Orient.

Surdam, Wayne Edward. 1984. See *Kriyākramadyotikā.*

Swaminathaiyar, U. V. 1994. *Ulāppirapantaṅkaḷ.* Cennai: Doctor U. V. Swaminathaiyar Book Depot.

Takashima, Jun. 2005. "Pratiṣṭhā in the Śaiva Āgamas." In *From Material to Deity: Indian Rituals of Consecration*, edited by Shingo Einoo and Jun Takashima, 115–42. Japanese Studies on South Asia 4. New Delhi: Manohar.

Thirumavalavan, G. 1991. *Political, Social and Cultural History of the Cholas as Gleaned from Ula Literature.* Thiruvathipuram: Ezhilagam.

Varadachari, V., ed. 1986–2002. *Descriptive Catalogue of Manuscripts in the French Institute of Pondicherry.* Publications de l'Institut Français d'Indologie 70.1–4. Pondicherry: Institut Français de Pondichéry. 4 vols.

Venkatesan, Archana. 2004. "Āṇṭāḷ and Her Magic Mirror: Her Life as a Poet in the Guises of the Goddess: The Exegetical Strategies of Tamil Śrvaiṣṇavas in the Apotheosis of Āṇṭāḷ." Ph.D. dissertation, South and Southeast Asian Studies, University of California, Berkeley.

Waghorne, Joanne Punzo. 1991. "Vahanas: Conveyors of the Gods." *Marg* 43, no. 2: 15–28.

———. 1992. "Dressing the Body of God: South Indian Bronze Sculpture in Its Temple Setting." *Asian Art* 5, no. 3: 9–33.

Wentworth, Blake. 2009. "Yearning for a Dreamed Real: The Procession of the Lord in the Tamil Ulās." Ph.D. dissertation, South Asian Languages and Civilizations, University of Chicago.

Wessels-Mevissen, Corinna. *The Gods of the Directions in Ancient India: Origin and Early Development in Art and Literature (until c. 1000 A.D.)*. Monographien zur Indischen Archeölogie Kunst und Philologie 14. Berlin: Dietrich Reimer Verlag.

Younger, Paul. 1995. *The Home of Dancing Śivan̲: The Traditions of the Hindu Temple in Citamparam*. New York: Oxford University Press.

———. 2002. *Playing Host to Deity: Festival Religion in the South Indian Tradition*. Oxford: Oxford University Press.

Index

abhiṣeka (consecrating bath), 28, 33–34, 70, 79–82, 118–120, 123, 124, 126, 128, 132, 134, 139, 141, 143
acalamūrtī (immobile body), 26, 37
ācamana (sipping water), 81
ācārya (preceptor, priest), 13, 20, 21, 75, 101, 119, 127, 134
  festival of, 44, 123–124
ācāryābhiṣeka (priestly consecration), 13, 21, 43, 79, 134
Ādhāraśakti, 77, 81, 100
adhivāsana (preparatory rites), 61, 71
Ādityas (group of twelve deities), 42, 53, 71, 86, 93, 118
Adiyulā, 52
Āgamas, 3, 23, 25
AGHORA mantra, 108, 120, 112, 125, 131
Aghoraśiva, 3, 7, 18, 31
  and his lineage of teachers, 6
  as author, 6–13, 21–24
  image of, 20–21
  vision of the festival, 52, 55–58
Agni, 36, 42, 53, 72, 90–91
agnikārya (fire rites), 77, 99, 129
āhvāna (invitation), 41, 88
Aiyanar, 54
Ajitāgama 4, 5, 25, 46, 47, 50
Alagappa Mudaliyar, Mayilai, 3, 4, 6, 9
alamkāra (adornment), 107
amāvāsyotsava (new-moon festival), 27, 141–143
Ananta, 42, 100
aṅgamantras, 72, 77, 85, 98, 119, 123, 129
aṅkurārpana (sprouting of auspicious seeds), 30, 51, 61–62, 70–71, 80, 89, 91, 117
annaliṅga (rice-liṅga), 27, 38, 89, 103–104, 122
anugrāha (grace), 35, 137–138
ārdra-paṅka (moist paste), 124–125
arghya (reception water), 72, 81, 131
āsana (seat, throne), 39, 75, 97, 121
āśīrvāda (blessings), 118
aṣṭamaṅgala (eight auspicious objects), 74, 93, 104
Aṣṭaprakaraṇa, 11–12
āsthāna-maṇḍapa (audience hall), 66, 101, 115
ASTRA (weapon) mantra, 33, 45, 77, 79, 88, 95, 103, 115, 127, 129, 137

astrayāga (Trident ceremony), 61–62
Asuras, 54
Aśvins (group of two deities), 86, 118
ātmārtha (on one's own behalf), 18, 26
ātmaśuddhi (purification of the self), 44, 72, 96
āvāhana (invocation), 76, 81

bali, balidāna (tribute), 33, 41–42, 48, 61–62, 81, 114
  procedures of, 101–106
balipīṭha (tribute pedestal), 89, 91, 103, 141
balivāhaka (tribute carrier), 50, 101, 104
Bhadrakālī, festival of, 65
bhaktotsava (festival of the Devotees), 45, 61–62, 134–136
Bhatt, N. R., 4, 14, 23
bheda (divisions of the festival), 29, 61–62
bherī (type of drum), 38, 42, 47, 70, 79–80, 83, 85–86, 101, 110, 115, 121, 127–128
  worship of, 87–88
bherītāḍaka (chief drummer), 47, 101
bherītāḍana (beating of the *bherī* drum), 30, 34, 46, 79, 115–116, 121
  procedures for, 83–91
Bhikṣātana (Śiva as Beggar), 19, 36, 38, 110
bhogāṅga (enjoyment position), 39, 122
Bhūdevī, 65
bhūśuddhi (purification of the ground), 65
Bhūsūkta (Hymn to the Earth), 70
bodhakas (scholars), 82, 124
brahmamantras, 36, 75, 77, 81, 85, 97–98, 100, 112–113, 119, 122, 129, 136
Brahman, 36, 42, 53, 54, 104–105, 126
  charioteer as, 127
  as Lord of the Site, 42–43, 84, 92, 95–96
  as Lord of *tattva* group, 68, 76, 77–78
  as World-guardian, 73, 89–91
brahmasthāna (central location), 31, 89
Brunner, Hélène, 6, 7, 14, 23, 26

calamūrti (mobile body), 26, 37, 65
Campantar, 16
Caṇḍeśa, 27, 31, 40, 41, 50, 65–66, 79, 84, 88, 107–108, 111, 121–122, 127, 133–134
  festival of, 34, 62, 120, 123
  as Gaṇeśvara, 96
  shrine of, 101
Candraśekhara (Śiva wearing the moon in his crown), 28, 143–144
catussamskāra (fourfold consecration), 87, 98, 116, 125
Cēramān Perumāḷ, 52–57
Chidambaram, 15, 21, 22, 24, 31, 78
  and Chola patronage, 18–20
Chola dynasty, 16, 17–21, 23
cūrṇikā (recitations), 88
cūrṇotsava (festival of powder), 32, 61–62, 110, 134
  procedures for, 114–117

daivajñā (astronomer), 47–48, 64, 66, 74, 79, 127
dakṣiṇā (honorarium), 44, 49, 119, 124
Dancing Śiva festival, 38, 51, 111, 122
  procedures for, 128–132
daṇḍa-bhaṅgi (stick method), 97, 130
Darasuram, 20–21, 22
darbhakūrcha (bundle of darbha grass), 69, 81
deśika (guide), 22, 82
  see *ācārya*
Devadāsīs (female temple servants), 46
Devī (the Goddess), 50, 88
Devotees, 31, 65, 101, 107, 111, 141
  festival of, 35, 134–136
dhūpa-dīpa (incense and lamp), 81
dhvajārohana (flag-raising ceremony), 30, 61–63, 121
  procedures for, 78–83
dhvajastambha (flagpole), 81
  see Flagpole
dhvajāvarohana (flag-lowering ceremony), 30, 34, 61–62, 117
  procedures for, 120–122
dīkṣā (initiation), 22, 43, 79

Kulottunga II, 18, 19
kuṇḍa (fire pit), 92

Lakṣmī or Mahālakṣmī, 43, 65, 86, 95, 97, 105, 133
Lakuliśa, 100
layāṅga (integral position), 122
liṅgapratiṣṭhā (establishment of the Śiva-liṅga), 44, 64, 67, 68, 75–77
Lokapālas, *see* World-guardians

madhutraya (three sweets), 129
Mahā-kriyākramadyotikā, 7–9
Mahāpadma, 87
mahāpīṭha (main altar), 68
Mahāśaivas, 51, 108–109
Maheśvara (Śiva as the Great Lord), 36, 129–130
Maheśvaras, 51, 70, 109
mahotsava (great festival), 3, 5, 22, 25–26, 29, 37
  description and history of, 15–17
  participants in, 35–52
  structure of, 29–35
  types of, 61–63
Mahotsavavidhi, 3, 5, 6–9, 17, 21–24, 29
  translation of, 13–14
Mahotsavavidhikrama Āgamaśekhara, 5, 6, 14, 35
maṇḍapa (pillared hall), 20, 65
Manonmanī, 42, 113–114, 117–118, 133, 137
māsotsava (monthly festival), 25, 27, 138–141
matsyalīlā (fishing festival), 28
mauktigrahaṇa (festival of gathering pearls), 28
maunabali (silent tribute), or *maunotsava* (silent procession), 34, 62, 121
modaka (sweet rice balls), 66, 70
Moon, 39, 42, 69, 70, 71, 81, 87–88, 126
Mothers (*saptamātṛkā*), group of seven deities, 42, 54, 84, 86, 87–88
Mount Kailasa, 52, 57
Mount Meru, 42, 57, 115
mṛgayātrā (hunting expedition), 32, 110–111
mṛtsangrahana (gathering earth), 30, 51, 70
muhūrta (auspicious moment), 48, 74
MŪLA (root) mantra, 77, 81, 95, 98, 100, 108, 120, 125, 129, 131, 133
muṇḍa-bhaṅgi (bald-head method), 97, 130
mūrti (manifest form), 35, 75
murtipa (image-protector, assisting priest), 44, 51, 82, 98, 119, 131
musicians, 46–47

nāda (primordial sound), 88
Nāgas (group of eight divine snakes), 42, 87–88, 101, 126
naivedya (food offerings), 81
nakṣatra (constellation, lunar mansion), 27, 29, 48, 144
  determination of, 63–64
Nandin, 27, 30, 31, 40–41, 50, 53, 56, 65, 79–80, 81, 82, 88–89, 95, 96, 107, 111, 121, 127
  festival of, 61, 71–78
Nandins (group of eight deities), 42, 72, 76, 79, 82, 121
nanditāla, 30, 88
Naṭarāja (Śiva as Lord of Dance), 36
  at Chidambaram, 18–20, 24
  festival of, 34, 128–132
  images of, 100, 109
  visualization of, 130
navasandhinṛtta (dance at the nine corners), 30, 83, 89–91 *see also bherītāḍaṇa*
nāyanmārs (Śaiva devotional saints), 18, 107–108, 116, 134–135
netronmilana (opening of the eyes), 48, 74–75
nidrākumbha (sleep pot), 75
nīrājana or *nīrāñjana* (illumination ceremony), 28, 32, 46, 51, 61–62, 91, 122, 141
  procedures for, 111–113
Nirmalamaṇi of Tiruvarur, 6–9, 22
nirodhana (protective encirclement), 67
Nirṛti, 42, 72, 90–91

nityahoma (daily fire-sacrifice), 7, 98
nityakarman (daily rites), 7, 22, 26, 78, 93, 96, 100
nityapūjā (daily worship), 7, 26, 36, 76, 82, 98, 106–107, 112, 113, 115, 120–123, 124
nityotsava (daily festival), 25, 26–27
nṛtta (dance), 82, 89–91
nyāsa (imposition of mantras), 72, 76, 126

oṣadhi-sūkta (hymn to the plants), 71
Oṭṭakkūttar, 19–20

pāda (word), 85
Paddhati, 3, 21, 23
paduka (Śiva's sandals), 27
pakṣotsava (fortnightly festival), 25, 27, 28, 141–144
Pallava dynasty, 16
paṇ (musical mode), 89–91
pañcagavya (five cow-products), 65, 74–75
pañcakṛtya (five fundamental activities), 137–138
pañcamahāśabda (five great sounds), 47, 89
pañcāmṛta (five nectars), 75
pañcāvaraṇa (five entourages), 98
Pandya dynasty, 16
paramaśāyin (design), 92, 94
parārtha (on behalf of others), 13, 18, 26, 44
Parameśvarī (Goddess in Supreme Form), 122, 130–131, 133
Parāśakti (Highest Śakti), 81, 133
paricāraka (temple attendant), 48–49, 70, 82, 95, 104, 116, 119, 124
pariveṣa (circling of light), 91
pariveṣaṇa (perambulation), 32, 61–62, 110, 128
parvan (juncture), 63
Pārvatī, 31, 36, 53, 84–85, 106, 131
paśu (bound soul), 138
Paśupati (Śiva as Lord of All Creatures), 26, 36
  meditation on, 103
paurṇamāsotsava (full-moon festival), 27, 141, 143–144
Periya Purāṇam of Cēkkiḻār, 18, 52–53
pīṭha (pedestal), 80
Planets (group of seven or nine), 42, 87, 131
pradakṣiṇa (circumambulation), 26, 31, 56, 66
praṇaya-kalaha (lovers' quarrel), 132, 134
prapā (temporary pavilion), 65, 118
pratiṣṭhā (establishment), 8, 37, 68, 71, 92, 103, 106, 127, 136
prāyaścitta (expiation), 82, 98–99, 136
Preceptors (group of seven), 43, 95, 97
priest, 38, 43–44, 51
  ascetic observances of, 61–62
  festival of, 34, 44
  images of, 20–21
procession, 14, 19, 24, 28
  in *Ādiyulā*, 52–57
  in *mahotsava*, 31–32, 50–51, 106–112
  in *nityotsava*, 26–27
puṇyāha-jala (auspicious day water), 126
puṇyāhavācana (declaration of auspicious day), 66
pūrṇāhuti (complete oblation), 77, 98–99

rāga (melody), 89–91
rājan (king), 49, 51, 108–109, 131, 134
Rājarāja II, 3, 18, 19
rakṣabandhana (tying on protective wristlets), 50, 100–101
Rākṣasa, 54
rakṣasūtra (protective wristlet), 31, 50, 68, 124–125, 128, 133
  rite of tying, 100–101
rāśi (sign of the zodiac), 127, 138
ratha (chariot), 65–66, 107, 124–128
ratha-kumbha (chariot-pot), 124–126
ratha-mārga (chariot street), 127
ratha-yātrā (chariot procession), 16, 32, 124
Rivers (group of eight divinities), 42, 113–114, 117–118
ṛkṣa (lunar mansion), 64, 144
ṛkṣotsava (festival with alignment of stars), 25, 27, 144–146

ṛtvij (assisting priest), 44, 96, 100–101, 116, 124
Rudra, 42, 68, 76, 78, 87, 100, 105, 115
Rudras (group of eleven), 86–87, 93, 118
Rudras (group of one hundred), 126
Rudragaṇikās (female temple dancers), 32, 46–47, 51, 70, 89, 108, 110–111, 113, 116, 124, 128

ṣaḍadhvan (six paths), 85, 97, 120, 121
Sadāśiva, 12, 35–36, 75, 100, 103–105, 113, 126, 133
  imposed on flagpole, 67, 80–81, 121
  visualization of, 127
Sādhaka (Śaiva adept), 51, 82, 124, 131, 134
sādhakābhiṣeka, 51
ṣaḍutthāsana, (sixfold throne), 72, 75, 100
Śailādi, 31, 107, 111
Śaiva brāhmaṇa, 13, 21, 51
Śaiva Siddhānta, 10, 13, 14, 20, 21, 23, 26, 35–37, 43, 57, 76, 88, 129, 137–138
sakalīkaraṇa (imposition of mantras onto body), 78, 113, 115
Śaktis (energies of Śiva), 35, 36, 76
  from Śakti to Śakti, 80–81, 121, 130
  group of eight, 113
  three forms of, 133,
  three principal Śaktis, 39, 69, 81
Śakti-pot (*vardhanī*), 95, 97
sāmānyārghya (ordinary reception water), 78, 96
samayadīkṣā (common Śaiva initiation), 51, 134
samhāra (destruction), 35, 137–138
samhitāmantras, 85
sandhyāvāhana (evening invocation), 88–89
saṅkrānti (solar transition), 27, 64, 138–139
śānti (pacification rites), 82, 136–137
śāntihoma (pacifying fire-rites), 82, 136–137
śāntikumbha (pot of pacifying water), 77–78, 129
Sarasvatī, 105
śibika (palanquin), 66, 107
Śilpaśāstra, 14, 48, 67
śilpin (artisan), 47–48, 67–68, 71, 74–75, 125–126, 128
Śiva, 18–19, 24, 26, 77–78
  forms of, 37–40, 76–77, 137
  icons of, 65
  theological character of, 35–37, 53, 56
Śiva-Agni, 40, 98–99
śivahasta (hand of Śiva), 124–125
Śivakāmī (Goddess as Śiva's Beloved), 41, 128–129, 131
śivakumbha (Śiva-pot), 39–40, 95, 97, 119
Śiva-liṅga, 26, 28, 34, 36, 37, 40, 72, 100–101, 106, 113, 116, 119–121, 130–131, 141, 143
  forms of, 38–39, 80
  see also *annaliṅga*
Śivapuram, 52, 57–58
Skanda, 31, 36, 40, 41, 42, 50, 54, 65, 84, 86, 87–88, 100, 106–107, 111, 122, 126, 127, 133
snāna-maṇḍapa, (bathing pavilion), 68
snāpana (bath ceremony), 28, 61–62, 141, 144
Somāskanda (Śiva seated with Umā and Skanda), 28, 31, 37, 50, 88, 100, 106–107, 109, 111, 113, 116–117, 121, 141, 146
  meditation on, 121–122
Śrīkaṇṭha, 76, 97
  impostion of, 97, 120, 121–122, 130
sṛṣṭi (creation), 35, 137–138
sthaṇḍila (ritual platform), 68, 74–75, 79, 84, 100, 113, 118, 123, 129, 137
sthiti (maintenance), 35, 137–138
śuddhanṛtta (pure dance), 46, 82–83, 89, 132
Sun (*sūrya*), 39, 42, 69, 81, 84, 86, 87–88, 95–96, 126
sūryapūjā (worship of the Sun), 7, 96
suvāsinī (married woman of good home), 51, 111, 113, 133

Takṣa (divine snake), 39, 81, 101
tāla (rhythm), 89–91

tattvas, three groups, 68–69, 76–78, 84–85, 100, 113
thirty-six, 68, 76
tauryatrika (triple symphony), 46, 66, 123, 128
tirobhāva (veiling), 35, 137–138
tīrthasamgrahaṇa (collection of holy water), 61–62, 113–114, 118
tīrthasnāna (final bathing rite), 33, 61–62, 117–119, 132
calculation of, 63–64
tīrthayātrā (pilgrimage), 33
Tirukkayilāyaññānavulā, 52
tithi (lunar day), 64
Trident (*triśula*), 27, 38, 40, 42, 65–66, 79–80, 89, 99, 101, 104, 113, 115–118, 121–122
ceremony for, 33, 49, 119
imposition of deities onto, 84–86
Tripurantaka (Śiva as Conqueror of the Triple City), 36, 38, 111
TRYAMBAKA mantra, 88, 100–101

uccāraṇa (ascending pronunciation), 77
ulā (procession poem), 19–20, 52
Umā, 40, 41
Umāmāheśvara (Śiva seated with Umā), 27
Umāpati, 24–25, 31, 78
upacāras (services of worship), 77, 107, 115, 121, 125, 128
list of five, 98
list of sixteen, 81–82
uṣṇīṣa (turban), 48, 79
utsava (festival), 25
types of, 25–29

vādya (musical instrument), 89–91
vāhana (vehicles), 15, 17, 32, 65, 109, 133
schedules of, 108, 135, 136
vaivāha (marriage ceremony), 34, 51, 61–62
procedures for, 132–133
vardhanī (Śakti-pot), 39–40, 95, 119–120
varotsava (weekly festival), 25, 27, 146
Varuṇa, 42, 53, 72, 90–91
vāstumaṇḍala, 39, 92
vāstuśānti (pacification of the site), 42, 92
Vasus (group of eight deities), 86, 93, 118
Vāsuki, 42, 87–88, 100–101
Vāyu, 42, 53, 73, 81, 90–91
vedikā (altar), 39, 68, 80–81, 92
vidhi (rule, prescription), 3, 13, 23
vidyādeha (body of mantras), 75, 78, 81, 96, 121
Vidyādharas, 54
Vidyeśvaras (group of eight divinities), 40, 42, 93, 95–96, 98, 113, 115, 119–120
Vikrama Chola, 18, 19
vinoda (entertainments), 47, 129, 134
Vīraśakti, 41, 133
Vīraśāsta, 65
visarjana (dismissal), 82
viśeṣabali (special tribute), 91, 105
Viṣṇu, 42, 53, 73, 87–88, 100, 104–105, 126
as lord of *tattva* group, 68, 76, 77–78
vṛṣavādya or *vṛṣanāla* (bull-roarer, instrument), 70, 82
vṛṣayāga (Sacrifice to the Bull), 61–62, 71–78
vyāhṛtis, 99, 125, 129
VYOMAVYĀPIN mantra, 85, 116

Weapons (*āyudha*), 95, 98, 101, 104, 117
World-guardians (Lokapālas), 33, 41–42, 43, 46–47, 84, 88, 89–91, 93, 95–98, 101, 115, 118, 122, 126

yāgaśālā or *yāgamaṇḍapa* (sacrificial pavilion), 32, 39, 42, 70, 113, 119, 123, 124–125
worship of, 61–62, 91–93
Yāgeśvara (Śiva as Lord of the Sacrifice), 39, 41, 95, 120, 125
Yāgeśvarī (consort of Yāgeśvara), 39, 41, 95
yajamāna (Patron), 49, 96, 116, 124, 134
Yakṣas, 54, 129
Yama, 42, 53, 72, 90–91
yānakrama (order of processions), 61–62
yātrā (journey, procession), 31, 80, 117
yātrādāna (gift at outset of journey), 80